you can't always get
WHAT YOU WANT

you can't always get
WHAT YOU WANT
my life with
the Rolling Stones,
the Grateful Dead
and other wonderful reprobates

SAM CUTLER

ECW Press

Published by ECW Press
2120 Queen Street East, Suite 200, Toronto, Ontario, Canada M4E 1E2
416.694.3348 / info@ecwpress.com

Published in Australia by Random House in 2008.

LIBRARY AND ARCHIVES CANADA CATALOGUING IN PUBLICATION

ISBN-13: 978-1-55022-932-5
Cutler, Sam
You can't always get what you want : my life with the Rolling Stones, the Grateful Dead and other
wonderful reprobates / Sam Cutler

1. Cutler, Sam. 2. Concert agents-Biography. I. Title.

ML417.G69C62 2009   782.42166092   C2009-905964-9

Editor: Jennifer Hale
Text Design: Tania Craan
Cover Design: Rachel Ironstone
Cover Images: Top front photograph by Bob Davidoff — www.palmbeachpopfestival.com;
Bottom front photograph © Robert Altman; back photograph courtesy Ray Slade.
Author Photograph: © Hudson Photo, 2009
Typesetting: Mary Bowness
Printing: Transcontinental   1   2   3   4   5

Mixed Sources
Product group from well-managed forests
and other controlled sources
www.fsc.org   Cert no. SW-COC-000952
©1996 Forest Stewardship Council

PRINTED AND BOUND IN CANADA

ECW PRESS
ecwpress.com

For Ella Louise Howard and all the musicians

CONTENTS

Every day

We murder our dreams;

Then pick them up,

Dust them down,

Adjust their silly hats upon their heads,

Kiss them on the cheeks,

And tell them how glad we are

That they're still alive.

– Sam Cutler, 1974

Let 'em bleed

In early December 1969, the Rolling Stones had just completed the world's largest-grossing rock'n'roll tour to date, playing to thousands of fans across America. The tour was a phenomenal success, but the band faced constant criticism from the media, who accused them of rip-off ticket prices. In response, the Stones had agreed to play a final concert in San Francisco for free. "What could be a better response to the accusations of rampant rock'n'roll greed than to play for free?" they had reasoned. Give the people some free music as a parting "thank-you" to America.

Thus we found ourselves at the Altamont Speedway, in the hills southeast of San Francisco, playing on a bill with the cream of the West Coast bands, and deeply mired in some unbelievable shit.

The Rolling Stones, like everyone else, got swept up in the maelstrom of a senseless and brutal confrontation between the thousands of people who had come to hear the music and party and a small group of Hells Angels wannabes who were attacking people for no apparent reason.

The initial beatific vision of the Stones and the Grateful Dead playing together was to turn into a nightmare that was to cost several people their lives, irrevocably damage many more, and serve to expose much of the West Coast's loving vibe as both a pitiless hallucination and a patent absurdity.

The Altamont concert was not organized by the Rolling Stones, or by me, their tour manager, but by a loose amalgam of well-meaning but ultimately irresponsible people from the community of San Francisco.

Needless to say, when the concert turned to shit, the Stones unfairly got the blame, and I have been living with my share of that opprobrium for forty years.

It's time to set the record straight and have my say. For the 300,000 people who were at Altamont, there could well be some surprises, for actual events certainly bore little relation to the stories that were later to appear in the American press.

But there's more to my story than Altamont. This is the history of my life on the road with two of the world's greatest bands: the Rolling Stones and the Grateful Dead.

CHAPTER 1

Busy being born

Unlike Michael Philip Jagger, who was born in a hospital, I was born in a stately home. Mick may have owned several stately homes, but darling, he was never *born* in one!

I was born in 1943 in Hatfield House, on the northern outskirts of London, in the county of Hertfordshire. The house was built in 1608 by Robert Cecil, the first Earl of Salisbury, and has been in continuous aristocratic occupancy by his titled descendants ever since. I hasten to add that I'm not one of them.

My arrival in such aristocratic surroundings was simply the result of Hatfield House being requisitioned by the government during the war and converted into a makeshift maternity hospital. This part of England was of little interest to the German Luftwaffe.

I was delivered into a complete shambles of destroyed buildings, shattered lives, millions of deaths, and general mayhem. It was the "crossfire hurricane" that Mick refers to in his song "Jumpin' Jack Flash." All of the chaos of the war was generously leavened by rampant promiscuity so that almost as fast as people were being killed, others were being born. It was a manic lottery in which the soldier and the newborn child had approximately the same chances of survival.

I was not to learn until I was fifteen that the woman who

gave birth to me was Irish, from a gypsy family out of Cork. She had worked as a government typist. My father had been a Jewish mathematician on active service in the Royal Air Force. Both were to disappear in the industrialized slaughter of the war. Talk about three strikes and you're out! In the blood of my veins I was Irish, Gypsy, and Jewish!

These three persecuted races commingled in me and were the perfect combination for a career in the entertainment industry, though of course I was unaware of this at the time of my birth. My heritage and the peculiar mixture of my bloodlines has always been a source of great comfort and pride to me, as from the very earliest age I was always convinced that whatever else I was, I was definitely *not* English.

A family friend helpfully described my early years to me when I was a confused teenager. My birth mother had tried to cope, he told me. She was a young and devoutly Catholic Irish girl with an illegitimate baby, and far from her family — who would have viewed the child she had borne with distaste and probably abandoned their daughter. Almost certainly her family back home in Ireland was not told of her pregnancy or my birth.

My mother had tried to raise her child in secret, alone in wartime London, but had been unable to manage the joint pressures of a war and trying to survive with very little money and a small baby. The friend of the family hinted darkly that she had selflessly given me up for adoption to help secure a better future for me, and that the man who had been her lover and my father had abandoned her and then died on active service.

I have always respected my birth mother's choice and, while it hurts to this day, I have never made any attempt to trace her or get in touch. I hope she found a better life than many Irish people who lived in London. I know her full name but I don't know whether she's alive or dead. If she were still living she would have to be at least in her eighties by now. Effectively, she died for me when I was a baby. Bless 'er.

In due course, I was packed off to Swansea in Wales, to a

Catholic children's home, and from that orphanage I was adopted just before the age of three. When I eventually found out that my birth name was Brendan Lyons and that I was Irish, all I could think was how grateful I was that I wasn't English and named Cyril.

My first memory is of being carried down the steps of a bomb-damaged Marylebone railway station by a nun, and being given to my new parents, Ernie and Dora Cutler. I sat in the back of their borrowed car and they told me that they had decided to call me Sam.

My adoptive mother says I bawled my eyes out throughout the journey, and when they finally got me home and my new father triumphantly placed me on the kitchen table for a group of friends to admire, he announced in a loud voice, to raucous congratulations, "Here's one we saved from the Catholics."

I was raised by my new extended family in the parliamentary constituency of Woodford, represented for many years by Winston Churchill, close to the epicenter of the vicious German bombing campaign that had destroyed London's East End. Dora and Ernie had seen firsthand what the nightmare of war had done to a once thriving community, and were unalterably opposed to war in all its forms. Dora, at the first available opportunity, called Mr. Churchill a "drunken old warmonger" to his face, and was banned from his constituency office.

My family despised Churchill and made their home available to serve as the campaign headquarters for the Communist Party candidate opposing Churchill in the elections. The communists, needless to say, lost. This did not endear my parents to the land-lord, whose politics closely resembled those of Attila the Hun.

From my earliest days I remember adults as people who were invariably reading, even when they were eating a meal. In my parents' house we had the collected works of Marx and Engels, Lenin and Stalin and Mao, every left-wing book club edition that was ever printed, and goodness knows what else. But we didn't have Trotsky, or the Bible.

People were constantly coming and going and there would have been Reds under the beds but for the fact that was where even more books were stored. We were host to an endless supply of transient members of the Party, who slept wherever they could find any space and debated the great questions of the day with skill and alacrity.

In addition to books and people, we had music. Music for the people, by the people, and performed by the people. My earliest memories are of wonderful parties where the assembled adults would drink homemade beer and enthusiastically sing folk songs, sea shanties, and political ditties. Where other children learned nursery rhymes, I was raised on union songs and paeans to Stalin and the Red Army. To these were added songs from the Community Songbook. My mother played the piano and all the adults gathered around and sang lustily late into the night. One would reasonably think that after countless acid trips and the experiences of the drug-fueled sixties, the words of obscure political songs would fade from my mind, but to this day they remain eerie reminders of that distant country which is my past.

My family always celebrated the memory of those people who had offered their young lives in the service of the Spanish Republic, fighting in support of the legitimate government of Spain, only to be defeated by the combined might of the German and Italian armies, who had intervened on the side of the fascists. Remembrance of the Spanish Civil War was treated as a sacred responsibility, and I can recall people raising their glasses to the republic and shouting "Viva!"

My adoptive family were "bloody heathens," as the landlord once memorably put it. I might add that we did not consider this a problem. Christianity in our house was considered a risible deception foisted on the gullible and defenseless. Christmas was celebrated in my childhood as an ancient and largely irrelevant pagan festival, but the adults boisterously celebrated the New Year. We were allowed to stay up until midnight before being rushed off to bed. Music played a central role in these celebrations and a highlight was my mother singing "The Socialist Sunday School," the words of which I can still recall.

The Socialist Sunday Schools were established to counter the Sunday Schools run by the churches. Classes were opened with the declaration: "We desire to be just and loving to all our fellow men and women, to work together as brothers and sisters, to be kind to every living creature and so help to form a New Society, with Justice as its foundation and Love as its Law."

At the end of the meeting there would be a further declaration: "We have met in love. Now let us part in love. May nothing of ours that's unworthy spoil the sweetness nor stain the purity of this good day, and may the time until we meet again be nobly spent in setting up the gates and building the walls of the city of the heart." I can't help but regret that I didn't open and close Grateful Dead meetings with those lines. It might have made a difference!

Dora raised me according to the precepts of the Socialist Sunday School, and I must admit that I have not lived up to their teachings, though I have tried. Nonetheless, they were to play a major role in my approach to life. The socialist precepts bear some repeating in this contemporary world of unalloyed greed, the pursuit of profit before all else, and the destruction of our beautiful planet:

> Love your schoolfellow, who will be your fellow work-
> man in life.
> Love learning, which is the food of the mind; be grateful
> to your teachers and parents.
> Make every day holy by good and useful deeds and
> kindly actions.
> Honor the good; be courteous to all; bow down to none.
> Do not hate or speak evil of anyone. Do not be revenge-
> ful, but stand up for your rights and resist
> oppression.
> Do not be cowardly. Be a friend to the weak and love
> justice.

Remember that all of the good things of the earth are
    produced by labor; whoever enjoys them without
    working for them is stealing the bread of the work-
    ers.
Observe and think in order to discover the truth. Do not
    believe what is contrary to reason, and never
    deceive yourself or others.
Do not think that those who love their own country
    must hate and despise other nations, or wish for
    war, which is a remnant of barbarism.
Work for the day when all men and women will be free
    citizens of one fatherland, and live together as
    brothers and sisters in peace.

My adoptive father, Ernest George Cutler, suffered from
osteomyelitis, a terrible bone-wasting disease, which in the days
before antibiotics caused great suffering and resulted in a very
unpleasant and painful death. His legs and his chest were covered in ugly scars where the surgeons had operated in a vain
attempt to keep the disease's ghastly ravages at bay. I can
remember my father showing me his wounded body as he gently
explained to me that his injuries were the reason he couldn't let
me get into bed with him and have a cuddle. He died in 1951,
when I was eight.

Immediately following World War II, antibiotics were available to those rich enough to pay for them. Working-class people
never had the luxury of such advanced medicines, and so my
father died, the treatment he needed available only to the priv-
ileged few. It was a cruel injustice that struck at my mother's
heart, for she had loved and supported this man through all of
his agonies and tribulations. Such iniquities helped to make a
revolutionary of my mother, but I was too young to understand.

For many years after his death I kept an old tobacco tin in
my father's memory. He smoked Balkan Sobranie in a large
wooden pipe and would have great difficulty in unscrewing the

lid of the tin because of his illness. His tin was one of my prized childhood possessions and for years I protected it fiercely and held it sacred to his memory.

My maternal grandmother was the only person in our large household who had any practical experience of how to raise children, having raised three daughters and a son. Everyone called her Tillie, short for Matilda. She smoked Capstan Full Strength, the strongest cigarettes then available, and had one permanently between her lips, its long ash drooping from the end. Her upper lip was stained a light brown and in the front of her silver-gray hair there was a similar stain, caused by the incessant cigarette smoke that curled over her brow. I have never known a person who smoked more cigarettes than my grandmother.

When I was very small she would give me a bath and even then she'd have a cigarette between her lips. She lived to be ninety-six.

My mother Dora worked for a trade union that represented employees of the British government. It was known as the Civil Service Clerical Association (CSCA). The CSCA was the first union in the western world to get equal pay for men and women, a fact of which my mother was extremely proud. She was the secretary to the editor of Red Tape, the union magazine. She was also the organizer of the union's annual conference, held in Prestatyn in northern Wales. Once a year she would disappear for two weeks for this get-together. Dora was devoted to the union movement and as radical a woman as one could ever hope to meet, but she had difficulties in expressing her affection for me. I can't ever remember my mother cuddling me, though I was sure she loved me in her own way. After Ernie, my adoptive father, died, Dora was forced to allow others to care for me, as she had to grieve for her lost husband while continuing to work. Ken and Joan Hoy, comrades of Ernie's in the Communist Party, became my surrogate parents. They lived four doors down in the same street, King's Avenue in Buckhurst Hill, Essex, east of London.

Ken had been a "tail-end Charlie" in the war, the man who sat in the very tail of the bombers and manned its most exposed anti-aircraft gun. They had the highest attrition rate of all Royal Air Force air crew. He never spoke about his experiences. I later read that the ground crew was sometimes forced to hose the remains of the tail-end Charlies from aircraft when they returned from missions, as the bodies had been rendered into virtual mincemeat by enemy fire. Ken knew he was very lucky to have survived. After the war he trained to be a teacher, and while he and Joan looked after me, he also used me as a model for the essays he had to write at his teachers' training college.

Ken was a knowledgeable amateur ornithologist. He and I would take day-long walks through the forest, wearing old World War II Air Force binoculars, which he'd kindly let me borrow. He would help me identify birds, badger tracks, and the plants that grew in hedgerows that could tell you how long ago the hedges had been planted. He was a source of fascinating information for a young boy. Ken was a gentle man, kindness personified, whose love of nature communicated itself to me and helped give my uneven life some stability.

Ken's wife Joan was a fashion designer who taught pattern design to people who wanted to enter the rag trade. I thought her very glamorous and she was generally considered to be an exceptionally bright and beautiful woman. Ken was her third husband, so Joan had broken a few hearts. She was as radical as my mother, if not more so, and I can remember her holding her own in heated arguments with other comrades and tossing her hair in annoyance if anyone so much as dared to patronize her because she was a woman.

Joan was a lady who fought for what she believed in. She took me on street demonstrations, where she was always in the vanguard of the protesters, shouting her slogans and encouraging me not to be afraid. I can remember being in London's Whitehall near the Cenotaph with her in the middle of a huge demonstration at the height of the Suez Canal crisis. The London Dockers, under their Communist leader Jack Dash, were fighting pitched battles with the mounted police and we were in danger of being trampled by the charging horses. Joan put her arms around me as she dragged me from the center of the stampeding crowd frantically trying to escape the melee. I was very scared, but Joan gaily laughed and told me to look at the Dockers — they were united and strong. She gently explained that each man was afraid; of course they were afraid! But with a comrade beside him, each man would subsume his fear in the interests of the greater good, and think not of himself but of others. "Remember, Sam," she would say, "remember this: unity is strength!"

I was twelve years old.

Joan was the first woman I loved, and in my adolescent fantasies I felt that she loved me. I lived for those happy moments when she would spontaneously crush me to her bosom in a wonderful friendly hug with gales of laughter. I worshiped her.

Joan and Ken were the most magnificent couple and I adored them both. Through their loving kindness I made the difficult transition from being a boy to being a man long before I reached my full physical maturity.

I was a lonely child and with the benefit of hindsight realize now that I had been profoundly disturbed and traumatized by my experiences prior to my adoption. While I could remember nothing of what had happened to me, I carried the scars of my previous life deep in the recesses of my heart. As an only child, surrounded mostly by adults, I longed for a brother, someone to play with. I never experienced the conventional play-centered life of most children. In many respects I was old even before I was a teenager, but I didn't really want to have much to do with adults.

Opposite Ken and Joan's house in King's Avenue was an Elizabethan hunting lodge that looked as if it hadn't been repaired since it had been built some hundreds of years earlier, when the area was covered in ancient forest. Elizabeth I had been at Hatfield House, the place where I was born, when she first learned that she was to be queen. She had hunted in the forest where I once played, and even stayed in the now almost derelict hunting lodge immediately across the street from where I lived. That the adopted child of a radical family should have experienced such synchronicities deeply worried me as a young child.

In the hunting lodge I would escape from the world. Every room was familiar to me, including the one in which the first Queen Elizabeth no doubt must have slept. I could never quite understand it, and the thought that I had been in the hunting lodge long ago, before I was born, made me feel decidedly uneasy. I found myself keeping a sharp eye out for my own ghost. Many years later it was all to become a little clearer to me when Elizabeth returned in somewhat incongruous circumstances: On a memorable acid trip at a Grateful Dead concert I began imagining myself in one of my previous incarnations. I was standing behind Jerry Garcia's amplifier, the band's money was safely stashed in my briefcase, and I could relax and get high. The acid began to play its merry tricks and I saw myself as a pirate returning to England with great treasure stolen from Spanish galleons I had raided and sunk. I gave half of the fortune to Queen Elizabeth, who was gracious enough to give me a knighthood and 10,000 acres in Buckinghamshire. Ah yes, those were the days! A likely lad could get ahead in Elizabethan times. Mind you, he could also often lose his head.

As I wandered through the rooms of that Elizabethan hunting lodge as a child, returning home to Ken and Joan at night, unbeknownst to me, my widowed mother had been seeing more and more of a man called Mel, a Welshman from Merthyr in the Rhonda Valley.

Mel had attended the University of Southampton and when the war intervened had joined up. He spent the war years firing a machine gun over the heads of nervous soldiers-in-training as they crawled up the cliffs in Ilfracombe, and advanced through the ranks to become a sergeant.

Following the war, Mel was active in the Communist Party and the civil service union, where he met my mother. They announced their intention to marry, and my mother saw this as an opportunity to reunite the family. She wanted me to leave Ken and Joan and return to the fold. She and Mel were planning to move out to the suburbs. I resented my mother's moving me from Buckhurst Hill and the people I loved with a silent fury. I became a morose type, a young man of few words — a typical teenager.

Teenagers were then a recently discovered species. Before World War II, there had been no such group of people in existence. We were a new breed, which, according to those in the know, had mating rituals and interpersonal relationships that were of unprecedented interest. We were widely studied and our sociopathic highjinks were much discussed in parliament. We had our own indecipherable patois that we spoke from the corners of our mouths so that none but our own kind could understand. We even had our own kind of music, guaranteed to disgust our parents. We became the incoherent philosophers of our day and, as far as we were concerned, anyone else who wasn't the same as us was dead, or they might as well have been for all we cared. Nothing much has changed; we just invented it, that's all.

Dora and Mel did their best to accommodate the unreasonable Martian living in their house, but I despised my new father and nothing he could do or say was acceptable to me. He was a decent man and had done little to deserve my antagonism, apart from contentedly singing the old music-hall song "Martha, Rambling Rose of the Wildwood" as he made tea in the morning. That was simply too much for me to bear.

Every day at exactly seven o'clock I would hear him walk downstairs in his slippers and put water in the kettle while singing that infernal song. I would squirm under my blankets with angry distaste. It was always the same song and always at exactly the same time. Monstrous! Needless to say I didn't like getting up in the morning and deliberately stayed in bed so that I wouldn't have to deal with my mother or Mel before they went to work.

I retreated to my room rather than participate in what I considered to be the charade of my mother's marriage and the family life they were attempting to construct for me. Like all newlyweds they were excessively solicitous of one another's little whims and desires, and watching them settling down together was sickening.

I longed to be an adult and loathed what was happening to me. I particularly abhorred the home to which I had been reluctantly forced to move. My parents' dream of owning their own house was certainly not a dream I shared, then or now. I have never owned a house in my life, though I've gone through enough money to buy several of the bloody things.

We had relocated to what felt like a tiny box on a suffocatingly small piece of land, a three-bedroom house in a suburban cul-de-sac in Croydon in the south of London. The houses on either side of us were no more than a meter from our own. The short, steep road ran between five houses on either side, all with little driveways that suckled at the street like dependent piglets on the teats of a sow. I hated the place with a coruscating passion. I hated home, school, and England and couldn't wait to leave all three.

Every book I read became an encouragement to go, to escape to where people lived with gusto, felt passion, and embraced the molten steel of conviction. *Red Star Over China*, *The Ragged Trousered Philanthropists*, and Willie Gallacher's *Rise Like Lions* were the siren calls that appealed to my developing political consciousness. The more I read the more cynical and depressed I became about England. I listened to American music and I read American books and I wanted so much to go there that it hurt.

My mother loved the works of American writers, and while we could barely talk to one another, we at least had the solace of being able to communicate about books.

"You should try this," my mother would say, and I would be given books like *Peekskill USA* by Howard Fast. I'd retreat to my room, where I would think myself very clever smoking cigarettes while hanging out the window in the belief that my mother wouldn't smell the tobacco. I wanted to see the meat yards of Chicago, go where author Upton Sinclair had been, meet the white men who had selflessly put their bodies between singer and activist Paul Robeson and the fascists at Peekskill so that he might sing for the people and not be harmed. I wanted to sing "Hallelujah, I'm a Bum" at the top of my voice and to rejoice in my freedoms. I wanted to bellow "Which Side Are You On?" and actually see a side that I wanted to join, for in England there was no side to anything that appealed to me.

Most of all I wanted to go to California and see what Woody Guthrie wrote about in his songs — that great and unimaginably vast land of dreams, those "Pastures of Plenty." Meanwhile, I was stuck in Croydon.

CHAPTER 2

Behind the beat

As the hairs on my groin sprouted and my hormones raged, I began to dream about girls. When I wasn't reading I was masturbating. When I wasn't masturbating I listened to music and played the guitar. Books, music, and sex were my all-consuming passions and my room became my refuge. I ached to leave home but first, whether I liked it not, the law said I had to finish school.

Alcohol and jazz saved me from going mad. On Saturday nights after work I'd meet up with my older mate Kelly in a pub in West Croydon, where we would listen to people like Humphrey Lyttelton and Ken Colyer, both well-known English jazz musicians. The local drink was a lethal mixture of Guinness and cider (aka Black Velvet) and with two of these under my belt I'd haunt the dance floor looking for dance partners. Kelly wasn't into dancing and became completely flustered if called upon to talk to the girls, so he'd hang out at the bar "getting them in," as he called it. This arrangement suited me, as I was legally not entitled to purchase alcohol, though I thought nothing of downing a few pints of beer on a Saturday night. At that pub in West Croydon, whose name for the life of me I cannot remember (The Croydon Arms?), I first saw English blues great Alexis Korner. He was playing banjo in Ken Colyer's band.

It was also the place where I first got high, and I have some musicians to thank for that. In the back of the pub was an enclosed yard stacked with beer barrels and tables that had been cleared to make room for the people who danced. It didn't take me long to realize that this was where the band hung out when they were taking a break. I would make my way to the yard as soon as the music finished and chat to the musicians and they would treat me with that detachment that all musicians employ when talking to fans. As I was far too young to be any kind of a threat, nobody worried about me and they would smoke joints as if it were the most natural thing in the world.

They'd pass the cigarette to one another and take a couple of tokes while continuing their conversation with nary a word being spoken in my direction. Everything seemed to be very relaxed, so I leaned my back against the wall and tried to give the impression of being totally at home. Whoever the man was who passed me the joint, he didn't even bother to look at me. He simply extended his hand with the goodies while maintaining an animated exchange with his friends. I accepted without saying a word and, following what I had observed of the protocols, took what I thought to be a reasonable time, had a couple of tokes, and passed it on. Nothing much happened to me and in truth I was a tad disappointed. Within minutes another joint appeared. This one seemed stronger and must have had more of an impact because when the musicians left me standing in the yard and went off to play, it took me a while to realize that everyone else had gone inside.

I sheepishly returned indoors to the pub to find Kelly. When I'd made my way through the press of people to the bar I found I could barely talk to him above the ambient noise. The band's music seemed incredibly loud and the room much warmer than I remembered, and there was a strange disconnect going on between my mind and my mouth.

Kelly and I sat at a table surveying the packed pub. As I looked at the dance floor my tongue felt swollen and I was overcome by an intense feeling that I was in the wrong place. The beer tasted dreadful, the women were not attractive, and Kelly seemed like a man from some distant planet. My nose kept twitching and I felt as if any moment I would sneeze. I breathed through my mouth and swigged disinterestedly at my beer. The whole place seemed to stink. Mumbling some unintelligible words, I wandered to the toilets to reassess the situation.

I stood beside some lump of a man having a piss and was shocked to realize that I could actually smell him beside me above the acrid stench coming from the urinal. I giggled to myself — my nose was as sensitive as a dog's — but I was shaken by the experience. I had to get out of the pub, into a space where I could breathe. The walk home was about four miles; making feeble excuses I left Kelly in the pub and headed for the street.

The taste of the beer in my mouth was horrible and I wished I could get a drink of water to wash it away, but as I gulped hungrily at the fresh air I began to feel more alive. As I made my way home I started to think. There was almost a year left of schooling, as my mother had extracted an ironclad promise from me that I wouldn't leave until I was sixteen. In the interim, before I left home, school, and England, I needed something to get into. What was missing in my life, I told myself, was pleasure.

My pace quickened and Croydon, which hitherto I'd loathed, all of a sudden didn't seem quite so bad. My spirits soared as I thought about being a secret smoker, though I didn't have a clue as to where I was actually going to get some of this new-found elixir. Never mind about that, I persuaded myself. At least I would have something to do, other than lounging about and drinking beer and dreaming about barmaids.

And so at a tender age I became a hashish smoker and to this day I remain convinced it was the only thing that enabled me to get through the tedium of my last year at school. I was in a holding pattern. I said little and read as much as I could, listening to music all the while. After jazz, I got into blues, quickly followed by Gene Vincent and Elvis Presley. With precious little effort I was finding my own way to what I loved.

I would visit a friend, bringing along my guitar. He was a great finger-style guitarist, and we would share a joint while he showed me how to play blues licks. He lived with his mother, Jeannie, a stunningly sexy lady of Anglo-West Indian descent who had once been a dancer at London's Windmill Theatre. She would come home from work to find us giggling and having fun.

She would sometimes dance as we played and my mouth would become dry as I looked at her body. I wanted her really badly but could not bring myself to talk about it with my friend. I wanted to learn as much as I could from him about the guitar without upsetting him. Somehow "I fancy your mum, how does an F7th chord go?" just didn't seem appropriate.

The only person who I wanted to tell about my mate's mum was another friend, a fellow called Brian, and soon I made my way to his house to tell him of my sexual awakening. We sat in his bedroom and while Brian rolled a joint I tried to tell him about Jeannie, but I could barely get a word in, as Brian wanted to tell me about a book. I listened as he described the characters and the plot. It was all about America and it immediately appealed to me.

He handed me Jack Kerouac's *On the Road*.

I made my way back home and settled down in my bedroom to read. It was an absolute revelation. For the very first time I read a book that described movement, that rejoiced in leaving and traveling, the very things I had wanted to do ever since I was a small child. It talked of jazz, sex, dope, and hope, and in its restless romanticism I felt sure that I had found a template for my future. I loved the book with a great and unbridled enthusiasm and thought it magnificent.

On the Road was the first book I read that described getting high, and I was comforted by the fact that others were doing what I was doing and writing books about it. I could tell that the book's narrator, Sal Paradise, an author, loved the flawed but magical Dean Moriarty. The book made me ache to find a man of such magical qualities in my own life. After making Dean Moriarty my hero, no man and no thing that subsequently happened to me ever really surprised me. Everything, simply, became possible.

This book made me want to stand on the edge of America travel coast-to-coast head west as far as one could go until the pacific ocean lapped at the ankles it made me ache to be in low bars get high with wild people move wherever whim took me wander without finite purpose simply experiencing sheer joy grooving on all I might discover and see — it made me want to drive to Mexico City. Here in this book the external journey, stumbling at great speed across America, became the metaphor for the journey within.

It remains to this day one of the only novels I have read from beginning to end, paused, and then read again — three times. After that I knew that I was a "Beat." Or, more accurately, I set out to become a Beat, guided by a book.

Years later I learned that *On the Road*'s Dean Moriarty was based upon Neal Cassady, the friend of author Ken Kesey, who'd been the driver of the Merry Pranksters' bus. (The Pranksters were a group of open-minded types who hovered around Kesey in the 1960s.) The Grateful Dead knew Cassady and held him in awe. I ended up looking after a band that had actually known Neal Cassady! I would have worked for them for free. But that was all in the future. *Becoming* was what immediately confronted me, and to do that I needed to leave school and get the hell out of England.

The prospect of being a wage slave like my latest father filled me with dread. As far as I could ascertain, my teachers saw me as a tradesman with great potential, something like a plumber, where other people's shit would provide me with a livelihood. I wasn't going for that, thank you very much. I cast about in my finest morose teenage manner for an alternative that would allow me to do as little work as possible. The alternatives to sex and song looked bleak, so I opted for the entertainment business. As far as I could tell it was dripping in sex and music — my favorites!

Music, the whole glorious gamut of guitars and glamorous girls, was where it was at as far as I was concerned and was surely the appropriate focus for my unrecognized talents. The music business, I assured myself, was made for me. It valued those golden attributes with which I had fortunately been born — native cunning, a measure of charm, the balls of King Kong, and more front than Brighton.

I never saw much point in aiming for the improbable, though, having had that conceit soundly thrashed out of me at a succession of appalling schools and, having made a cursory study of what passed in those days for the music industry, I gave up all thoughts of being a rock star. I was not much of a guitar player and certainly not good-looking in the conventional sense, so that option appeared unattainable.

I studied the rock stars of the day and it seemed to me that they were all over the place. Most had previously worked as barrow boys, builder's laborers, plumbers, or ditch diggers, and they were a bunch of ignoramuses. They had what the English quaintly call "humble beginnings." (Mind you, they may have been humble to begin with, but by God they weren't humble when they finally got on stage.) These people needed more than a bit of assistance. Rock stars were fragile, the poor dears, and there was my opportunity. I would become one of the willing helpers who looked after them. In other words, a kind of glorified "executive nanny," which is what the Grateful Dead called me years later on their *Workingman's Dead* album credits.

Little did I realize then, innocent that I was, that in a surreal sense other people's shit would figure large in my own life long after I had left school. Just as my teachers had confidently foretold, tons of shit became mine to deal with. When I got involved with the music business, other people's problems became ineluctably my own, illustrating with apposite clarity the old maxim: "It's all the same shit, just different flies!" Short of wiping their arses and brushing their teeth I did everything for musicians (though, as Chrissie Hynde and Marianne Faithfull would discover on tour in Germany, I drew the line at buying feminine hygiene products in foreign countries if I didn't speak the local language).

In the early days, though, I found the million and one things that go into making a successful gig infinitely fascinating and there in the production trenches I decided to make my bed. Being absolutely realistic quickly became my modus operandi, especially as most of the musicians I worked with barely knew what planet they were on, let alone what being "realistic" actually meant. After all, they had become musicians in order to pursue wonderful dreams, not to deal with the tedious requirements of reality. As we used to say, reality is for people who can't handle drugs.

I would eventually become the personal tour manager for two of the greatest bands of all time: the immortal Rolling Stones from England, headed by Keith ("The Man That Death Forgot") Richards, and the legendary Grateful Dead from California, reluctantly led by Jerry ("The Tainted Saint") Garcia. I am the only man to have ever worked for both bands in that role, and somewhat remarkably I have lived to tell the tale. Needless to say, my employment was a simple twist of fate — but I'm getting ahead of the story.

CHAPTER 3

No direction home

After leaving school I briefly escaped to Paris, thinking that my adventures were just about to start, but I was forced to return home by a bout of severe ill-health. I kept up my interest in music, but when I had recovered I decided to train as a teacher and, much to everyone's surprise, I passed the college entry exams. I found to my delight that almost all of my fellow class-mates were women. At times I thought I had more chance of getting a degree in gynecology than teaching.

During this happy period I ran a small folk club in a pub near the college. Paul Simon (among others) played there; I remember him as an arrogant little prick who'd just written "The Sounds of Silence" and played acoustic guitar better than me. I disliked him, he knew it, and the feeling was mutual.

I prospered at college, graduated with high marks, and went to teach in a special school for what in those days were called "maladjusted children." Disturbed children have few social skills, and the ability to slot their own individual needs into a social framework comes hard to them. They find it virtually impossible to think of anyone other than themselves. Above the noisy roar of their own rampant personalities, the tiny squeak that represents another person simply doesn't register. They are inherently alone.

Part of the secret of dealing with them is to find something that they want to be a part of and that they feel they have a direct stake in. Music is wonderful for such children and really seems to bring them happiness where virtually all else fails. I always thought these children, when they grew up, should start a rock'n'roll band. Let's face it, thousands have tried it and many have been very successful.

In the five years that I was a student and then a teacher — 1963 to 1968 — England's popular culture, the overall zeitgeist, changed dramatically. Ever since World War II, increasing numbers of young people had become sick to death of the boring reality of daily existence. They knew instinctively that the life they were expected to lead was no life at all, just an uninspiring crawl from cradle to grave. People despised what had been bequeathed to them by their parents' generation. By the time the 1960s arrived many were looking for an alternative.

Many began to investigate altered states of consciousness. It was as if revolution, normally conducted on the streets, had gone indoors. People decided to change themselves as a precursor to changing society. The best and the brightest took drugs and jumped merrily without a care into the fire of the unknown future. Fearlessly, with an open and receptive mind, I too joined in the grand experiment.

We all believed that some form of radical surgery on England's collective consciousness was desperately needed. The world had grown pale and sickly on a diet of Doris Day, Pat Boone, Winifred Atwell, Mary Poppins, Frank Sinatra, and *The Sound of Music*. The artists we loved — Bob Dylan, the Rolling Stones, the Beatles, Pink Floyd, and many others — were pointing their fingers toward other destinations. We followed their lead, not concerned that there was no direction home.

The possible annihilation of the human race through nuclear holocaust was a constant preoccupation in the postwar years, so when a specific drug appeared, considered by some to be the antidote to the insanity of our "mutually assured destruction," young people slowly but surely adopted it as their own. This drug was LSD, otherwise known as acid, and it was spread secretly, in much the same way that Christianity must initially have been spread during the days of the Roman Empire.

Underground chemists manufactured the drug in America, and their visionary compatriots declared that their purpose was to change the consciousness of the whole world. Psychedelic missionaries from California arrived with pure LSD and customs officials had no idea what they were looking for. It could be a clear liquid just like water, impossible to detect; it could be a crystal that looked like salt; it could be on impregnated blotting paper, or even on sugar cubes.

The powers that be were unaware of what was going on, and the genie of an alternative consciousness escaped from the bottle. Once it was out, it could never be put back in. Soon enough the postgraduate chemists of my generation would be manufacturing the drug in the laboratories of universities from Brighton to Liverpool and from Edinburgh to Oxford and Cambridge.

In their usual tired old colonialist manner, members of the establishment — that curious mixture of power and influence that had controlled England for generations — thought to make an example of those whom they took to be the "leaders" of youth, such as the Beatles and the Rolling Stones, who were influencing millions of kids. By prosecuting and imprisoning those whom they believed to be the leaders — for drug possession — it was reasoned that young people could be cowed into submission. This miscalculation only served to embolden the enemies of stasis and tradition.

The many-headed hydra of youth coalesced into an underground that had no real leaders and no definable center. It had disparate influences and its own little secret ways, impossible for the authorities to suppress in a conventional manner. They could not stifle what they could not understand. England had no one Timothy Leary, the American LSD pioneer — it had hundreds of them.

I was introduced through friends to one of the Americans who arrived with the new sacrament. He came from San Francisco. In a flat in Upper Montague Street, the "wizard" showed us his revolutionary wares. We sat around a small coffee table on the floor smoking hash as he told us what was going on in "Yankville, USA," how a new way of living was happening, and how the human race had to make a giant evolutionary leap in consciousness or be doomed to self-destruction. We were eager to learn.

He told of the underground chemists in America, who he declared had made millions of "trips" before the authorities finally made a law declaring LSD illegal. The CIA, he claimed, were in the thick of the drug's production and rogue agents were complicit in its distribution for reasons as yet unknown. His take was that various agents had tried the drug and then gone "off the reservation" as their experiences made them believe in the drug's benefits.

The strange little man with the Nepalese hat held us spellbound. He had five grams of crystal with him, he said, enough to make several hundred thousand trips. He was going to distribute it throughout Europe. We were suitably impressed and duly amazed.

It was September 1965, and memories of the Cuban missile crisis were still fresh in everyone's memories. The Vietnam War was increasing in ferocity. Dylan had released *Bringing It All Back Home* and *Highway 61 Revisited* in one wild creative explosion. Things were changing radically and we all wanted to be a part of it. I was twenty-two years old.

We thought of ourselves as pioneering visionaries, as young people often do. We were from widely different backgrounds. The flat was owned by a young and sexy gal who had invited me to London for the weekend; she was the daughter of a general. Several of us were students, and I remember that one of the men told us he was a journalist who worked at *The Times*, which surprised us all.

A doctor named Ronnie talked in a broad Scottish accent that was so dense he was virtually unintelligible. A couple of younger guys were from Hornsey School of Art and were accompanied by two exquisite girls, tall and languid. An older American lady sat in an armchair and smiled at us all indulgently like some guardian den mother. A very straight-looking man told us he was a solicitor's clerk. The plan was that we were going to take the drug and then walk in the nearby park.

We watched as the American solemnly squirted a drop of liquid onto each of the sugar cubes that were lined up on the table. I clearly remember him telling us not to be afraid, which made me rather nervous.

He said not to worry if we had a bad trip; he and the lady in the armchair would take care of us. I breathed deeply and prepared myself for whatever came next. Each of us took one of the sugar cubes, and waited for something to happen.

People settled down on cushions on the floor and Dylan's "Desolation Row" played over and over. None of us could believe the vast internal panorama of the song, its poetic imagery, its savage put-downs. Much of the music I had heard before now seemed hollow and meaningless — mindless pap designed for the masses. All that could be heard was Dylan's apocalyptic visions. We had gone way beyond words.

All that straight society held dear, everything that we had ever believed was recast, redefined, and radically re-remembered. Noah's great rainbow descended from the ceiling; people's faces dissolved and reformed; one of the girls cried vast sobs of happiness; and the little American smiled at us all benignly from behind his glasses.

I drank some water and it felt solid, like liquid lead. Its metallic molecules banged into one another and made strange noises in my stomach. I crawled to the woman sitting in the armchair and put my head in her lap and she stroked my hair. I felt like I was evaporating and the old me was simply no more.

I spent the night in Parliament Hill Fields with some of the others and shivered beneath the stars. I felt hungry and wanted to eat the Milky Way. I felt sad and the great cavern of the sky cradled me like a child in the sparkling arms of its benevolent immensity.

Every single emotion I had hitherto experienced came rushing at me with unbelievable velocity and just as quickly I discarded them all. What I had learned thus far in life, I told myself, had to be left behind like useless baggage.

I was absolutely convinced that a new and revolutionary sagacity informed my being. I ate some grass, to see what it was like being a cow, and it made me vomit. As a cold and damp London dawn broke we made our way through the empty streets and walked to Covent Garden. We went to a working-man's cafe and I remember sitting in its smoky interior watching people and thinking that I had landed on another planet.

I tried to eat some eggs but looking at the yolks I fancied that I saw traces of birds' wings flapping around in the yellow soup at the center. I couldn't bear the thought of putting it into my mouth. The tea appeared to be the color of blood and the toast felt like the thick skin of some unknown animal. I had to leave.

Somehow I managed to catch a train from Liverpool Street station back to where I was living. I walked through the streets as the church bells rang, my lips trembling and cold perspiration on my brow. No one bothered to look at me, which is the English way. I arrived at my small apartment and crawled into bed and stayed there secure beneath the blankets. After a trillion thoughts I eventually fell asleep.

The following day I simply couldn't face the idea of school, and decided instead to walk in the countryside. I needed to breathe fresh air and assimilate the most intense experience I had ever known. I walked through the narrow lanes of Essex and considered my future with a new-found clarity that amazed me.

I convinced myself that the trees understood, the plants of the fields were supportive, and that even the birds graced me with their tacit understanding. I felt more alive than I had ever been. I resolved to continue with my discoveries, and to keep going with music, and to apply all that had been revealed to me to my future life. I decided that an "altered state" was part of my destiny, a route to higher consciousness I had to explore. All over Europe and America young people were coming to similar conclusions.

CHAPTER 4

Standing in the shadows

The immediate effect of having taken LSD was a subtle diminution of my self-confidence. My own understanding of the world now seemed inadequate and I realized that I was misinformed about the essentially subjective nature of personal reality. It was as if my inner inmate had taken over the asylum of consciousness, and for a while confusion reigned as I struggled to reconcile what I had just experienced with my daily life as a teacher.

After a two-year struggle between my inner pleasure-demons and the outer reality of the daily grind, I left teaching because I couldn't live on the paltry salary — and I couldn't stand most of the other teachers.

To be frank, indulgence and hedonism seemed more attractive and much more fun. My initial enthusiasm and idealism had been blown away and had foundered on the inherently conservative policies of the educational establishment. The kids might have been interesting, but the adults were a bore. After I left, I missed the kids. I hope to think that the kids missed me.

I moved into a shared apartment with friends in Inverness Terrace in the heart of London and put my energies into music business activities and that vital component of a young man's life: having fun.

London was smoking, literally and metaphorically. My new

flat was round the corner from Queensway tube station and across the road stretched the green of Hyde Park. There I would notice small groups dressed like effete Regency dandies in multicolored clothing, lounging and discreetly smoking joints. It was easy to simply walk up to a group of strangers in the park, sit down and join the languid conversation. People were happy to share what they had as long as they didn't think you were boring — or that you were a police officer.

Richmond Park, to the west of London, had a large herd of deer. On the mornings after rain we would go to the park and search for psychedelic mushrooms, which grew on feces the deer had thoughtfully spread through the park. The small bell-shaped mushrooms sprouted, tottering top-heavy on a spindly stem. They were easy to find.

In the early morning mist, young people would tromp through the wet grass, laughing and giggling. The authorities were oblivious to the early birds catching these new worms.

People began to drive to Wales to collect mushrooms; there they grew in abundance. A substantial movement of young city-dwellers went to live in the Welsh valleys. Teepees sprouted between the hills, which had been depopulated for a generation as the farms had become economically unviable. Afghan and Lebanese hashish were readily available throughout London and the Home Counties, and as you walked in the Kensington Market or the Kings Road you could smell the joints being smoked. Fashions were getting wilder by the minute and the girls never looked more beautiful.

A generational shift was happening; those who had fought in World War II took political power. Student politics in England were abuzz with the events in Paris, where in May 1968 young people had been supported by trade unionists in violent demonstrations and in the seizure of universities and factories. American policy in Vietnam radicalized even jaded pop stars, and Mick Jagger, to his eternal credit, participated in a huge demonstration against the Vietnam War, where I walked holding the lead banner with my old friend from Paris, Hubert. The Campaign for Nuclear Disarmament symbol was everywhere.

In Notting Hill I could see the changes that were occurring. People seemed to have lost that grim unhappiness with which the English face the world. In the London streets strange slogans would appear on walls. I remember seeing: "If voting made any difference they'd make it illegal," and "Hashish is the new opium of the people."

Radical alternatives to the old systems were the subject upon everyone's lips and young people began to look at the music industry and speculate about a fresh approach. Old people, it seemed to us, ran the music business with their arrogant posing and big cigars. The Larry Barnes/Tito Burns/Larry Parnell school of management seemed hopelessly old-fashioned, with elderly "squares" in control. Some of the traditional managers not only had dubious business morals, but also came across as if they'd been doing things the same way for a million years. They appeared to us like living fossils.

We weren't totally naive. We knew that several of these men loved to control their artists in every sense, and were little better than sexual predators. Collecting a stable of young men to "groom" as stars seemed to be their main ambition. We viewed the whole thing as highly suspicious.

For a while it was all drainpipe trousers on good-looking boys with bulging crotches, who fed the masses a steady diet of musical pap that featured prominently on TV and in the charts. It was the "sore-bottom" school of rock; when we saw the "artists" we'd snigger: "One up the bum, no harm done."

None of this affected those who wanted to make alternative music: acts like the Soft Machine, Pink Floyd, and Arthur Brown, who led the Crazy World of Arthur Brown. Bands like these were far too "out there" for the older men who ran the music business. They were terrified that any involvement with druggy long-hair acts might bring a whiff of scandal into their otherwise socially acceptable lives.

Alternative music, initially at least, had to have alternative management, though it wasn't long before the professional sharks of the industry got their teeth into some of the psychedelic bands. Thankfully, by that time, I was happily in America.

All Saints Church Hall, off Westbourne Grove in Notting Hill, was one of the very first alternative music scenes. Musicians would play for fun and people would make a contribution to get in the door. I happily worked there for free, like everyone else. All Saints Hall became a legendary venue while it lasted, with people such as Arthur Brown, Charlie Watts, and many others playing for appreciative audiences who packed the place. It was there that I became friendly with Nick Mason, Pink Floyd's drummer.

For a while I thought I was madly in love with the sister of the woman who would eventually marry Nick, but then I was in love with most of the girls around the music scene. They were divine and desirable, and I wanted to love them all! I was effectively "in love with love," and still working out what I should do with my heart.

Pink Floyd always had the most spectacular women in attendance, especially their first singer and nominal frontman, Syd Barrett. Whenever I saw Syd, who could look like a frightened deer caught in a car's headlights, he would be accompanied by a delectable-looking creature who would waft about looking divine. We would all sigh happily for him and his good fortune. The girls around the Floyd were the perfect psychedelic companions for the journey; wonderful givers of love and light whom we would daydream about contentedly.

I used to watch as all these ethereal women, without exception, would initially set their sights on Syd. As far as I could tell, he paid them very little heed, occupied with his own whimsical inner workings, though it was plain that he was in need of their care. He was childlike, what we would unkindly call a "space cadet." I always doubted whether the man was capable of cooking himself a piece of toast, but when I first knew him he could play guitar quite well. I can remember him calling out chord changes to the band as they worked on new material.

There was no doubt that Syd was the first, albeit reluctant, star of the English psychedelic scene. He had a strangeness about him, and would stare intently and appear disproportionately interested in the most inconsequential thing. "Mad as a March Hare," my girlfriend at the time said (and she would have known, as she was resident at Kingsley Hall and being treated by Ronnie Laing, world-renowned psychiatric expert in "human madness"). Mad or not, Syd kept his guitar in tune, although sometimes he'd forget to play the bloody thing.

Friends told me how he took them to the country in his car, and on the way, Syd stopped and got out. He simply walked away. By the time they realized what was happening, Syd was unable to be found and they had to abandon the car. When they saw Syd again he had no memory of even going on the journey.

No one had the heart to give Syd a hard time because it was apparent that he had no idea what was happening. He was an innocent, Syd. The girls did their best to nurture and protect him, until Syd just wasn't "there" anymore, and there was nothing anyone could do for him.

The other guys in Pink Floyd were unbelievably kind to Syd, given the circumstances. What had once been a bright and shining diamond of a man devolved into a dull drugged-out pastiche. Everyone on the scene found it unbelievably moving and sad, yet there was no one who could have helped, though many tried.

I had been turned on to All Saints Hall by my crazy and wonderful girlfriend, and loved it so much that I took one of my own friends, Ron Geesin, to experience what was going on. Ron and I had met through a mutual friend and had hit it off immediately, which may well have been because I loved his music, a crazed twist on the theater of cruelty. He was one "out there" guy.

Ron was a skilled classical musician, but his personal tastes extended to manic instrumentals and odd sound effects, which he graced with absurdist lyrics delivered in an unfathomable Scottish accent. The whole effect was scary and disconcerting. To witness him play the piano with demented passion was to experience a vision of such deep alienation it made one pale with fear. Yet Ron was the most sociable of people, and once the musicians in the Floyd got to know him they loved him for his peculiar eccentricities. We all became firm friends.

Ron wasn't a drug user, refusing to even smoke a joint, but incredibly, he was able to relate to the Floyd's music, and soon became close to both keyboardist Rick Wright and bassist Roger Waters. Ron played a significant part in opening up the Floyd's approach to music, and his influence can be heard all the way through from their first LP, *The Piper at the Gates of Dawn*, released in 1967, to *The Dark Side of the Moon* (1973), *Animals* (1977), and *The Wall* (1979). *The Wall* may be credited to Roger Waters and the Floyd, but much of its alienated, angst-driven madness came from the early surrealist influence of my friend Ron.

Both Nick Mason and Ron Geesin were to help me with one of my own music projects, for which I was eternally grateful, as their involvement lent my experiment a certain gravitas. Some friends had decided to form a band called Screw, a punk band, more than a decade before Malcolm McLaren got involved with the Sex Pistols and well before anybody had a clue what "punk" actually was. Ron and Nick found it both awful and mesmerizing. The music we made was fun and irreverent and it sank without trace.

Screw was one of the only bands I have ever seen force an audience into dumb and befuddled silent surrender. After hearing Screw play, people simply didn't have a clue what to think, let alone say. Screw rendered them appalled and speechless. This was, we thought at the time, a considerable achievement.

Even John Peel, the well-regarded DJ who played all kinds of strange music on his BBC radio show, was dumbstruck by Screw. I invited John to one of their gigs and during the set, Chris

Turner, the harmonica player, overdid things a bit. Blood spurted from his lips, raining all over the stage. Pete Hossell, the lead singer, went to help and got blood on his hands and on the microphone. It looked pretty serious and afterwards a concerned Peel went backstage to see if he could help. He was shocked to see Pete Hossell washing Chris's bleeding lips with one of his dirty socks dipped in beer, swigging from the bottle as he did it, appearing totally unconcerned.

Chris was amazing: he played killer blues harp and sometimes spat out broken teeth and lashings of blood as he took his solos; audiences were suitably horrified. It often looked as if the man was bleeding to death while he was playing. Several times, Chris had to be revived on stage and a promoter once called an ambulance because he was convinced Chris had lost too much blood. (It was all an act, of course, with Chris chewing on blood capsules, but Screw was very convincing and few people knew the truth.)

The Floyd's Nick Mason helped to produce a few Screw tracks at Lansdowne Studios in London on May 13, 1969. The tracks then languished in a tape store for some thirty years. I no longer remember what it was I told Nick in order to get him to help with such an unlikely project, and goodness knows why Ron Geesin did the tape transfer and mastering. But Ron always had a soft spot for anything that was out of the ordinary and vaguely shocking. He was the only man I knew who liked the Dagenham Girl Pipers, a London-based band of female bagpipers.

Upon reflection, Nick Mason probably got involved because Screw represented a break from the complexity and cleverness of the Floyd. Their offensive approach was probably quite refreshing to Nick and a welcome antidote to Roger Waters continually telling him what to do.

I managed to get Screw on the bill of the free show the Rolling Stones did in Hyde Park (more on that subject later). At that gig the band played for some half a million people and

I remember jazz musician Alexis Korner watching them from the side of the stage and shaking his head in bewildered silence. Soon after I left for America, and thereafter Screw was other people's concern.

The band was way ahead of its time and suffered a miserable fate. Their co-manager went mad and tried to form a commune in Scotland that only had one devotee, whom he got pregnant. The lead guitarist, Al Kinnear, died young. The drummer, Nick Brotherwood, became a Christian minister. Pete Hossell ended up in São Paulo, Brazil, and Stan Scrivener, the bass player, was never heard of again. The record we made in 1969 was finally released in 2006, in a limited edition of 500 copies on the specialist Shagrat label. It sounded just as crazy as I remembered it.

Another of the London clubs central to the new musical culture was called UFO. It opened just before Christmas 1966, and was a bit of a pit, underneath a cinema in Tottenham Court Road. Pink Floyd and the Soft Machine would play there, and I would dress up in my psychedelic gear and attend with people who seemed to descend from all over England. A German fellow was the house drug dealer and I would sometimes smoke a few hash pipes, drop a trip, and watch black-and-white films projected on the walls all night. Stumbling up the stairs onto Tottenham Court Road at seven on a Sunday morning, still tripping, was quite a strange experience. I used to get away from the whole UFO scene as quickly as I could and go walking for miles through the deserted streets and watch the great city slowly drag itself awake.

As new clubs opened, new managers sprung up to take the place of those who had run the business for too long. Peter Jenner and Andrew King were in the forefront of this new guard and had founded a company called Blackhill Enterprises. I came to their establishment by a roundabout route.

It is a tradition in England that on summer weekends people leave the cities and go to the country, to a house party, or to visit friends. I was invited to spend a weekend at a huge house in the Surrey countryside. The house belonged to Nick Mason's father-in-law, a well-known and progressive architect.

We arrived somewhere south of Guildford to find forty or fifty people dressed in rainbow colors, all tripping like mad as they strolled through the formal gardens and lounged on the immaculate lawns of a monstrously large red-brick house. It was all terribly civilized in an English way. I remember meeting the owner of the house, who had a gray-white beard and was very gracious and thought that his daughter's friends were remarkable and interesting. I'm not sure what he thought of me, dressed in my most extraordinary clothes. With a lady friend, I was making clothing for some of London's new, trendy boutiques and we would buy furnishing fabrics at Liberty's, a huge shop which sold wild William Morris–designed nineteenth-century fabrics. The fabrics were intended as curtain material, or for covering chairs and furniture, but we used them to make bell-bottomed trousers and jackets for the Kensington Markets. I actually had a suit made from fabric with massive rhododendrons all over it. I'm amazed, looking back, that I was brave enough to wear it. We didn't sell many clothes, but it was fun.

On this lovely summer's afternoon in the depths of the English countryside, I talked with Nick Mason and Rick Wright about music, life, the universe, and the mad minutiae of it all, and somehow the subject of Blackhill arose. They told me it was a new company taking a very different approach to management in the music industry.

Blackhill's stance was that it all boiled down to a fresh approach to how musicians were managed and how their professional lives should be organized. Bands weren't going to take some aging, overweight, cigar-chomping member of the establishment telling them what to do. At the very least, the bands wanted to work with people who spoke their own language. They wanted to be represented by people who smoked dope, knew about alternative consciousness, and were prepared to operate on a different level. More than anything, bands wanted their affairs handled by people who were hip. Blackhill looked after the Floyd and glam rock star Marc Bolan and were at the epicenter of the rapidly emerging London music scene. I was keen to work with them, and Nick Mason told me he'd talk to Andrew King on my behalf.

Peter and Andrew ran a pretty loose ship. In a shop-front office off Westbourne Grove they presided over an enthusiastic, idealistic staff who organized tours and printed posters and generally did whatever was necessary to get shows on the road. People were made to feel welcome and allowed to hang out and were put to work. It was a wonderful time to be involved with music and London was abuzz with creative energy. I started hanging out there sometime around 1967 and picked up some work as a stage manager or roadie.

I found Andrew King to be very open and accessible, so in a spontaneous moment of recklessness I gave him a book of my neatly typed poetry (my only copy) that I fancied would make good lyrics. Andrew promised to take the poems with him to his cottage in Wales, where he could read them at his leisure. As he departed for a weekend in the country he absent-mindedly left the book on the roof of his car and somewhere between London and the provinces it was swept to oblivion and never heard of again. In the spirit of the times he never gave it a second thought, and after a brief pang of dismay, neither did I, until I sat down to write this book.

I watched with great interest as Peter and Andrew juggled "underground values" with the commercial imperative. Peter had been involved with the London School of Economics and Andrew had been in management at British Airways. They seemed, as far as I could tell, to practice a form of enlightened economic despotism, rather like the contemporary Chinese: capitalism with a lukewarm socialist face.

They delivered their new economic policy with dazzling smiles, chummy bonhomie, and some deft cunning, and were generally adored by all. Both very bright, Andrew and Peter were also possessed of a can-do attitude, something foreign to most English people, who at that time had difficulty appearing enthusiastic about anything.

Studied reticence and the stiff upper lip were still very much the thing in England; the breezy self-confidence of people like Peter and Andrew was refreshing. It's strange to think that enthusiasm in itself could be considered revolutionary, but it was in England during the 1960s. The last time the British had been enthusiastic about anything was in World War II, when they vowed to smash fascism.

We often forget that it was the young who did all the fighting in that war. People between eighteen and twenty-five bore the brunt of combat and casualties and it had exhausted them. Since 1946 the British had been asleep, to all intents and purposes. Now young people wanted the whole place to wake up and be (at the very minimum) a bit more alive. Rock'n'roll arrived just in time to save us from expiring in a fit of terminal boredom.

The music scene in London in the sixties was vaguely incestuous. It was easy to network and develop fast friendships because we all went to the same pubs and clubs and hung out in the same areas of London — and we took the same drugs. I met Alexis Korner one day in the Portobello Road and on the spot he invited me to visit him at his home in Queensway. Alexis laughed when I said I'd met him before, when he played banjo with Ken Colyer all those years before in Croydon.

Korner was graciousness personified and I was thrilled that he would even deign to talk to me. In his small flat we rapped about the blues and I was blown away to be told by Alexis that Big Bill Broonzy, Brownie McGhee, and all kinds of blues greats had actually sat on the sofa where I was sitting, and had stayed with him and his wife Bobby at their flat. I felt honored to be there. He thought it hilarious that I had first been turned on to hash by musicians and reckoned that if I picked up on getting high and the blues from musicians then I was a lucky boy. I agreed.

Alexis was the Big Daddy of the London blues scene. He was a small, wiry-haired Greek cat with an infectious grin and a head full of ideas as to who should be playing with whom and where the whole scene should be heading. Alexis was almost single-handedly responsible for the emergence of the English rhythm and blues scene with his great and massively influential band, Blues Incorporated. Cyril Davies, his harmonica player, was a kickass musician and adored by the punters.

There wasn't a musician in London who didn't know Alexis, except perhaps some people who played in the Salvation Army Band. Mick Jagger had sung in one of Alexis's bands, and Charlie Watts had been his drummer, prior to the founding of the Rolling Stones. Stones co-founder Brian Jones and Alexis were close friends. Guitar greats Eric Clapton, Jeff Beck, and Jimmy Page, as well as future Led Zeppelin singer Robert Plant, Davey Graham, bluesman Long John Baldry, the Yardbirds, band leader John Mayall — Alexis knew them all and they all knew him. In various incarnations they had all played in bands with him, or sat in on jam sessions that he coordinated. Alexis has never received the recognition he deserves.

Sitting in Alexis's flat made me feel connected to the great British blues revival, a musical movement that had developed from the traditional jazz scene into rhythm and blues and was to spawn many fabulous bands. We talked for the whole afternoon, smoking joints and drinking endless cups of tea, and I persuaded Alexis to come and play at All Saints Hall.

It was Alexis who made me realize that my place in the music business was as a tour manager, and he offered me a job to get me started. He was set to play a small festival in Holland and then some dates in Germany, and asked whether I'd like to come along. We would drive to the Hook of Holland and cross the North Sea by ferry to Belgium, then do the shows. He could cover my expenses and show me the ropes, and I fairly leaped at the opportunity.

We were away for six or seven days and had a lot of fun. I

remember leaving England on a ferry on a cold and dreary morning, having left London when it was still dark. I looked through the drizzle from the ship's stern and adored the idea of going off on a wonderful adventure, of leaving England to take music to other countries, not knowing exactly what was to happen — the idea of being on the road. I was far too excited to feel tired, whereas Alexis, a seasoned professional, slumped in a chair and was asleep before the boat had even left the dock.

Alexis was really shrewd when it came to money and with great patience and generosity he explained the intricacies of cash while not actually giving me any. Alexis would explain airily that we could eat at the gig — the promoter would feed us at his expense, thus saving our cash. A German autobahn on an empty stomach with the prospect of knackwurst, bockwurst, or any kind of "wurst" is not to be recommended to any but the fool-hardy. I'm tempted to describe it as the worst, but that would be too much. I survived and learned a valuable lesson from the experience: namely, don't rely upon promoters for food.

Alexis was the first to explain to me the whole business of voice-overs. He had a warm and mellifluous voice, rich and strangely reassuring, one that would make any housewife melt, and as a consequence his was the voice heard behind all kinds of TV advertisements. As soon as he told me that he was the voice in the Daz ads, and repeated the words "Daz washes whiter than white," we giggled like children as we roared down the autobahn smoking joints. I'd never met the voice behind an ad before. I was even more impressed by Alexis's explanation of residuals and royalties and how they worked. He was one clever cookie and I felt that if I wasn't seated at the feet of a master at least I was seated beside one.

Alexis had two guitars and an amplifier that I lugged around and set up on stage. I did the driving while he slept. I learned from him the wise practice of sleeping whenever and wherever one could when out on the road, for you never knew when the opportunity to rest would next arise.

The Dutch gig was a small outdoor festival where it rained continually and the roof over the stage leaked, but it was run with Dutch efficiency and the bands got paid, which in those days was something of a lottery. This led to the practice of the artists always insisting they were to be paid before they played.

Two of the German gigs were in small clubs and they were packed to the rafters with blues enthusiasts who smoked hash and drank beer in vast quantities. The gigs didn't pay very much, and to offset this we played in a club at an American army base in Frankfurt. I was amazed to see a fully equipped facility that must have held a couple of thousand people, with proper staging and lights. It was full of African-Americans and seemed like a Little America in the heart of Germany. We were paid in greenbacks and got to buy cigarettes and booze in the PX on the base. I brought home trophies: a bottle of Wild Turkey and a carton of Camel cigarettes.

By the time we got back home, thanks to this Greek cat who played the blues, I felt I knew what I wanted to do with the rest of my life.

CHAPTER 5

Free music, English-style

When we returned to England, Blackhill was representing Pink Floyd, but things rapidly changed. The Floyd had reluctantly retired Syd Barrett and replaced him with Dave Gilmour. Blackhill's Andrew and Peter had put their managerial energies into Syd, believing him to be the resident genius of the band, and I suspect they thought the Floyd didn't stand much of a chance of success without him.

Syd went sad and mad and the rest, as they say, is history.

Blackhill also represented Marc "T.Rex" Bolan until his premature demise. They clearly had bad luck with some of their artists. Managing bands always seemed to me to be a bit of a lottery, a business where one wasn't strictly in control of the outcomes. Many years later I was to learn at great cost how very true that observation was.

Back then, though, we were still idealistic, excited, and optimistic, with little thought of next week, let alone the future. Life was now; that was all that mattered.

Blackhill had very cleverly managed to swing a deal to put on music shows in London parks. I became a sort of production honcho, doing all the dirty work on site that the people in the office were far too busy to get involved with. All of the major London parks were nominally owned by Queen Elizabeth II, bless 'er, and were administered by a government department established for the purpose. I handled the mundane realities of staging and litter and vehicular access and 1,001 other boring but nonetheless vital details.

Without too much prior experience we managed to pull together some wonderful events. The English way of muddling through with gentlemanly good grace and the odd hash pipe to assuage troubled nerves generally sufficed, much to the authorities' surprise and our own smugly stoned satisfaction.

It all began in 1968 with a show entitled "The Midsummer High Weekend," which featured Roy Harper, Jethro Tull, and Tyrannosaurus Rex, with Pink Floyd as headlining act. The Royal Parks Commission had bravely given permission for the show; it was the first time anyone from the "underground" had managed to get such cooperation at a quasi-official level.

The show gained bucketloads of kudos for Blackhill, at the same time giving their artists tons of exposure. It is of some historic significance (and an interesting coincidence) that Pink Floyd introduced Dave Gilmour as Syd Barrett's replacement at that Hyde Park show in 1968, while the Rolling Stones introduced the replacement for Brian Jones at their Hyde Park show in 1969.

Not all of Blackhill's shows were roaring successes. Our biggest failure was a Fleetwood Mac show in Parliament Hill Fields. The gig was memorable for the thousands of empty beer bottles that were thrown at the stage. The band — at the time a pure blues act — was ready to play as I approached the microphone. As soon as I introduced them a veritable wall of glass missiles appeared, thrown by mods in the crowd; an unseemly rush to the only door at stage rear ensued, with all of us clambering over the drum kit to escape. Drummer Mick Fleetwood was not amused and it was something of a miracle that no one was injured.

After we'd swept the stage of glass I once more approached the microphone, keeping a wary eye on the crowd, and appealed to their innate sense of British fair play and justice. I asked the crowd — who were divided between old school rockers, mods, and dope smokers — to give one another cuddles rather than throw bottles. This absurd suggestion seemed to work, allowing a frightened and somber band to play a short set and survive the experience. It was a case of "stick 'em with the shit and split." Shortly after that show British-born Mick Fleetwood moved to Los Angeles, where I guess he felt he could expect a more civilized response to his music.

Other shows were less stressful, and it was with great excitement that we learned of a new supergroup to be formed by guitar hero Eric Clapton and drummer Ginger Baker (both from Cream), singer Steve Winwood (formerly of Traffic and the Spencer Davis Group), and bassist Ric Grech (Family). The group was called Blind Faith, and their manager was the all-powerful Robert Stigwood, who had managed Clapton and Baker in Cream, England's first supergroup. Somehow Peter and Andrew persuaded Stigwood that the best launch for Blind Faith would be a free concert in Hyde Park.

Mr Stigwood had a peculiar view of what constituted "free"; his office seemed reluctant to pay for anything. I was provided with a budget barely sufficient to feed a score of homeless people, let alone mount a major show, but high on the idea of being the first to present the new group, we soldiered on.

Somehow or other we managed to build a small stage, about a meter high. It was with considerable relief that I noted the day of the show was sunny and warm, as there had not been enough funds to give the stage a roof. Everything was in shape except for the arrival of Ginger Baker's drums. These showed up on the morning of the concert in unusual fashion.

A truck pulled up to the rear of the stage and four beefy roadies unloaded the drum kit, which was completely assembled and nailed down to a plywood riser. They simply dragged the kit out of the truck and plunked it down on the stage and Ginger was ready to roll. I almost expected him to be seated at the drum kit in the truck. With Ginger Baker, a wild man with an equally wild shock of red hair, all things were possible.

Many of London's rock glitterati, including Donovan and Paul McCartney, had turned up, and were sunning themselves behind the stage on this glorious English summer's day. Mick Jagger was wandering about with Marianne Faithfull.

The Stones hadn't gigged in almost three years and felt that they were in danger of being forgotten, but at that Blind Faith concert Mick saw firsthand the way for his own band to play for free and re-establish themselves. At that time, "free" was a wonderful statement — placing the *music* first, not the financial imperative, defying the corporatization of the whole scene. We had a long and earnest discussion about the logistics involved in setting up such a show. Mick hated the stage we'd built so hastily, as did I. We both agreed that a roof was essential, as no one in England could ever be certain that it wouldn't rain, even at the height of summer. I stressed repeatedly to Mick and Marianne that "free" was a concept that cost money — someone somehow had to pay for the production. Mick nodded sagely, and I explained about Alexis and me being friends. Should he want to discuss things further, I told him, all he had to do was reach me via Alexis or get in touch with Blackhill. He wandered off deep in conversation with Marianne. Blind Faith played the Stones' "Under My Thumb" that day as a nod to him.

The show was in many respects a breakthrough. A free concert of such size had never been attempted before, but the band insisted that they didn't want to be introduced: it was about the music, not an ego trip. Everyone sat on the grass, smoked joints, and enjoyed themselves, and there were no arrests; the police deemed it prudent not to bust people. The 150,000 punters enjoyed themselves, and generally the event was considered a roaring success.

The music, however, was not very good. The band was obviously under-rehearsed and Clapton, pale and diffident, looked like he was having drug issues. Winwood did most of the vocals;

he looked so frail that I remember thinking he should get a decent meal. Ric Grech, the bass player, appeared to be on a different plane, and Ginger Baker played a fifteen-minute drum solo, as was his wont. It all seemed like Cream Mark II, which was what Clapton didn't want to happen.

With one American tour following this debut, the band simply disintegrated. Can't say I was surprised. Blind Faith was a perfect example of "take the money and run." Too bad, and too sad, because if they'd been given the time to write some interesting music they had the makings of a truly wonderful band.

On the day following the Blind Faith show, the *Daily Mirror*, one of Britain's largest dailies, opined in an editorial, "There aren't many countries where 100,000 youngsters could get together so peacefully and give the police no real worries. [It was] one of the most remarkable and amiable gatherings of young people ever seen in this country." Of course we never got a word of thanks from the musicians or management, but it didn't matter. We had proved a point. Free concerts in London parks were eminently doable; people were interested in the music and they knew how to behave. It was as simple as that.

CHAPTER 6

Thou art that

Two days after the Blind Faith show, Rolling Stones Mick, Keith, and Charlie Watts drove to Cotchford Farm, where Brian Jones lived, and told him he was fired. Mick Taylor, Brian's replacement, had himself replaced Peter Green in John Mayall's band and was known in London musical circles as a sophisticated blues player. He was young and fresh and a killer guitarist, just like Brian had been in his heyday. Most importantly, unlike Brian Jones, he had no drug convictions that would count against him getting a U.S. work visa.

When Mick and the band told Blackhill they'd decided they wanted to play in Hyde Park, and to use the gig to introduce Mick Taylor, I jumped into the project with manic energy and began work on the central components of the show: the site, the stage, and the PA system. It was firmly established that a budget was an absolute necessity, and the Stones arranged for Granada Television to make a documentary of their performance, with the television company covering the costs of the production.

Financing the event by selling the rights to make a film was Mick's idea and had never been attempted before, at least not with a live rock'n'roll show. Such was the attraction of the Stones that a major television network was prepared to offset the costs, intending to recoup their investment by broadcasting the subsequent film and through ownership of the film rights. Mick was to take this idea and modify it when it came to the Stones' American tour later in the year.

Hyde Park is as fundamental to London as Central Park is to New York City. We chose to build the stage beside the Serpentine, a lake that sits in the middle of the park. The backstage area looked out over the water; in front the ground rose gently in a massive bowl, so everyone would have great sightlines.

I designed a stage that would look positively rudimentary by today's standards, but was one of the largest stages ever built for an outdoor rock show at the time. It also had a roof and was two meters high — people in the audience would be able to see, but they couldn't climb up on it to get close to the band. Security would be virtually unnecessary.

The largest public address system company in England at the time was WEM, run by an affable gent called Charlie Watkins. He was considerably older than most of the rock'n'rollers who were working on getting the gig together, but like everyone else he loved the Stones and relished the challenge of bringing the sound to the hundreds of thousands of fans expected in the park. There was also the technical problem of how the soundtrack for the film would be recorded; in the end Mick sang through two microphones taped together. Funky, but it worked a treat.

To accommodate an unprecedented number of PA speakers, we included separate scaffold towers in the stage design. I worked with Charlie Watkins on calculating the weight, so that the stage was strong enough to take the load.

I got a call from my close friend Chesley Millikin, the former European head of Epic Records. He invited me to accompany him to Heathrow, where we were to collect an American friend he wanted me to meet. Though I was madly busy, Chesley wouldn't take no for an answer and he duly arrived in his wonderful old Bentley and we drove to the airport in magnificent style, smoking a large joint.

We talked about Brian Jones, who was in some respects a little like Syd Barrett. He just didn't possess the self-control not to be greedy. Not all people can handle a prodigious drug intake, and Brian was one of them. He took drugs with reckless abandon and as his consumption increased they destroyed his talent, turning him into a nasty piece of work.

The only time I ever saw Brian Jones in a studio, he resembled a catatonic patient in a psychiatric ward and was studiously ignored by everyone. The police were constantly harassing and busting him at every opportunity. It was certainly no fun being Brian Jones.

As we bowled along to the airport I was a little surprised when Chesley told me that we were actually heading to Feltham police station, close by the airport, but thought little of it, and we merrily continued on our mercy mission. There had been some small kerfuffle, Chesley told me in his wonderful Irish brogue, that I really needn't be concerned about. His friend had been caught with thirty trips of LSD, but what did I care? My thoughts were consumed by the forthcoming show in the park, though I was vaguely surprised that the cops were allowing this person to enter the country.

At the police station we collected Chesley's friend, who turned out to be Rock Scully, one of the managers of the San Franciscan band the Grateful Dead. I must say I was impressed. Rock was a good-looking man dressed in denim from head to toe and wearing expensive-looking cowboy boots. I was particularly impressed when the station sergeant returned Rock's belongings, and, reading from a long list, actually said: "One eagle feather." He then handed Rock a whole sacred eagle's wing bound in exquisite Native American beading. On the ride back into London we became friends.

Over dinner, Rock reminisced about San Francisco and the American music scene and I was enchanted. Tales of "acid tests" and the Grateful Dead, beautiful California girls, and other attractions spilled happily into our conversation. When we talked of *On the Road*, Rock described Neal Cassady and his relationship with the Dead and the Pranksters in the most magical terms. I was reinforced in my determination to discover America for myself. Rock seemed to be a born romantic, living the California dream, and I effortlessly fell for his wonderfully high-energy rap.

He told us about the free concerts held in Golden Gate Park, close to the heart of the alternative culture in the Haight-Ashbury district of the city. Rock said many free concerts had been played in this area and there had never been any problems.

It was all so simple: the bands would play, the people would have a good time. The Hells Angels would hang out by the generators so people left them well alone and the electricity supply remained uninterrupted. All was peace and love. If there was the occasional problem, it was nothing more serious than a bad acid trip, and these unfortunate folk were dealt with by specialists skilled in supporting the temporarily deranged through their terrors.

It sounded incredible.

Rock was to swan around London and I saw very little of him, but he met up with Keith Richards, having been introduced by Chesley Millikin. It was at that meeting, at Keith's house in Cheyne Walk, that the idea of the Stones doing a free concert in California was first broached. No one seemed too enthusiastic as far as I could tell, but the idea would eventually come back to haunt the Stones.

A couple of days later I was at dinner with Chesley and Jo Bergman, who managed the Stones' office. Chesley was the personal manager of Terry Reid, who, although he was still very young, was in many people's opinion one of the greatest vocalists England had produced. Chesley was talking to Jo about the possibility of Terry getting a support slot on a Stones tour of America. The Stones were getting a lot of pressure from their record company to cross the pond.

I liked Jo Bergman. She was pretty and wore long skirts that came down to her ankles. She was a short and finely featured woman with a mop of frizzy hair that spread in all directions like a mad Jewish Afro. She was highly intelligent and possessed a steely togetherness. We all laughed when I asked her by mistake if she was Mick's right-hand man. "Of course," she replied without blinking an eye. I told her that Alexis Korner was an old friend, and the evening passed pleasantly.

CHAPTER 7

The Stones in the park

On July 2, three days before the Hyde Park concert, Brian Jones died in mysterious circumstances, apparently having drowned in his swimming pool. The police made a complete shambles of the investigation and the coroner eventually ruled that Brian had died through "death by misadventure." One could reasonably conclude that all unnatural deaths are misadventures.

Many older people in England were not at all sympathetic to Brian and basically thought that as a drug-taking rock star he had got what he deserved. They were jealous of his wealth and lifestyle and generally scandalized by what they saw as his unbridled hedonism. The English in their quiet and undemonstrative way can be savagely cruel. I like to think of them as the Japanese of Europe, but I digress.

All that I know is that the day after Brian's death a certain person took a truck to Cotchford Farm and removed everything of value; none of Brian's belongings have been seen since that day. Valuable guitars, clothing, furniture — the lot was simply stolen. While this was going on, every scrap of paper that made reference to financial matters was burned on a bonfire in the garden. This happened in a place where someone had died in suspicious circumstances less than twenty-four hours earlier. The police didn't even bother to secure the crime scene.

The person who removed the articles was a close friend of Frank Thorogood, the builder whom many suspect of murdering Brian because he was there at the scene. Thorogood is supposed to have made a deathbed confession to Brian's murder, but this was in front of only one witness, and those who know both the witness and the history of his relationship to the Stones remain unconvinced. What is beyond dispute is that several people who were present when Brian died were subsequently threatened and forced to leave the country so that they had no input into the enquiries made by the police or the coroner. This information didn't surface until years after Brian's death.

The coroner was unable to establish who was present on the night that Brian died. No blood test results were produced in court. The whole case for his cause of death seemed to rest on an asthma inhaler conveniently found beside the pool; the coroner found that "on the balance of probabilities" Brian had died from an asthma attack while swimming. No one who knew Brian, or knew the people who were around him at the time of his death, believed the verdict for a minute. I am firmly convinced that he was murdered.

Jo Bergman called and asked me to see her. I went to the Stones' office in Maddox Street for the first time. The office occupied the top floor of a nondescript building. It felt more like the interior of a Cotswold farmhouse than the office of one of the largest bands on the planet. There was virtually nothing to signify that it belonged to the Rolling Stones: no pictures of the band, gold records, nothing. It had the decor of a typical middle-class home in the London suburbs.

Mick arrived and we were joined by Les Perrin, the band's publicist. Mick seemed genuinely distressed, and freaked out that Brian should have died so soon after being fired. The band had had a meeting, he told me, and they had decided that they would still do the Hyde Park show and make it a memorial.

I asked Mick who had been looking after Brian. Surely he'd

had someone taking care of him? Mick slagged off Brian's minder, who apparently wasn't at the scene when Brian died. This man had worked previously for Keith, who had fired him for some financial irregularities.

Mick told me he remembered being on tour in Australia, when they were all at Bondi beach, and Brian had swum so far out to sea that no one could see him. Brian was a strong swimmer, and it was simply inconceivable that he could have drowned in his own pool. Mick then sat in stunned silence, until eventually we decided to get on with the details of the forthcoming show and to concentrate on the future.

Mick wanted pictures of Brian to be put on the stage and Les Perrin said he'd source them for me. We talked of releasing white doves, which was dismissed as being too corny. Then Mick came up with the idea of butterflies being set free. He saw this as an ironic reference to a *Times* newspaper editorial, written following a drug bust on Mick and Keith, which had asked, "Who breaks a butterfly on a wheel?" I promised to do my best to find some butterflies and we left it at that.

Mick was most concerned that he should have fresh bottles of water to drink and that there should be no backstage area as such. He wanted the band to arrive, go on stage, play their music, and then split. If anyone famous wanted to see the show they could watch it from the front like everyone else.

A long discussion ensued about other bands taking part in the show and I pointed out to Mick that people would be assembling in the park as soon as it was daylight and we couldn't just leave them sitting there. The crowd would need to be kept happy until the Stones finally hit the stage. Mick agreed, though he didn't want any bands on the bill that would detract from their set.

The whole business of who else would play was left to the people at Blackhill. Mick wasn't that interested in the details, but he and I agreed that Alexis Korner should definitely be offered a spot on the bill, as he and Brian had been extremely close. After thirty minutes or so Mick wandered off to take care of other things, and the rest of the arrangements I made through Jo Bergman.

The morning of July 5, 1969, began at dawn for me. I joined the several thousand who had slept overnight in the park. The fans woke to a warm and sunny summer's day and by around 7 a.m. there were many tens of thousands of people there. The largest free concert in England was about to get underway.

Les Perrin had managed to acquire two giant pictures of Brian, but they were a somewhat unfortunate choice as they showed Brian in dissipated splendor, completely off his head. They were massive prints taken from the photo shoot for the *Beggars Banquet* album. At the last minute the stage was "dressed" with the pictures and a whole slew of artificial palm trees and flowers we had rented from a set designer.

Ten thousand cabbage white butterflies in cardboard boxes were collected from Paddington station. I stashed them under the stage out of the sun and prayed that some of them would survive what was going to be a very long and hot day.

Tom Keylock, the Stones' "security man" and apparently a former member of the parachute regiment, briefed a bunch of motorcycle riders with hand-embroidered "Hells Angels" signs on their backs on how to deal with "screamers," girls who might try to get at Mick on stage. Most of the bikers were no more Hells Angels than any other young rock'n'roller in England. They were a joke. In fact there was no officially sanctioned Hells Angels chapter in England in 1969, just a bunch of risible wannabes who were barely old enough to know how to shave. Tom was deputized to look out for these wannabe bikers.

The leader of the pack was a man in his thirties who went by the name Wild Child. He wore a Nazi helmet and struck me as being singularly unintelligent. Keylock, in an absurd expression of macho naivety, asked the phony Angels to behave themselves during the performance, and then offered to have a punch-up with them after the show if they wanted a bit of action. No one took him up on his silly suggestion.

The phony Angels were to be paid with free cups of tea, dispensed by a film location catering van, which everyone thought a righteous remuneration for standing about and looking suitably moody. Everything was peaceful and calm. Horse riders trotted at their morning exercise in the park and there wasn't a policeman in sight. The young bikers preened themselves like peacocks in the early morning sun and, like everyone else, began to get excited at the prospect of seeing the Rolling Stones play.

As late morning arrived, the first of many bands took to the stage. Over a quarter of a million people were already in the park. Equipment was shuffled and various minor technical difficulties were sorted. Most of the rock'n'rollers had mercifully left their egos at home. Bands played and no one took much notice, but civility and good manners were the order of the day. Everyone was waiting for the stars of the show. A fierce sun blazed over the crowd.

The medical facilities consisted of four rather elderly ladies from the St John's Ambulance brigade. They dealt with the dehydrated by giving them a cup of tea and a biscuit in timeless English fashion. A doctor was on hand but his skills were never called upon, and eventually he removed his stethoscope, as he felt a bit silly. The whole event had the surreal character of an English garden party.

The Stones arrived mid-afternoon in a World War II ambulance that drove slowly through the gathered masses. It was the largest crowd they had ever played to. In fact, it was the largest crowd London had seen since the spontaneous celebrations that greeted the end of the war. Over half a million people had come to hear the Stones.

Jeff Dexter, a well-known DJ, was supposed to be the master of ceremonies, but there was no sign of him, so I took over microphone duties. King Crimson played. Alexis Korner's band played. There was still no sign of Dexter. I had never spoken in public before, but didn't give it a second thought and prattled away in hippie-speak to the assembled masses, reminding them not to damage the trees and to be nice to one another. I was surprised at how easy it was. I felt like I had a half a million friends.

I was soon summoned backstage to talk to Mick. He was dressed in a white suit by Mr. Fish, a famous fashion designer of the day, which struck me as rather silly, but of course I didn't express my opinion. In the caravan backstage, which was serving as the Stones' dressing-room, Mick explained that he wanted to read from a Shelley poem, "Adonaïs," in memory of Brian, and he asked me to quiet down the crowd so that the poem would be heard. I assured him that he had nothing to worry about.

We rapidly came up with a spare microphone Mick could read into, and I introduced the Stones to thunderous applause. Mick asked for quiet and then read the piece from Shelley:

> Peace, peace! he is not dead, he doth not sleep —
> He hath awakened from the dream of life —
> 'Tis we, who lost in stormy visions, keep
> With phantoms an unprofitable strife,
> And in mad trance, strike with our spirit's knife
> Invulnerable nothings. — We decay
> Like corpses in a charnel; fear and grief
> Convulse us and consume us day by day,
> And cold hopes swarm like worms within our living clay.
>
> He has outsoared the shadow of our night;
> Envy and calumny and hate and pain,
> And that unrest which men miscall delight,
> Can touch him not and torture not again;
> From the contagion of the world's slow stain
> He is secure, and now can never mourn
> A heart grown cold, a head grown grey in vain;
> Nor, when the spirit's self has ceased to burn,
> With sparkless ashes load an unlamented urn.

The massive audience received the words of England's great poet in reverential silence. We tipped the butterflies from their baking boxes and those that had survived flapped weakly into the stifling heat and tried to escape. The stage was soon littered with their corpses. Brian, a groggy butterfly himself, would have liked that, I'm sure.

Mick then led the band into playing and used the wrong microphone for the first number. I had told him about the different mics, but such was the tension of the moment that he had forgotten. I had even made a joke of it: "One for the Shelley, two for the show." He had smirked and probably thought me a complete prat. Anyway, he forgot and I had to creep on stage and remind him. Then, in recognition of his mistake, he smiled, took his silly jacket off, and got down to the serious business of playing properly.

Nobody cared that the musicians were out of tune, and sometimes out of time. Everybody on that day simply loved the Stones for surmounting all the problems that had beset them and giving the people something for free. It was a powerful statement and it showed the establishment that the Stones, who had been mercilessly targeted by the police, were wildly popular. There was not one arrest; in fact there were no police present to make any arrests. It is significant that after the Hyde Park show the police in England were never again to harass the Rolling Stones.

The Parks Department had been somewhat concerned about the litter left behind after earlier concerts, so after the show I organized a clean-up. Literally hundreds of garbage bags were handed out to the crowd and thousands of people spent a few hours filling and returning them to a collection point, where we gave them a copy of a Stones record for their efforts. It worked a treat: a veritable pyramid of garbage was collected, and the park was left pristine. It was something of which I remain extraordinarily proud. We had managed both to have a good time and to clean up our own shit afterwards.

Exhausted and exhilarated, that evening I managed to slip away to the Albert Hall and catch Chuck Berry and the Who in concert. Mick was there with Marsha Hunt and gave me a cheery smile and a thank-you backstage. He'd had, he told me, one of the best days of his life.

CHAPTER 8

Firing Allen Klein

My next contact with the Stones came about a month later, when Mick was in Australia making the movie *Ned Kelly*. Bob Dylan was going to be playing the Isle of Wight in a few days' time and some of the Stones wanted to go. Jo Bergman asked me if I'd accompany the guys, nothing official, all very discreet. I was hip to the festival site and knew the Gunnell brothers who ran the place. It took me at least a second to say yes.

Dylan's set was not that impressive. After a long delay, The Band came on alone and played a forty-five minute warm-up that didn't gel with the crowd. Finally, Dylan slipped onto the stage in almost apologetic fashion. He only performed for just under an hour, and his set was greeted with steely silence at its premature end. His white suit made him look like some kind of salesman and he didn't appear comfortable. Some Beatles and a few Stones were down the front and perhaps this had an inhibiting effect. Two weak encores and he and The Band were gone. They had bolted like frightened rabbits.

The Great White Hope in his great white suit actually seemed a bit tame. People remembered the amphetamine attitude he'd had on his tour three years earlier, and the new laid-back Dylan just seemed to lack any kind of bite. He appeared to take a savage delight in diminishing his own "rock god" status, frustrating the expectations of his fans and coming on stage looking like a Nashville car sales worker.

After the show, the Stones and some friends wanted to visit a local restaurant for a meal. This was easier said than done. Every decent restaurant on the island was booked out, but with a few frantic telephone calls and some help from the Gunnell brothers, I managed to find a place. I'd earned my first brownie points.

The meal progressed at a lazy pace and people ordered food and plenty to drink. I had a pleasant time arguing with Charlie Watts about the peace movement and what bands could do vis-à-vis the Vietnam War. At the end of the meal, when most of the people at the table were drunk, I asked for the bill. A huge argument ensued with the restaurant owner, who had blatantly overcharged our party. In the end I made a deal and I saved our table a bunch of money, pleasing everyone.

After returning to London I was once more invited to dinner with Jo Bergman and we discussed the Stones' forthcoming trip to America. Having sworn me to secrecy, Jo explained that Mick wanted to do the tour using Ronnie Schneider as the "money man" and that the box office income was not going to go through Allen Klein's office in New York, but directly to the Stones.

Klein was, at that time, managing both the Beatles and the Stones and had frankly overstretched himself. The Stones were heartily sick of all the money hassles they'd had with Klein and were adamant that they would control the tour's box office takings. Schneider was Klein's nephew and had left Klein two weeks before agreeing with Mick that he would handle all the money transactions on behalf of the Stones. I knew nothing of these internal politics, as Jo was the height of discretion, and the band's business affairs in any case were no proper concern of mine.

This new arrangement was bound to create difficulties, Jo explained. As Klein was currently in London, a meeting had been organized. Keith would meet Klein in the Maddox Street office. Jo wanted me to collect Keith and to be there when it happened. I looked forward to what I anticipated would be a great confrontation, a moment of rock'n'roll history. I wondered if Klein had any inkling what was about to happen.

I knocked on the door of Keith's house and told a suspicious-looking little man that I was from Keith's office and had come to take him to a meeting. I retreated to the car and settled down to wait. Keith duly appeared, looking frail, stumbled down the front steps, and slumped into the back seat. I thought he was being very brave in the circumstances. It takes balls to stand up to Allen Klein, and Keith was "clucking," as we say in London, meaning he was in need of some kind of self-medication.

We arrived at the office and I went into the meeting with Keith. We sat at the pine table in a room with a pine dresser and pine chairs — pine was in fashion at the time — and awaited the man's arrival. Keith sipped a cup of tea and placed his chair so that his back was to the wall — a wise precaution, though it was well known that Klein would as soon give it to you in the front as the back. Everyone was afraid of him. I consoled myself with the grim thought: What can he do — shoot us?

A nagging voice in my head answered: "Yes, that's a distinct possibility."

Klein duly arrived and it was as if an angry elephant had suddenly appeared in the room. He bellowed, "What the fuck is this with Ronnie? Ya fuckin' know he's my family, dontcha?"

Keith looked steadily at Klein and replied, "Ronnie's going to work for us on the tour."

Klein visibly darkened. "You're taking my own fuckin' nephew from me? What the fuck are you talking about? Where's Mick?"

I calmly explained that Mick was in Australia.

Klein gave me a withering stare. "Who the fuck are you?"

"I work for the Stones," I airily replied. "Mick's away, so I'm here with Keith."

Klein leaned across to me. "I don't give a fuck *who* you are."

"Allen," said I, all sweetness and light, "you just asked me who I am, and all I did was tell you."

If looks could kill, I was a dead man. Poor Allen, I reasoned. He's a little upset. I thought it might be best to appear level-headed. "Allen," I said, "Keith wants to tell you something."

Klein fixed his malevolent stare on Keith, who stared right back: "We're going to work with Ronnie on the tour."

Klein was fit to burst. "We'll fucking see about that. No way!"

"Allen," I said, "surely Ronnie can work for whoever he likes?" I was grateful there was a table between us.

Klein stood and wagged a fat finger at Keith and me. "Ronnie ain't working for you, and the tour ain't going to happen without *me*. Forget it!" With that he stormed to the door, looked back, and snarled at me: "You, you little prick, you better watch your back!" Then he was gone.

I smiled at Keith. "Nice guy, eh?"

"That motherfucker has been dicking us around for months. Enough is enough."

I told Keith that I thought he was great standing up to Klein. "Weren't you scared?" I asked.

Keith gave me a wicked grin. He pulled out a switchblade from his pocket and stabbed it into the top of the pine table, chuckling merrily. "Fuck 'im," he said, and we both grinned like naughty schoolboys.

We left the office, Keith happy to get home as soon as possible to take the antidote to whatever it was that ailed him.

Over a late pub lunch I sat quietly trying to digest what had gone down in the meeting. The word on the street was that Klein was definitely not to be messed about. He had, shall we say, some unsavory associates.

A journalist friend of mine was working on an exposé of Klein, with some help from a disgruntled Paul McCartney, who was appalled that Klein had taken over the management of the Beatles. My friend said he'd seen a photo of Klein posing with a lupara, the four-barreled shotgun favored in Sicilian assassinations. I resolved to watch my back, and my front.

On the following day, Jo called me and offered me the job of personal tour manager for the Stones. My primary role would be to look after Mick and Keith and Mick Taylor at a house in Los Angeles, and to look after all the musicians while on tour. The rest of the details would be sorted when we got to America.

I was thrilled and hurried to the American Embassy in Grosvenor Square to get my visa. A wonderfully friendly and remarkably compliant Mrs. Worthy immediately installed the document on the spot. All of my dreams were coming true.

Even before we left London, I began to get some idea of the way the press hounded the Rolling Stones. It was at the band's Maddox Street offices that I first observed Mick's skill at dealing with hostile questioning up close. A journalist asked Mick whether he used cocaine. All of the people in the office felt uncomfortable and wondered how he was going to answer.

Mick paused theatrically before saying that he'd just seen his hairdresser and the man had offered him a line of coke. The presumption of the man! Mick assured the journalist that if cocaine was now so widely popular that hairdressers were even using it then, darling, it certainly wasn't his cup of tea; it was far too common. Of course it was all bullshit but the journalist was convinced. Nice one, Mick, I thought — but there was a lot more of this sort of thing to come.

I had a few loose ends to tie up in England before leaving. I worked on the Rugby Rag Blues Festival in Warwickshire in September 1969, featuring Pink Floyd, Free, the Nice, and Roy Harper. There was a recording session for Screw, as well, and a luscious girlfriend to deal with, who was as mad as hell and couldn't understand why I would choose the Rolling Stones and America rather than her delights.

High with the excitement of landing the job, I went in a limousine to see my mother. I thought I'd make a good impression, and show her that at long last I had "arrived." In the living room of her house in Raglan Court I sat with her and my step-father and explained all about the Hyde Park show and what a success it had been. My mother sniffed and said the Chartists had many more people at demonstrations in London in the nineteenth century. I decided not to argue the numbers point and told her instead how peaceful and decorous the crowd had been.

The fact that so many people had been well behaved was in itself unremarkable, my mother said. "After all, that's what people are supposed to do." I dropped my little triumphal presentation and explained what my new job entailed. I told her of the fabulous amount of pay I was to receive; she and her husband seemed singularly unimpressed. When I asked if she was happy for me, she gave me an almost apologetically weak smile and said: "But it's not a proper job, is it?" That was the last I was to see of my mother for a few years.

CHAPTER 9

Hurry up and wait

I flew to America with Keith Richards and Mick Taylor on October 17, 1969. Keith was happy to be on the road but sad at leaving his lady Anita and his new son, Marlon. As soon as he got onboard Keith banged down a few drinks and before long his sleeping pills had kicked in. I covered him with a blanket and made sure he was left alone. We next spoke just before we arrived in America. "Welcome to the good old U.S. of A." I said. He didn't look like he cared at all.

Mick Taylor was reading a book, so I got mildly drunk with Chrissie Shrimpton, Mick's ex-girlfriend, who talked of the different music scenes in America, and of how Americans were different to the English. She also told me some wicked gossip about Mick that doesn't bear repeating — a perfect illustration of the old adage: "Hell hath no fury like a woman scorned."

We knew about America in general terms. The Sharon Tate/Charles Manson murders had recently made headlines. Martin Luther King, Jr. had been assassinated and in response, the black ghettos of America had been razed in massive urban unrest. The Vietnam War was raging and America was divided. The Monterey Pop Festival, Woodstock: there was a new American music scene — that much we understood, but not much more. We also knew we were heading into the usual media-driven

Rolling Stones hysteria, but everyone was happy that finally the American tour was underway. Mick was in great shape and leading the charge.

Jo Bergman had rented a huge house for the Stones on Oriole Drive in Los Angeles. It had many bedrooms, an enormous swimming pool, and tennis courts, and was intended to serve as Mission Control throughout the tour. From the main living room you looked out a huge window down over Los Angeles. The view was better at night, as you couldn't see the yellow smog haze that hovered over the city by day.

It was an unsuitable location for Mick and Keith to live, though, too accessible to the public, so the singer Stephen Stills of Crosby, Stills, and Nash rented us his own house. It was ideal, hidden away at the top of Laurel Canyon.

Mick and Keith decided that they would live at the Stills house with me, and that initial rehearsals would be held in the place's converted basement. Charlie Watts and his wife Shirley, along with their lovely baby Seraphina, would live at the Oriole Drive house. Bill Wyman and his lady Astrid would stay at a hotel.

Mick Jagger decided that Mick Taylor should live with us; he was new and needed a paternal eye kept on him.

The Stills house was perfect. It came complete with Phil Kaufman installed as majordomo and general in-charge good guy. Phil had worked with everyone in the Los Angeles music business as tour manager and go-to man and, while he was geniality personified, he still took no shit from anyone. He'd looked after the Byrds and Stephen Stills and knew his way around famous musicians. He and Gram Parsons of the original Byrds were as close as any two men could be. Thanks to Phil's skilled understanding of what was required, the Stills house became a home away from home for us all.

Sharing a house with Mick, Keith, and Mick Taylor sometimes felt like living with three English gentlemen in a sedate country hotel. Most of the time the house was very quiet and that was the way everyone liked it. The house served as a retreat for Keith and Mick to write music, rehearse, and spend time together. They needed to bond musically and socially as they had, to all intents and purposes, been leading very separate musical and "pharmacological" lives of late.

I was mildly amused to note that the wild image of the Stones was at odds with their essentially English version of domesticity. We had, in effect, created a little bit of home in a foreign field, which is what the English do whenever they travel. It was all very civilized and Mick and Keith (bless 'em) were as undemanding and understated as could be.

As local guides and good-vibe factotums we had lovely twins staying at the house. Exquisite California girls who were good fun to be around, they were dubbed the "Dynamic Duo." They were supplemented by an ethereal blonde we called "Angel," who was so beautiful that she was assigned no particular role other than to sit like some delicate orchid, stunning and overwhelming one and all with her radiance. The twins adored Mick and waited on him hand and foot while Angel loved everybody and smiled to such glorious effect that we were all speechless. Everyone settled down together into that dreamy and domesticated version of satisfaction unique to the West Coast. The ladies read the tarot and gave wonderful back rubs and, if one were fortunate, offered a gentle cuddle to shoo away the blues.

In the main room of the Stills house, overlooking the pool, was a grand piano. In front of a wonderful log fire, Keith and Gram Parsons would sit at the piano and run through a massive catalog of country songs, crooning moody duets late into the night. It was one of my great privileges to see them together, happy as sandboys, singing about the despairing poor of America. I almost cried in my beer.

The Stones had originally approached country music with a certain tongue-in-cheek disdain. Gram was responsible for changing that. As he taught Keith a thousand and one country tunes, the music clearly resonated with a lonely man who was missing his lady and son back in London.

The rehearsal room in the basement had been draped with blankets to deaden the sound and was suitably funky; the musicians felt at home. Ian "Stu" Stewart, the Stones' long-time roadie, had brought over Keith's guitars and some amps and all was set for some serious work. Initially, however, nothing much happened, which was often the way with the Stones. We lounged around the pool and worked on our tans.

Mick Taylor did some guitar parts for the *Let It Bleed* album, which was being completed, but these didn't take much time. He quickly learned that being a member of the Rolling Stones can involve a lot of waiting. I set about learning my way around Los Angeles so that I wouldn't get lost when we drove down to the Oriole house for various tour-related meetings. Other than that I hung out and sampled the delights of California grass and the twins, who were patiently waiting for Mick to show them some attention.

Driving on what for us was the wrong side of the road presented no problems, though it was firmly established by Mick and Ronnie Schneider that none of the musicians were allowed to drive alone. Insurance considerations simply didn't allow for such recklessness, and in any case Keith was known to be an eccentric driver, to say the least. Keith might survive the experience but the car would inevitably suffer the consequences. I drove Keith wherever he wanted to go.

Keith would get dressed up, decide we were going to some club, announce the intended destination, and then flop out in the back of the car — out to the world. On our first such foray, Keith was passed out on the back seat and I was driving down Sunset Boulevard on the way to the Ash Grove club on Melrose. Suddenly, Keith sat up in terror and screamed, "You're on the wrong side of the road!" I screamed right back, "Keef, this is America!" He flopped back down and was asleep before his head hit the seat. The human riff possessed the ability to fall asleep in any position anywhere and at any time, but once in a while he had nightmares. My driving didn't help.

The Rolling Stones had pretty much been away from the music scene for three years. At the height of their fame, their concerts would last for perhaps twenty minutes before the stage was swamped by screaming teenagers and the show would have to be abandoned. A Stones show in the U.K. invariably ended in a full-scale riot. The band often played in inappropriate venues with terrible PAs and their equipment was frequently wrecked.

Production values seemed to be of little concern, as no one expected their gigs to last that long — and hardly anyone came to Rolling Stones concerts to listen to what they were playing. The forthcoming American tour, the Stones soon realized, was going to be different; they were going to have to deliver the goods. In America, people actually listened to music.

Mick handled all the planning with practiced aplomb. I never once heard him raise his voice, though occasional flashes of impatience sometimes surfaced. He would have made a perfect diplomat, such was his self-control and grasp of the essentials. He assumed his role as the general in charge of the rock'n'roll army without batting an eyelid. He was one impressive cat.

As I watched Mick operate, I couldn't think of anyone, other than jazzmen Duke Ellington and Count Basie, who'd exercised such control over their musical and business affairs. The bottom line loomed as large in Mick's calculations as the performance. The emphasis was on the music, but he was also very much concerned with "a fair day's work for a fair day's pay." And the Stones needed the money.

This tour was going to be unlike any the band had ever done. They would travel with their own PA, which was a first, and for once Mick would have foldback speakers that enabled him to hear what was going on as they played. Their amplifiers would be capable of projecting their sound to the largest auditoriums. Each show would have the same production. The stage would be dressed with its own carpet, and this, like everything else, would travel from show to show. The production for the tour was put together by the Bill Graham organization, in the shape of Chip Monk, and was handled with a professionalism that the Stones had never hitherto experienced.

Chip Monk, known by all as "Chipmunk," was the master of minutiae; no production detail escaped his attention. It was interesting to watch him gently guide Mick through what was necessary to making shows a success. Lighting was of vital importance to the overall effect, and Chip explained the nuances to Mick with an authoritative voice. Mick soaked up Chip's suggestions with eager enthusiasm; I kept my mouth shut and learned from a master.

Ronnie Schneider was an interesting man. He looked as if he didn't belong on a rock'n'roll tour and dressed like he was about to play golf, but he was smart and tough. No one fucked with Ronnie, including his uncle Allen, who had conceded that Ronnie could work for whoever he liked. Ronnie smiled a lot in private and was suitably heavy in public, which was reassuring. I liked him immediately. The Stones needed a heavy when it came to money matters, and Ronnie should have received an Oscar, he was that impressive. Mick trusted him, and what's more, secretly adored him.

When I first met Ronnie, he looked up as I came into the room. "You got any money?" he asked me.

"No," I said, as no one had thought to give me any. "Have you?"

Ronnie smiled and took me off into the corner and gave me 500 bucks, telling me to be sure, if I could, to get receipts for whatever I spent. I signed for the money. How could I not like the man? I resolved from the outset to work closely with him and knew instinctively that our getting along was vital to the tour. Ronnie took care of the money and I took care of delivering the musicians. It was not a problem; we made sure of that.

Klein was nominally still the manager of the Rolling Stones and yet he had nothing to do with the tour. I just assumed that Klein's contract with the group did not cover personal appearances and gigs. There was no question that he was persona non grata on the tour, and as far as I know no one from the Stones spoke with Klein or his office on tour matters. Ronnie was solely responsible for the funds that went to the Stones' own company, which had been specially set up for the tour.

There was a standing instruction from Mick that the telephone at the Stills house was to be answered only by Phil Kaufman and that Mick would talk to no one but members of the band and Jo Bergman. Klein called several times and left messages but never got through. Everyone, Mick demanded, had to leave a message, with Kaufman telling one and all that the Stones were "unavailable." The phone never stopped ringing and we just learned to ignore it. Klein might have had more chance of talking to the pope than he did of talking to Mick.

A bodyguard duly arrived, an affable African-American named Tony Funches. He was a former boxing champion of the U.S. Marines, and was, as Mick remarked, a magnificent specimen. He must have felt like a spare prick at the wedding, though, for the biggest threat to anyone's safety was the occasional horny lady who was desperate to give whatever she had to whoever in the band was prepared to take it.

The two Micks, Keith, Gram, and I would regularly go to L.A. nightclubs without bodyguards before Tony arrived, and never had any hassles. But everybody felt comfortable around Tony and he slowly became part of our little entourage. His presence seemed to make the musicians feel secure, though in my innocence I asked myself: Who needs protecting from women? Little did I know! The one time we did need protection from a woman, poor Tony was at a loss to know what to do.

We were staying at a hotel in New York. Mick and I descended to the lobby, where we met Tony, and set off toward a waiting limousine. An elderly woman, who had to be in her seventies, approached Mick, saying, "I want to show you something." Mick, ever the gentleman, stopped to speak and the woman pulled out a Polaroid of herself, lying naked on a bed, legs akimbo. She thrust it into Mick's face.

Mick shrank back and muttered, "That's disgusting," where-upon the woman lunged and managed to grasp his hair in both hands. They collapsed to the sidewalk, Mick frantically scream-ing, "Get her off me!" What was our brave bodyguard Tony to do? Knock her out? It was an absurd scene: the pin-up boy of rock'n'roll grasped tightly by a demented and very determined grandmother.

Yelling "Don't hurt her!" as loudly as I could, I managed to get one of her hands off Mick while the woman struggled and hung on tightly with her other hand. It was ridiculous, but finally, after much shouting and screaming, with Tony hanging on to the hand I had managed to get free, I gave the old lady a mild Indian burn and a frightened Mick was released. He scampered into the limousine, horrified, and I must say he had my sympathy.

Meanwhile, Tony stood on the pavement and held the old lady, who was kicking and screaming in the air. After that Mick didn't stop to talk to anyone, especially elderly women. The former U.S. Marine was a great guy but he wasn't much use when it came to a demented granny; a trick learned in a school playground was a better option than a punch.

Before long I would learn just how much trouble the Stones had with women. Girls would do literally anything to get to the band. In a very drunken moment late one night in a hotel bar, Bill Wyman suggested that when I was approaching various ladies at Rolling Stones concerts I should conduct a survey of their morals, or more accurately their *lack* of morals. Bill was a good man to share a drink or three with, and definitely loved the ladies — he was in many respects a man after my own heart. It was his jovial suggestion that I inquire of the fairer sex, "How would you like to meet the Rolling Stones — and fuck me?" When the tour kicked off, I gave it a try — and lo and behold, at least 90 per cent of my subjects of interest agreed with alacrity and were quite prepared to consummate the deal upon the spot. Never being one to disappoint a fan, I did my best and gave as good as I got. It was all great fun and seriously exhausting.

CHAPTER 10

Play that country music, white boy

While we planned the tour, Keith and Mick supervised the completion of *Let It Bleed*, to my mind one of their greatest albums.

I had watched Mick at Olympic Studios in London, talking with the choir who sang on "You Can't Always Get What You Want," and had been amused at the choir's very English pronunciation of the word "want." Mick wanted it to come out sounding like "wa-ant" rather than the usual crisp English pronunciation. He struggled for hours with some uptight vocalists who seemed to think the whole thing was beneath them.

He finally surrendered and went with what he got — an English choir that could never bring itself to sound American. What they delivered vocally seemed oddly unsuitable to the song, and yet here in Los Angeles, with some judicious mixing, producer Jimmy Miller and Mick made it work. The choir, in a fit of pique, demanded to be removed from what they thought to be a degenerate example of popular culture but somehow or other their contribution remained intact. In many ways it made the track.

Let It Bleed's "Country Honk" was a fun track, and I got to be directly involved. Gram Parsons had recommended that a superb country fiddle player called Byron Berline do the overdub, and everyone was amazed when this country gentleman in a beautifully cut western suit and a huge Stetson hat arrived at the studio. He talked with the deepest of southern accents, slow and deliberate, and Mick had to call up his considerable diplomatic reserves to deal with him. Straight bluegrass musicians weren't often found hanging out with the Stones in the studio, and this was a first for all concerned.

The existing track was played while Mr. Berline (no one called him Byron) listened. Mick explained where he wanted the solo and what kind of feel he was after. In due course the track was recorded. Mick wasn't happy; they changed the microphone, yet once more it lacked that certain pizzazz. Mick suddenly had a flash of inspiration: the violin should be recorded in the control booth rather than in the studio proper, so we tried that.

Mr. Berline stood beside the mixing desk and listened to the playback at what must have seemed to him like earth-shattering volume and appeared to grimace. Encouraged by Mick, he once more gave the track his best effort, but the results were unsatisfactory. Mick then suggested very respectfully to Mr. Berline that what he really wanted to do was to record the violin in the open air. The country gent graciously allowed what he probably thought to be a bunch of slack English rockers to have their way. He seemed grateful to be going outside.

A long microphone lead was strung out and the fiddler stood by the studio's back door and recorded the track. Passing traffic could clearly be heard on the take and Mr. Berline was very unsure as to its suitability, but Mick assured him that he loved it so much that he now wanted him to stand right beside the road, outside the studio, so that we could record the sounds of Los Angeles along with the fiddle. He must have thought we were mad. A microphone was set up beside our limousine, which was parked in the street, and Mick stood in the doorway of the studio.

Then a further "flash" from an enthused Jagger: he wanted me to sit in the driver's seat of the limo and press the horn when he gave the signal. Mr. Berline, wearing headphones and a grim expression, stood on the curb and gave it his best shot. With Mick gesticulating theatrically, I pressed the horn at his command.

The results can be heard on *Let It Bleed*. Funky as hell and the car horn was played with expressive timbre and perfect control, I must say.

Needless to say I didn't get any credit for my invaluable contribution.

Let It Bleed was due to be released in November and there were lots of overdubs to be completed. The local branch of the American Federation of Musicians in Los Angeles complained about the Stones working in the studio, as their work visas were strictly for concerts. A visit to the Oriole house by some union heavies — who met a couple of band members and received some signed albums, plus front row seats to the band's L.A. shows — seemed to do the trick.

CHAPTER 11

The greatest
rock'n'roll band in the world?

Apart from the music, there was only one other major problem
for the Rolling Stones, and that was the press campaign waged
over ticket prices for their concerts. For the shows scheduled at
the L.A. Forum prices ranged from $5.50 to $8.50, which com-
pared unfavorably with the $7.50 top price charged for Blind
Faith or $6.50 for the Doors. The Stones' Los Angeles concerts
alone would have an expected gross of $275,000.

No sooner had the tickets gone on sale than respected *San
Francisco Chronicle* journalist Ralph J. Gleason began a one-
man campaign against the Stones, a campaign I always believed
to have been initiated at the behest of promoter Bill Graham,
who resented the Stones' demands for a larger-than-usual share
of their box office returns.

In his column, Gleason suggested that the Stones had a bad
attitude toward their public, and asked whether any band could
need so much money. He disingenuously suggested that as virtually all the riffs the Stones played were based upon black
music, then surely they should share the money with the black
artists they had on the bill.

Mick sneered at Gleason's criticisms during a press conference in the Beverly Wilshire Hotel. "Either you're going to sing
and all that crap or you're going to be a fucking economist . . .

I really don't know whether this is more expensive than recent tours by local bands . . . I don't know how much people can afford. I've no idea. You tell me."

Ticket scalpers in L.A. were already moving the $8.50 tickets for $40. People wanted to see the Stones. They were more than happy to pay the ticket price, even more if necessary, but the press refused to let the matter drop. Mick rather defensively suggested that the Stones might be open to doing a free concert that would go some way to mitigating the perception they were only doing this for the money.

Rock Scully's proposal had now made its way from London to America and had perversely insinuated itself into the debate about ticket prices.

Gleason, like every other journalist who criticized the Stones, received money for the words he wrote, and the irony of his attacks upon the Stones for wanting to be paid for the work they did seemed lost on everyone. Mick commented to me, "The Americans don't do irony; it's simply an alien concept for most of them, poor dears. They're an unsophisticated lot."

Gleason's irrational attacks were to have a far-reaching effect. The Stones felt vulnerable to the suggestion that they were somehow being greedy. This in turn led to the idea that they "owed" their American public. The Stones bought into the idea that by playing for free they would be giving something back to their "exploited" fans.

It was stinking thinking, unrealistic and too convenient to be true. It would also have dire consequences, but unfortunately we didn't see the disaster coming.

As the opening tour dates grew closer, the sense of anticipation within the band morphed into growing concern about the state of the music they were playing. Keith was occupied playing the "white man's blues" with Gram Parsons. Mick spent most of his time on arrangements for the tour and on finishing *Let It Bleed*, while Charlie had his wife and child to keep him busy. Bill Wyman hung out with Astrid and played tennis.

We'd been in America for two weeks and although everyone realized the band wasn't in good shape, no one had actually played together yet. Rehearsals began at the Stills house and were off-limits to everyone but the band, Ian "Stu" Stewart, and myself.

They certainly didn't sound like "the greatest rock'n'roll band in the world" — far from it. They all sounded like they needed a good kick up the bum, and they knew it. Jamming in the basement of a house in Laurel Canyon is not the best preparation for playing at Madison Square Garden; it soon became painfully apparent to Mick and Keith that full rehearsals under concert conditions were needed.

A soundstage became available at the Warner Brothers film studios in Burbank, and Chip Monk and the production crew reproduced a full stage as it was to be used on the tour.

Rehearsals duly began, and I have never seen so much aimless hanging around in all my life. With the tour just around the corner, no one seemed to be in any kind of hurry. I'd be with the two Micks and Keith up at the Stills house and gently remind them that rehearsals were to begin at a certain time; we'd eventually arrive some three or four hours late. It was then that I realized Charlie Watts and Bill Wyman had to be the most patient people in the history of rock'n'roll. Bill and Charlie accepted their bandmates' tardiness with a good grace bordering upon saintliness.

The Stones have always been what I call a "pressure" band — when they are finally backed into a corner, with only hours to come up with the goods, then they finally find it within themselves to deliver. It should also be remembered that after three years of not playing live, it was a miracle that anyone could remember the songs, let alone play the bloody things.

As the tour got closer, the band slowly but surely dragged themselves into shape. Within a week they sounded as if they had played together all their lives. Keith sorted the band, Mick sorted the vocals, Charlie sorted the beat, and Bill followed it.

Mick Taylor followed Keith's lead. If one discounts the days spent mucking about while personnel were located and lighting cues were established and equipment hassles resolved, the entire musical content of the 1969 tour was worked out and rehearsed in the equivalent of about three days of serious work.

It was rough but it was ready. Supremely vulnerable and so very mortal, it felt as if it might fall apart at any moment, yet it struggled and fought its way to a wonderful cohesion and vitality. Seeing the Stones getting their music together was like watching a baby being born. It was messy but somehow it was miraculous and most importantly, it lived.

In the course of all this activity, various people had been renting cars and some of these cars had been misplaced. A quick audit came up with the alarming reality that some seventeen cars had been rented, yet we could only find three sets of keys. Into this conundrum stepped a man whose participation in the tour was to have catastrophic effects. Where he came from, and how he got involved, was a mystery at the time, but with the passage of years his genesis has become clearer.

This paunchy character called himself John Jaymes. This was not his proper name. He told us that he had been sent by the Chrysler Corporation, a tour sponsor, to sort out the car mess. Meanwhile, he told Chrysler that he worked for the Rolling Stones.

Jaymes's persuasive skills fooled everybody, and overnight he had insinuated himself into the heart of the tour arrangements.

When we complained about the Stills house being virtually overrun by teenage girls, Jaymes became a "security consultant" and a group of moonlighting NYPD detectives appeared. They were armed to the teeth and scarily heavy, though they proved to be hopeless at keeping girls away from the Stones.

The cops couldn't believe their luck at having such a groovy assignment, and many a middle-aged policeman thought he'd died and gone to heaven as sweet young things offered him anything just to get close to the band. When I complained, one of the cops shrugged and explained that none of his men could resist the charms on offer. These were hardened policemen who were quite prepared to shoot someone if necessary and yet they couldn't refuse sexual favors — it was pathetic.

John Jaymes now sat at the center of operations with a bunch of heavies who were answerable solely to him. No one had hired him, the Rolling Stones were not paying him, and yet he seemed to have limitless funds and endless influence. There were now more than 100 people directly involved in the tour. It had become the largest operation ever mounted by an English band in America.

Jaymes assured me that no one would get busted while he and his men were around and of course this was music to our ears. Little did any of us know that our involvement with him would have bizarre and long-lasting consequences.

The coordination of the huge numbers of people involved in the overall production was left to Chip Monk and Bill Belmont, who had been seconded from Bill Graham's outfit to take care of the hotel arrangements.

The musicians took care of the music and had little to no idea of who individual people were and what their role on the tour was. I was in the same boat. It was as if we were traveling around America with a few familiar faces sprinkled among an anonymous group of strangers. When the band members were traveling no one approached them; I interacted with the outside world on their behalf and dealt with anything that arose.

Charlie was the only one who seemed to take any interest in who was who. Once, on a crowded tour bus headed to an airport, Charlie pointed to Jaymes and asked me, "Who's that man?" I explained that he had been sent by Chrysler to sort out the rental car mess. Sitting next to Jaymes was an old lady, who looked completely out of place — absurdly so. I had never seen her before. Charlie asked who she was, so I went to find out. We were introduced by Jaymes, who told me it was his mother. The woman didn't say a word and looked decidedly uncomfortable.

I was shocked and amused. Here was a little old lady with her gray hair and handbag sitting in the middle of a bunch of armed off-duty NYPD narcs on a bus with the Rolling Stones; it was too incongruous for words.

Charlie grinned and shook his head in that bemused wonderment which is his personal trademark, and asked, "Why would you bring your mother on tour with us?"

It was strange, but we could handle strange.

In addition to the growing numbers of crew and support staff, the tour had its own "writer in residence," Stanley Booth, and a photographer, who were granted all-areas access.

Stanley Booth wrote a Stones book that is considered a classic by some. According to this book I am supposed to have made love ten times in a day to a woman who was working at the Stills house. Now I know why Stanley always looked at me so strangely — he was jealous! I have read hundreds of pages of stuff written on the Stones and most of it is absolute tripe. The Stones gave up reading books about themselves in the mid-'60s.

Ethan Russell was the tour photographer. Everyone loved Ethan and the Stones knew him well, so he was free to shoot whenever and wherever. An event happens, the picture gets taken, and the camera rarely lies — a photographer's work is so much simpler than a wordsmith's. Ethan's pictures captured the tour's triumphs and disasters and they stand as a testament to an historic event. His pictures are immortalized in *Let It Bleed*, the most beautiful (and expensive) book of photographs ever produced on a rock'n'roll band. I'm proud to have recently received a signed copy from Ethan.

The first date of the tour would be on November 7 at a sports arena in Fort Collins, Colorado, home to a university and thousands of nubile youngsters. They would be a perfect first audience for the Stones. Everyone in the touring party nevertheless viewed the upcoming date with some trepidation, for at the very moment when it had all more or less come together we had run out of time for further fine-tuning of the show.

I stood with Ronnie Schneider and a few others in L.A. and watched the last rehearsal. It was good but it wasn't great.

I was wondering whether the music would cut it when I saw a couple of young Hollywood girls watching the proceedings. I walked over to them and asked them what they thought, and one of them replied, with stars in her eyes, "Oh, they're the greatest rock'n'roll band in the world!"

I didn't argue with her, but laughed cynically inside and began to worry that maybe we would be in the horrible position of delivering shit and pretending it was sugar. I reminded myself that the Stones absolutely thrived on pressure.

On the plane to Colorado, Ronnie and I went over the details of the show, and we realized that one simple fact had been overlooked: there was no one to introduce the band. A quick word with our beloved leader soon sorted that one out. Mick suggested that I do it, and (of course) I agreed.

I sat thinking about what I was to say when the vacuous comment of the girls at the rehearsal came to mind: "The greatest rock'n'roll band in the world!"

That would make the band work ferociously hard.

At the show that night, an expectant audience of around 10,000 students sat sedately on their chairs, greeting the opening acts with subdued enthusiasm.

It was time to stir things up a little, so when I walked out on stage, I grabbed the mic and screamed, "Ladies and gentlemen, the greatest rock'n'roll band in the world: the Rolling Stones!" There was thunderous applause. Without looking at Mick, I ducked to my position at the side of the stage and left the Stones to do their thing.

The show was hard going, yet Mick worked his butt off and in the end the students responded and crowded to the front and yelled delightedly for more. I led the band back to the dressing room, Keith and Charlie in earnest discussion about the correct feel for various songs. Mick fixed me with a baleful stare and said we had to talk.

"Sam, when you're introducing the band, *please* don't call us the greatest rock'n'roll band in the world."

I replied like some London gangster: "Well, either you fuckin' are or you ain't. What the fuck is it gonna be?"

Mick said nothing as he pondered the two alternatives. He looked a trifle gloomy, so I left him alone with his thoughts.

Whether Mick liked it or not, I used that intro for every date of the tour, and for a few glorious weeks in 1969 that's what the Stones became — the greatest rock'n'roll band in the world. Fuck it, this was a rock'n'roll show, there was no time for being coy. In the world of rock'n'roll dreams, only the best will be remembered. All the others fade into lonely obscurity.

I said nothing further on the subject but was secretly rather pleased at my little dabble in reverse psychology and was inordinately proud to be working for a band that actually knew how to aspire to greatness.

CHAPTER 12

Los Angeles

The L.A. Forum seated close to 18,000 people. Two Forum shows had been sold out in eight hours and the Stones were only to receive twenty-five complimentary tickets for each show, which was absurd. The number of people hanging around the tour easily exceeded that. A lot of friends of the band were going to be very disappointed.

Those who had no tickets began to devise strategies for getting into the Forum on the night. One method was to ride in the limousines with the band. The limos would drive straight into the facility and deposit one and all backstage. I managed to smuggle in several friends of the band this way.

Of course there were other slightly less conventional ways of gaining access to a Rolling Stones show. There's many a surprised security man who can testify that the ladies would do anything to gain admittance. I mean *anything*.

One very strange man managed to get himself and several friends inside in a very unique way. I had met this man twice before at various gigs we had attended in Los Angeles, and he was a good friend of the Grateful Dead. Everyone called him Goldfinger, though not to his face. His real name was Ken Connell and we were eventually to become firm friends.

Goldfinger and I had first met at the Ash Grove, where I had taken Keith and the two Micks to see blues great Taj Mahal. The hottest band in the world were seated in a small booth and enjoying themselves as I wandered to the bar. I had just ordered a drink when a man with one arm and a shock of flaming red hair sidled up to me, grinning broadly. He introduced me to his two stunning lady friends, who positioned themselves on either side of me as I tried to pay attention to what Goldfinger was saying while keeping a wary eye on my band.

With the ladies in tow, we retired to the manager's office for a chat. With his one good arm, Goldfinger pulled off his large shoulder bag and dumped a veritable treasure trove of drugs onto the desk. One-handed, he flicked open a large buck knife and chopped some massive lines of coke for the girls and me to snort. Making my excuses, and now pleasantly high, I left to rejoin the group.

The Stones were watching the show and oblivious to the fact that I had been missing, but Keith spotted the white powder on the end of my nose and demanded to know where I had got it. He wanted to go to the office, too. I got everything arranged in double-quick time.

Within five minutes I was back in the small office with Keith and Goldfinger and the two lovely ladies. I introduced Keith to Goldfinger, who grinned sheepishly and once again dumped the contents of his bag onto the desk.

Our new best friend produced a giant rock of coke and with his buck knife skillfully managed to split the rock in two. He picked up half and gave it to Keith, who slipped it into his waist-coat pocket with a grin and a "thanks, man." We were all happy to get acquainted.

The girls eyed Keith with suitably predatory smiles, and I considered leaving him to it. But Keith wasn't interested; grinning, he told them, "Ladies, I gotta hear the music. Taj is a friend." He left to go back to his seat while the ladies shrugged and attacked the remaining lines on the desk.

Goldfinger wanted to talk and I gave him the number at the

Stills house. I told him to say that his name was Ken and he was to ask for me. If anyone asked who he was and how he got the number, he was to say that he was making tour clothes for Keith. He was staying at the Chateau Marmont and invited me to drop by after the gig. First, though, I had to see everyone safely home.

Goldfinger, like everyone else in Los Angeles, wanted tickets to the Forum show, and was heartily disappointed that I couldn't oblige. I repeatedly told him that I had no tickets and that I couldn't get any, for love or money, both of which he offered in copious quantities, until I finally made him understand my predicament.

On the night of the Forum show we eventually managed to get the band together in one place, plus as many others as we could squeeze into the cars, and a veritable fleet of limousines left for the gig. Unbeknownst to me, or to anyone else, Goldfinger, accompanied by four beautiful women, simply added his limousine to our fleet. Keith and I chuckled as we got out of the limo to see Goldfinger and his pretty girls arranging their clothes and getting ready to party. I found him a spare room backstage in which to hang out and went to sort out some passes.

The promoter gave me twenty from a huge pile he had on his desk and I returned and gave five to Goldfinger. He was delighted and rewarded me with my own little packet of goodies. I left to take care of business and immediately ran into Keith and Gram Parsons.

Keith wanted to know where Goldfinger was and I took him and Gram to the room where I had him stashed. With one of John Jaymes's cops standing guard outside, the two musicians, like naughty reprobates, made their way into an L.A. version of paradise and emerged a few minutes later wiping their noses and grinning. It looked like it was going to be a good night.

There had been considerable discussion among the tour party about how onstage security was to be handled. In the past, the Stones would play, the kids would go crazy, the cops and security would get nervous, and before you knew it a full-scale riot had erupted. Mick was determined that he didn't want this to happen in America, that it would look bad if the band played behind a phalanx of uniformed police, and that we would handle the onstage security.

It was decided that I would be stage left, behind the PA stack, and Tony Funches would be stage right. The stage would be built as high as possible so that it was difficult to access from the front, and if anyone managed to get onstage, I would grab them and lead them off with the help of the crew. If things looked like they were really getting out of hand, Tony would intervene.

It was also my job to hold a basket of rose petals that, at a suitable moment in the show, Mick would toss by the handful into the audience.

The Stones finally hit the stage two hours late and the audience went ballistic. I marveled at how the band had managed to pull it all together. The L.A. shows were a triumph. The Stones took everything that their fans wanted and served it up as hot as possible. Mick was stunning, a frontman without peer, an entertainer, dancer, vocalist, and focus of attention who had no equal (except, perhaps, for opener Tina Turner, who outdid him in the animal magnetism stakes). The Forum shows were a taste of things to come, with thousands of people leaving their seats and rushing forward to get as close to the stage as possible; no amount of security could control that craziness.

Still, for a band that had been used to having their clothes ripped from their backs and having to flee for their lives at most of their shows, the Forum was a revelation — people were actually listening to what they were playing.

There was one slightly disturbing moment between shows when John Jaymes told me he had to talk to me in private. Did I know this guy with the red hair and the girls, he asked? Yes, I knew him, he was a friend of the band, I lied. Jaymes looked very worried. But did I know who he was? No, I replied disingenuously, he's just another one of the band's unusual friends. Jaymes gave me a withering stare. "That man is a drug dealer!" I feigned astonishment. Jaymes continued his rap with a strange intensity.

"Not only is he a drug dealer, he's a well-known drug dealer and every cop in California knows him. The Feds are after him." I stared hard at Jaymes. "Well, why don't they arrest him?" I asked in theatrical innocence. Jaymes sighed. "Sam, you don't understand" — which was true — "we simply can't have him around the band; it don't look good and is going to cause endless hassles for everyone. Get rid of him."

I wondered why a man who said he came from Chrysler would be so bothered about such a thing. As far as I could tell, one half of Los Angeles was made up of drug dealers, while the other half was made up of drug consumers. It all seemed pretty normal to me. America was awash with drugs and they were the least of my concerns. I had a band to take care of; the drugs could take care of themselves. I filed away Jaymes's preoccupations and decided to address the issue when we had more time. There was the Forum show to complete and on the following day we were to be in Oakland.

CHAPTER 13

Bill Graham

Bill Graham had wanted to promote all the dates on the tour, but Ronnie, in consultation with Mick, decided that different promoters should be involved. Bill Graham liked to think of himself as the greatest showman on earth and had an ego that would have dwarfed Napoleon's. Most of the Stones found him to be insufferably arrogant, though everyone conceded that his production crew was the best in America.

Graham was unhealthily obsessed with the Stones and felt wounded at not being given control of all the dates. In spite, he formed an alliance with journalist Ralph Gleason. Bill was a schmuck, and lest anyone think I'm speaking badly of the dead, there are many people who will testify that I regularly called him a schmuck (and worse) to his face. I detested the way he did business and I thought that his attitude to other promoters, bands, managers, and agents was predatory — what *Peter Pan*'s Captain Hook would call "poor form."

The Oakland Coliseum gig on November 9, 1969, brought Bill Graham into direct confrontation with the Rolling Stones, and I'm proud to say the band won that particular battle. Graham rarely got bested or beaten, but in this particular case he was thoroughly humiliated and it was something for which he never forgave the Stones or me. He held me to blame for his comeuppance. Later disasters, confrontations, and bad-tempered miscalculations can be directly traced back to that night.

The Oakland show was sold out, and it was the custom at the time to "turn the house," which means that two separate shows were scheduled for the same evening. After the first show there would be an interval as the audience for the second show entered and were seated. The first gig was really good, except that Keith's amplifiers quit toward the end and in sheer frustration he had pushed the whole stack over, signaling a not totally satisfactory end to the entertainment.

Various equipment guys from the Grateful Dead were present backstage as supplementary crew for Bill Graham, and they volunteered to race across the Bay Bridge to Marin County and bring some of the Dead's equipment for Keith to use in the second show. We settled down for what would prove to be a long wait between shows.

The dressing rooms at the Coliseum were very basic, like the locker rooms for a football team. There were hard wooden benches along the walls and strip fluorescent lights that bathed the whole area in a harsh glare. The Graham organization had provided a buffet of cold cuts and salad that sat on a series of long trestle tables covered in white tablecloths. None of the band was happy and Keith was completely outraged at the equipment failure.

No one was to be allowed into the dressing room and a succession of Bay Area music stars who wanted to say hello were kept well away. There was some serious sulking going on. To break the monotony, I walked to the backstage area with Charlie Watts to see how things were progressing with the replacement gear, which was frantically being assembled by the Dead's crew.

A man was kneeling on the stage with his back to us; he slapped a girl who was trying to get up onto the stage apron. "Who's that guy?" said Charlie. "Look at what he's doing to that bird! Get him off the stage right now; we can't have people behaving like that."

I walked from behind the back line of amplifiers and approached the man, who was still on his hands and knees trying to push the girl back down into the front row seats. I grabbed his shoulder and pulled him to his feet. "Leave it out, mate, she's not a problem. Just get off the stage and we'll deal with it. If there are slappers to be slapped, we'll do the slapping."

He went ballistic and started screaming, much to the audience's amusement. "Who the fuck do you think you're talking to? I'm Bill Graham, the promoter of this show; this is my stage." It was the first time I had actually set eyes on Graham.

"This is the Rolling Stones' stage, mate," I said, and threw a wild punch at him. Graham was obviously not too popular with the audience and people booed and yelled like a crowd at a dogfight. In the full glare of the house lights and spurred on by the jeers of the crowd, punching and scratching like two women having a cat fight, Bill Graham and I rolled under the piano with various members of our respective security details trying to separate us. It was not a pretty sight, though I must say that the audience loved it. Bill Graham was being challenged on his own turf and I suspect that most of the crowd thought it was about time.

In due course we were unglued and with a burly security guard's arms around him, Bill stood and screamed that the second show would not happen while I remained in the house. He didn't care how much money it cost him.

This was the promoter? I was flabbergasted.

In the dressing room Charlie told the other members of the band what had happened and everyone shrugged. Big deal!

Then Graham came shouting at the door, which Tony was guarding under strict instructions that no one was to enter — especially Graham. I decided to confront him and get the bullshit over with. Ronnie Schneider came to my aid.

Outside the dressing room, in a narrow corridor, two sets of armed heavies eyeballed one another as Ronnie and I slipped into the narrow space between them and tried to make peace.

Bill pointed at me and demanded hysterically that I leave the building or the second show was not going to happen. We tried to explain that canceling the show would produce a first-class riot but Graham refused to listen.

Finally, Ronnie had enough of the histrionics and swung his briefcase with a well aimed blow at Bill's family jewels. The two bunches of heavies intervened, tackling Ronnie and Bill, and at that moment I was grabbed by the scruff of the neck by Keith Richards, who dragged me inside the dressing-room. "Stay in 'ere, don't get involved," Keith ordered. I did what I was told. Two minutes later, a flushed and angry Ronnie made it back through the door and we considered the situation.

Mick, having been briefed by Charlie as to what had happened on stage, seemed singularly unimpressed with Graham's bluster, but his attitude changed when Ronnie reported that the rival groups of heavies were looking like they were about to do some serious damage. We could still hear Bill screaming outside the door and I begged Mick to talk to him to calm him down.

Bill was let into the dressing room and his eyes immediately alighted on me. He let out another torrent of foul abuse, quite literally foaming at the mouth, while Mick sat waiting for the storm to pass.

At last Graham ground to a halt and Mick gave him one of his most withering haughty stares. Then, in his finest English accent, and with a slightly surprised look on his face, he asked Bill, "Who are you?"

Poor Bill. I almost felt sorry for him; he worshiped Mick.

"I'm Bill Graham," he stammered, "I'm the promoter."

Mick looked at him like an Englishman looks at his dog in a park when it's taking a shit.

"Bill Graham," Mick replied in a we-are-not-amused tone. "Didn't I speak to you on the telephone once?"

Bill was mortified. "Yes, I'm the promoter. I spoke to you when you were in London."

Mick gave a little toss of his head, puckered his lips, and then let out a long and theatrical sigh. "Yeeeees," he said, and gave a little shudder.

The room was completely silent.

Mick continued with his regal tone. "I remember you. You were rude to me on the telephone; you yelled at me from San Francisco. I simply cannot bear people who shout on the telephone; it's appallingly bad taste. I most certainly do not want to speak to you until you've developed some manners."

With that, in his finest camp manner, Mick turned his back on Bill Graham, picked up a makeup stick, and busied himself applying rouge to his cheeks. Talking into the mirror, where he could see Bill's stupefied reflection, Mick made his final pronouncement: "We'll be on in a few minutes, Mr. Graham. Now please don't be so dreary, you know of all people that the show must go on. Sam works for me, he's a naughty boy, but he does work for me, not you. I'll decide what happens to Sam."

Mick then swiveled round and stared at Bill with savage intensity and growled: "The show will go on."

Bill was ushered speechless from the royal presence. Mick gave me a wink, and I was overcome with gratitude. Keith grinned and walked to the table covered in food, picked up a paper plate, and proceeded to smear some ghastly potato salad all over a picture of Bill Graham which Graham had thoughtfully put up on the dressing-room wall.

Order had been restored.

Bill realized that it was time to get the boys on stage immediately and to save his personal hostility to me for another day.

Keith left to go to the stage and check his replacement equipment and I sat down for a moment to gather my thoughts. Were the Rolling Stones responsible? Whenever people dealt with the band they seemed to lose all restraint and decorum. It was all so tacky, so vulgar. It worried me deeply, but I then received a message to go to the box office and had to get back to business.

America was a pretty crazy place.

On the way backstage from the front of the house I ran into

a very worried-looking Ian Stewart. "Oy, Sam, those weird bloody Grateful Dead people are smoking this gear that makes the amps go all funny and people fall over."

I laughed at Stu and gently explained that nobody had gear that made you fall over. He then said that the amps were behaving strangely and giving off a weird smell. I asked Stu if he'd smoked some of the stuff, but immediately regretted it. Stu didn't smoke anything and held pot-smoking hippies in utter contempt. He gave me a withering stare and I decided that I had better investigate what the hell was going on.

We were running three hours late.

Keith was standing on stage with a stack of Jerry Garcia's McIntosh amps wired together with a total power output that would have been five or six times anything Keith had ever seen before, let alone played through. He was strumming the odd chord on his guitar and looking at the amp stack with nervous bewilderment while Ramrod, the Grateful Dead's main equipment man, was frantically trying to modify the output to his liking.

Right behind Keith's stack of amps was a funny-looking man, short and stocky, with rimless glasses, surrounded by some ten people. Some were standing, some were lounging, some were lying flat on their backs, and there was the most awful smell of burning plastic in the air. This was unusual, as normally when the Stones played no one was allowed to be on the stage, let alone within touching distance of the amps.

Keith was trying to get used to the amps, but the sheer power of the McIntosh gear was blowing him sideways. The sound was too clean, he wanted a dirtier sound, and this was almost impossible to achieve. He looked at his guitar, looked at the amps, and then looked at the strange people behind his stack. Then he caught sight of me and began frantically gesturing in my direction.

A strange blue smoke was curling over Keith's amplifiers and we thought the stack might be about to burst into flames. I marched up to the little man who seemed to be at the center of all this and said: "What the hell's going on?"

He simply plugged my mouth with a small wooden pipe. In an instinctive reaction I inhaled, and crashed to the floor. It was the strongest, strangest shit I had ever smoked. Stu was right, you could smoke stuff and fall over, and you might say that I fell corrected.

In a second I came round and tried to recover what was left of my dignity. Stu had pulled me upright. "You fuggin' idjit, I told you what would happen. Look at you; you're as much use as a porn star's morals."

I remembered there was a show about to begin, and thankfully I also remembered that I had to introduce the band. I composed myself and headed for the dressing room with Stu behind me raving about the absurdities of drugs and useless fucking hippies.

Tony stood impassive at the dressing room door and gave me a silent nod as I went inside. The two guitar players were jamming as Charlie kept time on the table with his drumsticks. Mick had found his Uncle Sam hat; we were ready to rock-'n'roll. Holding two guitars, I led the way through the building and onto the stage. Bill Graham and strange drugs notwithstanding, the show had to go on.

CHAPTER 14

By the time we got to Phoenix

John Jaymes's paranoid preoccupation with Goldfinger worried me. Why was this man, sent by Chrysler (so he claimed), so interested in just another drug dealer who happened to like the Rolling Stones? Everybody liked the Rolling Stones. Go to a Stones show in Los Angeles or San Francisco (or any other town in America for that matter) and half the drug dealers in town would be present.

I had filed away Jaymes's warnings, and when the opportunity arose I had decided that I would investigate further. In a hotel bar in Phoenix I got my chance to talk with two of Jaymes's cops, Ray and Brad. They knew all about Goldfinger and a lot more.

Guarded by the cops, we had our very own (in-house) drug dealer on tour. In *Old Gods Almost Dead*, a book by Stephen Davis (Aurum Press, 2001), it is asserted that this man was Fred Sessler and that he was a businessman who had "a legal license to import pharmaceutical cocaine from a Swiss drug company." Wrong. The drugs on tour were not pharmaceutical cocaine, they were the finest Peruvian flake, with large rocks, and Fred Sessler, whom I have met, was not the man distributing them. He wasn't even on the tour, though he came to the New York gigs. Sessler, a lovely man, is now dead, so I take this opportunity to defend him. Anyway, the supply came from the off-duty cops. In Phoenix I found out all about it.

The two off-duty cops and I sat in a booth in the hotel bar over some drinks. I started out cautiously, and reminded them of Goldfinger's appearance in Los Angeles. Why was a man with a missing hand and piles of drugs such an issue? Then the cops explained.

Goldfinger's real name was Ken Connell and he was a marijuana smuggler of some renown, responsible for flying tons of the stuff into the United States. He had lost his limb in an accident in Mexico when he had walked into the prop of a plane loaded with drugs; it had chopped off his lower right arm just above the wrist. Goldfinger had ordered the loaded plane to be stripped of its cargo, which was dumped on the runway, and instructed his pilot to fly to America. He had put his limb in a plastic bag, and with this grisly package clutched in his remaining paw, made it to San Diego, but surgeons had not been able to re-attach the mangled body part.

It was obvious from the cops' attitude that they held Goldfinger in grudgingly high regard. I shrugged and tried to look unconcerned. So what did this have to do with us, I demanded? The off-duty police officers explained that they were "moonlighting" and had taken their annual leave to act as our security. The man dishing out drugs on the tour was one of their people. He was a man from Brooklyn, recently released from jail, who was doing the cops a favor.

All the NYPD cops were making sure the in-house dealer was safe from local police looking to bust the Stones. It had nothing to do with the Stones and was all part of the "service" John Jaymes had established to keep everyone happy. I don't know about happy, but he had certainly managed to keep everyone stoned out of their brains. All one had to do was ask, and a film canister full of Peruvian flake would be handed over. You want it? Here. I was kept busy throughout the tour ferrying empty canisters to the main man for resupply.

And Goldfinger? What was the problem with him? The cops sighed. Goldfinger was undoubtedly being trailed by feds. If they were watching him, they might get wind of what our security was up to and this could lead to some nasty complications. While our security could protect everyone from local police in the different towns we played, there was no way they had any pull with the Feds.

I had a sneaking feeling that I was finding out stuff I'd really rather know nothing about. Why didn't the Feds simply arrest this man if he was such a big dealer? The cops went into an elaborate explanation about surveillance that was lost on me, and as we were now well away from the West Coast and unlikely to ever see the mysterious Mr. Connell again, I relaxed. None of this seemed like a direct threat to the Stones — we were not paying for the drugs, and we were not paying for the off-duty cops to act as security. We were simply enjoying what there was on offer. Temporarily satisfied that no one was about to be hauled off to jail, I left the cops and went up to my room.

Lying in bed, I wondered about the cops. Who were they working for? John Jaymes was obviously fronting for someone else, but who? What was his angle? How come he seemed to have such a huge, virtually limitless budget? How come he could get cops "on side" in any town in America? Who was this man?

The overall planning of the tour was something of a shambles because the lines of command and control were not always clearly delineated. Ronnie Schneider handled the money (along with Mick) and Chip Monk was in charge of production of the actual shows, in consultation with Mick and the band. Tony was personal security, and yet we had half-a-dozen off-duty cops who also covered the tour. Where they came from, who was paying for them, and their specific mandate remained obscure.

John Jaymes simply dubbed himself "the man from Chrysler" and no one other than me seemed to give it a second thought. The crew and promotional people from the record company also seemed to change with bewildering regularity. I looked after the band, and was frequently unsure who I was answerable to on the tour.

Mick liked to think of himself as being in charge but he was no more in charge of the '69 tour than the pope is in charge of the Catholic Church. Basically he was a titular figurehead with only a limited idea of what was happening. Mick was a romantic, and had little connection to the reality shared by the masses. It had been many years since his life could be described as ordinary. He had made the passage from middle-class obscurity to rock icon seem like a transit from unholy innocence to holy ignorance.

Mick hardly knew who most of the people on the tour actually were, and really didn't care, as long as the Stones weren't paying them. To him it was all a lark, the rock'n'roll circus writ large upon the American stage. A few cops and a few gangsters — what did he care?

Mick slept well and looked after himself, with particular concern saved for his vocal cords. He was a singer in a rock-'n'roll band, he assured himself. His minions could care for all the other stuff. The only problem was that the minions were getting stoned and laid and were not necessarily on top of what was going on.

Nothing in my background had equipped me to deal with American cops and gangsters. The band's survival was paramount, but I liked to think that it was not part of my employment description that I should die on the job. Paranoia was starting to affect me, just as it was affecting everyone else. The 1969 tour was a coke tour, not sponsored by the soft-drink company, but by a bunch of serious-looking, heavily armed cops. Without a gun I felt naked. I decided to get "tooled up," just like the rest of America.

Ray and Brad, my new best friends, came to my rescue. After much discussion — for I had never actually held a gun, let alone fired one — I was given a small .32 caliber derringer. A woman's gun! Two shots fired at close to point-blank range would at the very least stop an assailant. I prayed that if I had to fire the bloody thing it wouldn't kill anyone. The gun, which sat comfortably in the palm of my hand, could be concealed by stuffing it in the top of my boot. That's what the cops called it: a boot gun. I felt better for having it and was sworn to secrecy by Ray and Brad.

In Dallas, where we played the Moody Coliseum, the cops handed it to me, in a dressing-room deep in the bowels of what looked to me like a cow barn, while the band was busy with sound check. I asked the cops to stand outside and I fired both barrels, aiming at the toilet door in the corner of the room. The noise was deafening and two rather satisfying holes appeared in the door. The cops rushed in. What the fuck was I doing? "Trying it out," I sheepishly replied.

After they showed me how to reload the thing and made me promise not to fire it again (or we'd all get busted), they left me, shaking their heads and muttering about dumb Englishmen. I looked at the door — the holes, about six inches across, were proof that I was now equipped to do some damage if required.

It was a sobering thought. I imagined that this was how most Americans felt when they persuaded themselves that being armed increased their personal security.

I was not completely happy, but I was happier.

CHAPTER 15

Mick Taylor

By the time we hit Dallas, the band were playing as well as they ever had. Mick Taylor was proving to be an inspired choice on second guitar, playing with a deftness that belied his age. He was a great blues player and his self-effacing surety of touch added immeasurably to the band's overall sound. Keith was re-energized after several years of having to carry the load, and once more the "dueling guitars" at the center of the Rolling Stones' sound led the charge.

Mick Taylor was an interesting study in what happens to a man who joins the Rolling Stones. He was an all-round lovely guy, without a hint of arrogance or ego. I did my best to ease his transition, but the Rolling Stones put him to work, swallowed him up greedily, and were eventually to spit him out a wasted and hollow man.

Taylor's bottleneck guitar made him the equal of Brian Jones, who had been one of the greatest bottleneck guitarists Britain had ever produced. Keith and Mick used Taylor to great effect on tunes like "Love in Vain" and "Midnight Rambler." On the 1969 tour, Taylor was one of the stars, as musically eloquent as the great B.B. King, who opened many of the shows. The man could play.

Taylor and his girlfriend Rosie were a loving and devoted

couple. What they must have gone through in the midst of the debauchery which is a Stones tour is hard to describe, but afterwards these two lovely people (like the rest of us) were never quite the same again.

In some respects, Mick Taylor was a typical olde-worlde Englishman: reserved and respectful to those he met, solicitous of other people's feelings, shy and self-effacing. He was absolutely aware of his own talents but at the same time modest to a fault. When I first met him I found it difficult to believe that he had been in one of England's finest bands, John Mayall's Bluesbreakers. All of this changed, of course, the moment that he had a guitar in his hands, whereupon he played with an authority and power that was both subtle and mesmerizing.

Mick had started playing guitar at a really young age, and was brought up in Hatfield on the northern outskirts of London, the same town where I was born. When he was sixteen he attended a Bluesbreakers concert, when Eric Clapton was lead guitarist for the band. Clapton was a no-show and during the interval Mick talked John Mayall into letting him sit in. Mick actually got to play Clapton's guitar, which was sitting on stage. It must have been one hell of a show, for Mayall remembered the brilliant young kid, and when Peter Green quit he asked Mick to join.

Where Keith was brash and loved the sheer vulgarity of guitar riffs, Mick went for a more subtle feel, intricate and urbane. The pair managed to marry their individual styles and produce some wonderful musical offspring.

Mick barely drank alcohol, though he smoked cigarettes and had the odd puff on a joint. In the beginning that was pretty much the extent of his indulgences. John Mayall had a reputation for running a tight ship and it may well have been his influence at work. Taylor was self-disciplined where most rock musicians are reckless.

Mick ensured he ate a balanced diet, which to us was virtually unheard of. He didn't chase pretty girls (or boys), something we considered extraordinary. No sex, no drugs — we wondered if the man was human!

One of the first things that Mick Taylor discovered is that there's a huge amount of time spent just hanging about waiting for either Mick or Keith to show up. No disrespect, but the so-called Glimmer Twins had an approach to work that had no relationship to clocks and time-keeping. Mick Taylor seemed to settle into the routine effortlessly. He'd simply curl up somewhere comfortable and happily read a book until it was time for him to do his thing.

The general public would be very surprised if they knew how polite the Rolling Stones were in their dealings with one another and their employees. Mick Taylor was no exception to this rule. He was always the epitome of English good manners, using the words "please" and "thank you" at every opportunity. Simple courtesy is the sign of a certain type of upbringing. It has something to do with the fact that almost sixty million English live together on a tiny island.

Rosie was a delicate slip of a girl, excessively shy and definitely not the kind of woman one would see hanging around Mick and Keith, who specialized in demonic dragon ladies who could eat most men for lunch. I felt sorry for Rosie, having to withstand the rude stares of the Rolling Stones' menagerie while in America, and did my best to make her feel welcome and safe. She was not, strictly speaking, my responsibility, and neither was Shirley Watts, but they were so obviously central to their partners' lives that I felt obliged to watch out for them. There were some people on the Stones' tour who were wholesome and pure of heart, so it was a joy to play Uncle Sam on their behalf.

Mick Taylor's innocence regarding drugs changed very quickly. Mick soon got into the marching powder like everyone else. It was unavoidable. It did little to help his relationship with his lady, and when Rosie visited the tour, it was obvious there was tension between them. It was sad to see. Nonetheless Mick was sorry to see her go, just as Charlie was devastated when

Shirley and his daughter departed as the tour continued. Rock'n'roll is blisteringly hard on the hearts of those who love one another.

The long-term effects that touring with the Stones had upon Mick are difficult to quantify, but it is well known that he had major issues with addiction that took him some years to get over. His creativity was at its peak on the 1969 tour of America and he contributed substantially to various tracks on Stones albums, but the sad truth is that Mick never received the creative credits that he felt he deserved. He and the Stones eventually parted company after the 1973 LP *Goats Head Soup*.

Perhaps things might have been different had Mick Taylor partaken of some of the more esoteric delights that surrounded the Stones and stayed away from the hard stuff. There were ladies aplenty, sufficient to stimulate the most jaded palate, and some of them would have been pleased to make his hair curl. For example, Dallas, that supremely vulgar manifestation of the Texan dream, possessed its own little star that rivaled those from other cities. Chicago may have had "The Plaster Casters," but Dallas had "The Butter Queen."

The Plaster Casters specialized in facsimile reproductions of rock stars' penises, which they covered in Latex in order to make a mold and then poured plaster into the receptacle. They claimed to have "done them all," from Jim Morrison to Hendrix, though they never managed to do the Stones. The Butter Queen was a girl of infinitely more esoteric taste, and was disconcertingly bizarre.

I was told of her presence by one of the crew and went to a suite where some of the production guys were partying. The Butter Queen was holding court. With a body like Jayne Mansfield's and a brain to match, it would be ungallant of me to describe her as not particularly attractive; but truthfully, she was not very attractive and she was not very bright. Her specialty involved a similarly complex series of maneuvers to the Plaster Casters', but differed in that her description of the process was likely to make the recipient collapse in gales of hysterical laughter.

She had arrived at a suite in the hotel, and the entire band was otherwise engaged in their rooms. There was time to kill and what more pleasant way to spend it than in the elaborate company of the weirdest representative of the dairy industry you are ever likely to meet? The girl had a thing about butter (don't we all?) and what she required was this. We listened to her explanation while trying to keep a straight face. We all fixed looks of solemn attention on our faces and tried hard not to giggle.

The Butter Queen demanded that she be allowed to perform her specialty for one of the members of the band, if not all of them; but I assured her this was out of the question. With as straight an expression as I could muster I explained that The Rolling Stones were vegans and would have nothing to do with animal products; consequently butter was out of the question. The explanation didn't so much go over her head; it didn't even enter her head. She shrugged in blank incomprehension and decided that one of the crew was the next best thing, as she was in a bit of a hurry and had a kid to go home to. I quite understood her predicament and several members of the crew were eager to volunteer.

She had certainly arrived equipped to do the business. She spread a rubber sheet on the bed and took out a small electric hot-plate which she proceeded to plug into a socket in the wall. A volunteer would have to be naked, so in front of his dubious colleagues a roadie duly obliged and lay on the bed with a large vodka and tonic and fortified himself for the ordeal ahead. The rest of us watched in subdued silence, with barely suppressed grins. Dairy Girl rummaged around in her large bag and produced a huge block of butter which she chopped into small lumps and popped into a saucepan on top of the hot plate.

As the butter slowly melted, Dairy Girl, the Dallas Butter Queen, proceeded to get excited and stared into the melting butter like some veritable witch from Macbeth. People began to laugh as she stirred and this produced a string of foul epithets of such ferocity that everyone immediately lapsed into stunned silence. This girl was not to be messed with. The recipient of her favors lay back and wondered what the hell was going to happen. Was he to have boiling butter poured on his body? We held our breath while the roadie held his hands like a protective cup over his family jewels and began to look a bit concerned.

From the saucepan she poured the butter into what looked like a copper tea-pot and then she got down to business. We all tried to be as serious as she was, for this was obviously a serious business. Slowly and carefully she poured a stream of clarified butter onto the roadies' exposed nether region and began to lick, so that as she poured she consumed and he was cleansed. It was a strange production made all the more strange by her obvious excitement brought on by the process.

As she poured and licked, she became more and more aroused and then she began to climax in a series of convulsions, for which only one metaphor seems appropriate — it was positively bovine.

A low and resonating groan emerged from her chest, a perfect reproduction of the sound a cow might make when it is separated from its calf. It was simply too bizarre for words and the molten butter was licked and consumed with a gusto that was frightening in its intensity and very unsettling. Nobody said a word and we looked at one another uncomfortably as the woman groaned and moaned throughout the procedure and had what appeared to be the longest orgasm in the history of dairy farming.

The whole event must have taken around half an hour and it was so singular and bizarre that the roadie, who was a veteran of some of the strangest sexual encounters known to man, couldn't bring himself to consummating the strange ritual by having sex with her. Shaking his head and grimacing sheepishly, he wandered to the shower and left her to the other people in the room, all of whom seemed quite keen to replicate his experience. I smiled inwardly and wondered at this strange lady.

How had she first got into this? Where had her preoccupation with molten butter come from? What on earth made her think that other people would find this erotic?

Perhaps Dallas ranchers with tens of thousands of head of cattle enjoyed this kind of thing, I mused. I walked out of the hotel suite with The Butter Queen hard at work on her next grateful recipient. Can't say it did that much for me, except to reinforce my belief that the human race can be fascinating: infinitely strange and decidedly perverse. I wandered off to my room, smiling to myself and somewhat unsettled by the absurdity of it all.

It was something I would rather not have witnessed; after all, I've always been a margarine man myself.

CHAPTER 16

Trust me, I'm a pilot

We were due next in Auburn, Alabama, and there had been much soul-searching as to whether the band should play the Deep South at all. Mick had insisted that the gig be integrated and this clause had been inserted in the contract for the show.

We flew to the nearest airport in a DC3, the only private plane that the incompetent John Jaymes could find. It was a relic and, as it sat on the runway with its engines spluttering, memories of the crash that killed rockers Buddy Holly and Ritchie Valens swarmed in my mind. A nagging voice kept saying, "Don't get on this bloody crate, Sam — find another way."

The plane should have been in a museum. The seats were cracked plastic and the window shades were primitive contraptions; only a few of them actually worked. The band, seemingly unconcerned, took their seats while I took a deep breath. The pilot, who was as much of a relic as the aircraft, revved the engines, and with clouds of black exhaust smoke billowing behind us, we took off. The acrid smell of burnt aviation fuel filled the cabin, and I said a silent prayer.

As we gained altitude, the fumes became stronger and we began to feel alarmed. I went forward to talk to the pilot. He nodded when I told him about the fumes and said it was probably because the air vents were open. "Air vents?" I queried.

He explained that there were air vents in the floor of the plane, between some of the seats; all we had to do was close them. I went and began a search for the mystery vents. They were open. Unfortunately, they wouldn't close. They had obviously been stuck in the open position for so long that they'd been rendered inoperative.

We chugged along and the temperature began to drop. A small group of skinny Englishmen hardened to all the excesses of touring were simply not prepared to freeze to death in the air over America. Once more I went forward and demanded that the pilot turn on the heating. "Heating's already on," he told me. I noted that he was wearing a quilted jacket and a scarf.

Mick and Keith were not amused. Charlie was turning blue and I rubbed his feet to ward off frostbite. John Jaymes sank lower in our collective estimation as the temperature plummeted along with our expectations for the coming gig.

As we screeched to a halt on the runway, we noticed that it was snowing. I peered into the darkness trying to spot the limousines that were supposed to meet the band. The airfield seemed deserted, and everyone was shivering alarmingly. As the door opened, I looked at Mick and my beloved leader's expression said it all. I headed for the terminal to look for the cars.

When I finally found the limousines waiting outside the terminal, I got permission for them to drive up to the plane. I noted that each of the drivers was a uniformed African-American gentleman, and asked them very politely to turn the heating of their cars up to the maximum. The band, I explained, were freezing cold and in danger of contracting pneumonia. One of the drivers told me that he loved my accent and I gave him what passed for a smile as I bundled the band into the warm cocoons of the cars. Everyone was pissed off, though the heated vehicles went some way toward thawing out the frosty atmosphere.

Things didn't improve when we arrived at the sports arena at the University of Alabama. The limo drivers were the only black faces we were to see the whole night. In front of the band there stretched a sea of young, white students. Crewcuts were the preferred hairstyle.

Mick screamed for the promoters and in due course we were shepherded into a cold dressing-room by two young men who would not have looked out of place in an army boot camp.

"The show was not to be segregated," said Mick. "Why are there only white people here?"

The promoters couldn't understand why this was a problem: there were no black students on the campus.

At that moment, Chuck Berry arrived, to high fives all round, but he looked like a man who had been booked to play a gig in hell. He smiled at Mick. "Welcome to the south," he said and announced that he'd play a shortened set and get out of there as soon as he'd finished. He was accompanied by a white couple and looked distinctly uncomfortable about being in Alabama. This was not going to be an easy gig.

The arena was half-empty, and Terry Reid began proceedings.

It happened that November 14, 1969, was Terry's twenty-first birthday. It was not a happy day for Terry, or for anyone else. Chesley Millikin, my dear friend and Terry's manager, had managed to get Terry on the Stones' tour as the opening act, and from the very beginning he had been treated shabbily. The pressure of getting several bands on stage before the Stones' set meant that Terry's forty-five minutes on stage had slowly been whittled away; by the time we reached Alabama he was expected to play for twenty minutes, thirty at most. The embarrassment I felt at having to explain this to an artist of Terry's talent has never left me, and I'm sure that to this day he has never forgotten the humiliation.

This was the man who had turned down the chance to be the lead vocalist of Led Zeppelin before the job had been offered to Robert Plant. He was being treated abominably, but Terry was forced to take the rough end of the stick right where it hurts. He deserved better. Where most men remember their twenty-first birthday for the rest of their lives, I'm pretty sure that Terry is one of the few who would rather forget it.

I didn't bother to wish him happy birthday; he would have killed me. His performance went down like a man jumping from a high building. It was fast and the result was terminal — Terry died right there on stage. The crowd didn't have a clue that they were listening to one of the great rock'n'roll voices of their day. Chuck Berry turned in a half-hearted effort and then the Stones took the stage.

It all fell rather flat and produced a muted response. A half-empty auditorium of rednecks simply didn't get Mick prancing about in an Uncle Sam hat and flowing scarf. The girls, decked out in white, tight-fitting sweaters that matched their complexions, seemed a little more enthusiastic than their dates, but were unsure how to respond to the music.

Mick left the stage after the first show muttering, "Terrible, that was terrible." The girls and boys strolled out into the night to do what I guess good girls and boys do in Alabama: namely read the Bible and protect their virginity at all costs. The sixties, it seemed, had passed Alabama by.

As the audience filed in for the second show, the two Mutt and Jeffs who'd previously explained why there were only white people in the audience came to speak to us. We had a problem: there was not enough time left for all the acts on the bill, as the female students had to be in their dormitories by midnight.

We laughed in their faces. If this was the case, the band would simply refuse to play the second show. I told the promoters that they'd better get in touch with a higher authority. With laughter all round I suggested that, as everybody was so devoutly Christian, perhaps a call to "Him upstairs" might be in order. It was going to need divine intervention for the Rolling Stones to play and watch all the women leave.

Divine intervention or not, within minutes the organizers relented, informing us that "the authorities" had granted a dispensation and the girls were now allowed to stay out past their bedtime. It was the closest the Stones ever got to playing in a kindergarten.

With time pressures mounting, and the hall slowly filling, something had to give and that something was Terry Reid's set. I had the unenviable task of explaining to Terry what was to happen. Terry didn't take it well and neither did Chesley. Thus it was on his twenty-first birthday that Terry Reid got bumped from playing on the bill with the Rolling Stones, and I've wanted to apologize to him ever since.

I made my way back to the dressing-room to face a seriously unhappy Mick. The exposure to the cold air in the plane had affected his throat, and this had been exacerbated by going from the cold plane to the heated limousines. With a steely glare, Mick told me that the Stones would do a shortened set and the minute we finished we were leaving. We were going from the campus to the airport, he explained, and then flying straight to Chicago. I reminded him it was snowing, but he didn't care. We were leaving and that was that.

I hurried to make the arrangements.

The second show got off to a good start with a complete idiot of an announcer (not me!) telling the girls that they could all stay out late. Mick gave me an ironic smile. He pranced on stage and worked his butt off trying to get the crowd aroused, with limited success, and I worked the phones trying to find another plane so we could fly to Chicago. None was available; in fact there was a good chance that owing to the weather, the airport would be closed.

I really didn't want to fly on the DC3 if it could be avoided, but as the Stones' set progressed I realized the old clunker was our only option. More images of Buddy Holly's death crowded uncomfortably into my mind.

After a lot of argument I managed to get the three limousines inside the sports arena and positioned backstage, engines running and heaters on full blast. I rummaged around and found a bunch of blankets and Alabama football team jackets that I appropriated and stashed in the limos. If the plane crashed, I told myself, the press would claim that the bodies belonged to the football team of the University of Alabama. I didn't find that amusing.

The band ran from the stage and we sped into the night, the windshield wipers thrashing away at the snowflakes battling to obscure the windows.

We scrambled aboard the DC3, having been given a somewhat grim welcome by the pilot, and as he revved the engines, everybody snuggled as best they could into the jackets and blankets. Those among us of a nervous disposition moved our lips in silent prayer. Not a word could be heard from anybody.

We were flying to Chicago in the same old plane that had flown us from Dallas to Alabama, and I felt that we were seriously at risk. I went forward to talk to the pilot and came right out with what everybody was thinking. "Are we going to make it?" The pilot gave me a look of contempt. He had flown DC3s all over the world, they were the world's safest airplane, and there was no way he would fly the damn thing if he thought he was putting himself or his passengers in danger. Please, would I mind sitting down and letting him get on with his job?

I walked back to the rear of the plane, trying to look cheerful. I settled in my seat next to Charlie and looked out of the snowflake-encrusted window as the now-familiar stench of burning aviation fuel assailed my nostrils. There are certain times in rock'n'roll when one is forced to lie back and accept what's coming.

Everyone was mightily relieved when the plane managed to take off in the teeth of a howling gale. I tried to ignore the insistent voice in my head that kept repeating, "What goes up must come down, what goes up must come down." The temperature began to drop, and the snowflakes that were actually coming into the aircraft via the air vents did nothing to relieve our anxieties.

Some thoughtful soul had equipped the plane with airsickness bags, which we stuffed into the open vents and secured in place with some cutlery we'd found on board.

Several miserable hours later, we arrived in Chicago. We had all draped our legs across the aisle so that those sitting opposite could rub our feet to keep them warm. It was absurd.

When the plane landed we greeted the happy event with ironic cheers and bundled into the waiting limousines, with some of our number, no doubt, re-acquainted with the notion of an almighty, all-powerful, and compassionate God.

Keith summed it up perfectly: "We made it! Thank fuck!"

I vowed that I would never again allow myself to get on a plane. That solemn promise lasted just under three days.

The next couple of gigs were at the University of Illinois, and a happier experience than Alabama — both had a racially mixed and enthusiastic audience and the girls didn't have to be in bed by midnight. As the Stones took to the stage many of the students fired up joints, so at least we weren't playing for rednecks. The shows were a stunning reaffirmation of the Stones' musical powers and a great preparation for Chicago itself, a town for which the Stones had always felt a musical affinity since their earliest foray into the blues.

Chicago was an important gig in one of America's major cities and the band was determined to give the shows their very best shot. Everyone was well aware that some of the Stones' musical idols might well pop in to say hello, or be in the audience. All this meant our arrival at the Chicago gig was initially a letdown. What an awful venue!

Located in the middle of the stockyards, the whole place stank of slaughter and old meat. It also retained the emotional stench of the 1968 Democratic Convention, at which the Chicago police had brutally beaten protesters and innocent bystanders.

I noted with concern that the number of hefty Mafia-types in our entourage had increased exponentially. "Our" cops were busy fraternizing with the Chicago cops and the whole place felt like a police academy reunion. John Jaymes was in his element and I became more and more alarmed at his growing and insidious influence. He was definitely getting too big for his boots.

The Stones, for the first time on that tour, were truly magnificent, and Chicago, one of their favorite cities, got the goods. While Tina Turner was always electric on stage, in Chicago, Mick and the Stones seemed positively nuclear.

Chicago was also fun for Terry Reid, which gladdened me, though I doubt whether anybody else gave a rat's arse. The Chicago audience finally took to Terry's voice and he came off stage (at last) with a bit of a grin. It sure is no fun opening a bill for the Rolling Stones, B.B. King, and Ike and Tina Turner, yet for once Terry made it work.

Before we knew it, we were on our way back to L.A. and the mansion on Oriole Drive, where we now had to stay. Stephen Stills had reclaimed his house, which we would miss. From here on in, the Stones would experience as much privacy as Los Angeles grants any of its stars, which is to say bugger all.

John Jaymes and the hired thugs now endeavored to turn Oriole Drive into an armed camp: we were to receive twenty-four–hour security. We sprawled on the sofas at a meeting in the living room with its splendid views over Los Angeles while Jaymes, the pompous ass, described how secure we were going to feel. The band yawned, but I thought it would be fun to make a surprise tour of the house, grounds, and the troops.

Jaymes and I found our off-duty cops sitting in a summer house by the tennis courts playing poker, perspiring in their shirtsleeves, and draped in guns of every conceivable type and size. As I passed I cheerily waved. Six podgy hands waved merrily back as I sighed and went on my way. This lot seemed incapable of protecting their families, let alone the Stones.

CHAPTER 17

A free concert

The following day we met with Rock Scully to discuss the free concert idea. Rock brought a friend with him named Emmett Grogan. Grogan was one of the founders of the Diggers Collective in San Francisco, an anarchist community organization that provided free food, medical care, and shelter to people in the Haight-Ashbury district and also put on free concerts. In later years Grogan would write a wonderful autobiography called *Ringolevio*, before succumbing to life's unkindness by overdose on a New York subway.

With several members of the band sitting round, Rock explained what was going to happen and we took it all in like children entranced by the promise of candy. Emmett sat mutely, with an unreasonably stern expression. He and Rock were a study in contrasts: Rock every bit the successful Californian manager and Emmett looking like a street tough. Where the glamorous manager talked of the media, the streetwise Digger spoke of how the kids would get fed and watered. We should have been listening to Emmett, but we were foolish, and wanted so much to partake in the dream of ending the American tour on a wonderful high. "Practical realities," Mick airily opined, could "be addressed at a later stage."

The concert would now take place at Sears Point, Rock said,

as Golden Gate Park in San Francisco, where so many wonderful shows had been staged, was not available. Bill Graham had put pressure on the mayor's office and had off-the-record contact with local journalists, deliberately sabotaging the plan. His ally Ralph Gleason was among several prominent citizens of San Francisco involved in this campaign.

There had never been any trouble at any of their free concerts, Rock assured us. The electricity would be provided by generators, guarded by the Angels, as had happened so many times before. We didn't imagine that the Angels would present any kind of a problem. They loved music, we reasoned, and there was to be a veritable cornucopia of the finest music the West Coast had to offer.

We asked about medical people and toilets and those kinds of concerns, but really didn't pursue such mundane details with great enthusiasm. Instead we sat listening to Rock's tales of the Haight-Ashbury, the Grateful Dead, and the wonderful sense of community that existed in San Francisco. He explained how a new paradigm was evolving on the streets, with people throwing off the old ways and freeing themselves from tired postwar constraints. It sounded too good to be true, and in the end, that was what it would turn out to be.

Rock outlined the state of play for us. Everyone wanted to be on the lineup. There would be a huge stage with ample sightlines, a backstage area, and all the necessary accoutrements of a major show. It would be the crowning highlight of the Rolling Stones tour. Mick gave it his imprimatur and even Ronnie Schneider seemed enthusiastic, though I noted that he didn't actually give his direct support. He nodded and waited for Mick to tell him in which direction he would like the vessel to head. Ronnie had a great rock-politics brain, and like all good generals, made damn sure he didn't get in advance of his troops.

We asked a few questions, but nothing that would tax anyone beyond ten years of age. No one thought to inquire what the temperature might be in December. It simply didn't occur to us.

On their way out, I asked Emmett if he thought everything was cool. He shook his head, muttering, "I don't know, man, I don't know." I wish his skepticism had registered.

The first public airing of the free concert idea was at a press conference at Los Angeles' Beverly Wilshire Hotel.

Ralph Gleason had accused the Stones of "despising their own audience" and Mick was confronted with this criticism. What did he have to say? Was it true that the Stones were thinking of doing a free concert at the end of the tour?

Mick stalled for time: "There's been talk of that," he replied. "I should think toward the end [of the tour] . . . We'll have to see how things go . . . I don't want to plan that right now, because we're going to be here some while . . . We've got time for all that . . . I don't want to say that's what we want to do or not do . . . I'm leaving it rather blurry . . . I'm not committing meself."

Immediately following the press conference, the radio reports began. Within hours, the prospect of a free concert morphed from possible to probable. Within twenty-four hours, everyone the Stones met could talk of little else but the free concert, and when it was going to happen. When — not if.

The alternative site at Sears Point, north of the city, could accommodate up to half a million people, and looked promising. Then the owners got wise to the fact that the Stones were not only filming the whole of their American tour, but wanted to film the free, tour-ending concert. They demanded a slice of the film action.

A famous and well-connected lawyer had been retained to represent the interests of the Stones, but someone from the Stones' inner circle needed to go to San Francisco and get a clearer picture, so that Mick and the group could make some firm decisions.

We all gathered back at the Oriole Drive house for supper and to discuss things. A free concert seemed such a perfect and gracious way to thank America. We had several days off and we needed to know if the free gig was to be more than just a hippie pipe-dream. Who was actually going to be organizing this thing? Who were these Grateful Dead people? What specifically were they proposing? Did Rock Scully even manage the Grateful Dead?

Ronnie Schneider thought that someone related to the drummer managed the Dead. Warner Brothers had told him that Lenny Hart was the manager of the Grateful Dead and that Rock was their record promotion man. One of the crew from Bill Graham's outfit said that Rock used to manage the Dead along with a guy called Danny Rifkin. Mick asked me to travel up to San Francisco, get a handle on things, and report back to him within forty-eight hours. He and Keith, meanwhile, would be overdubbing at Sunset Sound.

CHAPTER 18

What you see is what you get

The following morning I flew to northern California to meet the Dead, see the Sears Point site, and to meet a Mr. Mel Belli, the lawyer for the Stones. When I had finally got to meet the Rolling Stones it was one of the great moments of my life, but the prospect of meeting the Grateful Dead filled me with even more excitement. Memories of reading *The Electric Kool-aid Acid Test* crowded into my mind.

I would be meeting Captain Trips (Jerry Garcia) and Mountain Girl, and maybe I'd even meet the legendary Cassady. I spent some time on the plane composing myself and trying to ensure that I was in a cool space. There was a lot riding on this meeting. I didn't want to blow it.

At San Francisco airport, I boarded a helicopter, which landed in Novato, a town in Marin County, over on the northern side of the bay. In a small building next to the heliport the Dead maintained their rehearsal space and their offices. The first person I met was their manager, the Reverend Lenny Hart. He stood unsmiling at the entrance to the building, proffered his hand, and embarked on a nervous speech.

He was, he assured me, the manager of the Grateful Dead. He was a Christian minister, he was at pains to add, but looked and behaved like no reverend I had ever set eyes upon. He was wearing cowboy boots and a suit cut in the western style. As his secretary made me a coffee, I looked around the office. There was a Bible on his desk.

On the walls there were psychedelic posters, and helicopters could be heard outside. The place struck me as very noisy for either an office or a rehearsal facility. I asked to see where the band practiced and went on about the Stones having a similar rehearsal space in Bermondsey in an old warehouse.

Lenny marched me into a part of the building adjacent to the office where some space had been converted to use as a rehearsal studio. There I met Ramrod, the Dead's equipment guy, who had helped us out at the Oakland gig. Ramrod gave me a welcoming smile while Lenny hovered about. I was pleased when Rock Scully showed up to rescue me from Lenny's forced friendliness.

Scully and Ramrod took me into the crew's hang-out space and rolled a big spliff and explained what was to happen. Everyone was going to meet at noon in the barn at the ranch of Mickey Hart, the Dead's drummer. Yes, the Reverend Lenny was his father. I just couldn't get my head around a preacher being the manager of a famous psychedelic band.

Ramrod and Scully were much more my kind of people and I was thrilled to hear Ramrod tell me that Ken Kesey had given him his nickname. To be hanging out with someone named by Kesey was an honor. To celebrate, I chopped out some lines of Peruvian on the table and we snorted ourselves into band-meeting mode. Then we jumped into Ramrod's truck and headed for the ranch.

Just outside Novato we pulled across a cattle grid and entered a small property nestled below some sunburnt hills. A huge barn stood there, a gigantic and weather-faded Stars and Stripes flag nailed to its wall. Outside the barn there were vehicles of all shapes and sizes and a couple of horses were tied to a hitching rail. Chickens were pecking away at the dirt. Several kids played on a rope swing.

We were greeted by the sight of Mickey Hart careening to a dusty halt on a white Arab stallion right in the middle of the parked cars. He slid expertly from the saddle and walked straight up to me like a character in some Western. "You the guy from the Stones?" I nodded and without a word he signaled for me to follow him into the barn.

About sixty people were seated on chairs, hay bales, broken sofas, buckets, and whatever they could find. Everyone was busy talking and not the least concerned about my arrival. I asked Rock to point out who was who. Various names were mentioned, people vaguely introduced, others nodded to. Men, women, children, dogs, and a horse tethered in the corner vied for my attention. I noticed Jerry Garcia to one side, dressed in a light-blue poncho and looking slightly bored. I asked, "Who are you all?"

A girl in jeans and cowboy boots with a pleasant face smiled at me and said, "We're the family."

Someone said, "What you see is what you get." And we all laughed.

I was handed a joint, and asked Rock to tell me how this free concert was going to work.

No sooner had Rock begun talking than twenty people started giving him a hard time. He didn't seem to me to have much support, and the dialogue went round and around. Everyone wanted a free concert, yet no one seemed clear how it was going to be brought into being. No one here seemed to have any more status than anybody else and frequently people would talk at cross-purposes, and over each other.

"Participatory democracy, northern Californian style," I told myself. The Grateful Dead and the Rolling Stones occupied different planets. On Planet Dead everyone could think and act like a leader. On Planet Rolling Stone there was really only one leader.

A young man in dusty overalls and a torn T-shirt asked if he could make a suggestion. All would be easily sorted out if the

Rolling Stones simply came and hung out at the ranch. Crosby and those guys did it (meaning Crosby, Stills, and Nash); the Jefferson Airplane did it; shit, even Janis did it. They would see how it all came together.

This impractical suggestion received universal approval. I explained that I was here to talk on Mick and Keith's behalf, and people snorted in derision. The musicians needed to be here so that they could understand what San Francisco was about, so that they could feel what people wanted. People nodded their heads again, and I realized that we were going round in circles.

The Rolling Stones were interested in playing for free, I said. We wanted to play with the Grateful Dead, and all the other bands. We wanted an idea of how this thing was to be organized; we couldn't simply show up and play from the back of a truck. Why not, several people asked. I pressed on. There had to be a plan, and we would need to know who was going to be responsible for what. It was my suggestion that Chip Monk be in charge of all things technical. That proposal went through with general assent, and I felt like we were getting somewhere.

Who was going to represent the Dead? It was decided that Rock would be the main man, as he'd already been to London and Los Angeles to talk to the Stones and it was, in a sense, his baby. I wearily decided we'd leave it at that, as further progress seemed improbable with so many competing voices, and the meeting was adjourned.

I couldn't quite work out what had actually been achieved, though everyone seemed positive. I wasn't worried, just mildly mystified.

Later, as I sat in the parking lot of the office smoking a doobie with one of the office girls, I heard the sound of a Harley approaching. A man with long hair dressed totally in black parked his bike. To a skinny little runt like me he seemed like a giant of a man. It was whispered to me that this was Terry the Tramp, a famous Oakland Angel.

Tramp wasn't impressed by the Stones, but we shared a

laugh about my fight with Bill Graham at the Oakland show. Tramp had been in the third row of the audience. "Is that the way you English fight?" he laughed. He clearly thought I was something of an alien.

"You gonna play this free concert or what?" he demanded.

"That's what the musicians want, so I guess it'll happen," I replied.

Tramp stared hard at me. "It'll be a fuggin' mess, man, too many people, too many hassles. I won't be there. I got better things to do than go through that bullshit. All the people who want this to happen are loco and that Bill Graham's an idiot." He wandered off into the rehearsal space.

The girl I was with said nothing. Tramp then re-emerged, told the girl to "tell the Bear I came by" and roared away.

Another girl from the Dead's office borrowed a car and took me to see the site at Sears Point. We drove north for about half an hour, through rolling hills, and arrived at an isolated site. It seemed ideal. It had good access to the main north-south highway and enough parking spaces for 100,000 cars. To one side of the racetrack there was a huge natural amphitheater. I walked around its perimeter to a point on its ridge where a stage could be erected.

I could see for half a mile, in an arc of 180 degrees. It was a perfect spot for a concert. Nobody from the company that owned the site was in attendance, just a caretaker who knew nothing of what was going on. With a clear picture of the site's possibilities I returned to the Dead's office to meet up with Rock.

He and I talked about the Angels. We decided it would be good politics to go and speak with someone from the San Francisco chapter, as the free concert would be held on their turf. That evening we met with Pete Knell, a member of many years' good standing in the Frisco chapter, and a friend of Rock's. Pete couldn't talk on the Angels' behalf, he explained, but he wanted me to know there was no way the Angels were going to police anything.

"We ain't no cops," he said.

"We don't need cops, we have our own. Plenty of 'em."

We talked about the concert and Pete spoke of how the Angels loved to be at any party. They would drink beer and do whatever they did, he said, but one thing was certain: there was no way they would act as cops. Again I repeated my assurances that we had cops of our own and that we didn't need cops.

The question of beer arose, and it was agreed that the bands would provide it and that the Angels could drink where they always did, beside the generators. It was agreed that the bands would provide $500 worth of beer. I told him I couldn't give him the money as I didn't have $500 with me, and in any case I'd have to clear it with my people first. Nothing else was either discussed or agreed. Rock left to go to a gig and I checked into a hotel.

It was just a small meeting, but one which was to have endless ramifications. Unbeknownst to me, I had met with someone who was not an officer of the club and who therefore had no right to talk on the Hells Angels' behalf. Regardless of how long he has been a member, no man has the right to talk on the club's behalf — unless he is an officer.

CHAPTER 19

The king of torts

Rock had briefed me in a cursory fashion about Mel Belli, so I knew that he was one of America's most famous tort lawyers, renowned for his eccentricity. He was also rich, successful, and very well connected in San Francisco. I made my way to his office in Montgomery Street, and entered a surreal-looking building beneath a striped awning. It looked like the exterior of an expensive New York restaurant.

I found myself in a large waiting area that had a massive table and a grandfather clock, and was greeted by a stunningly good-looking woman in one of the shortest miniskirts I have ever seen. I told her I was from the Stones and was here to see Mr. Belli and she gave me a smile that would have melted even Mick's cynical heart. She asked me to follow her.

She tottered along with me behind her, my eyes glued to one of the most glorious bodies in Christendom; she made the girls who hung around the Stones look positively plain. She seated me outside Belli's office and entered the great man's lair with another radiant smile. I sat down feeling weak-kneed, with my mind on anything but the coming meeting.

I looked around. The place resembled an expensive brothel, and it had the ladies to go with the decor. Blondes and brunettes and glorious redheads in daringly short skirts and high heels strode about the place. As each of them passed me they would flash me their sunny smiles.

I was startled to hear a voice yelling, "Come in, come in," and entered the great man's office. He was seated behind a huge desk piled high with a chaotic mass of papers, stroking his receptionist's leg while looking at something in front of him. Without looking up he told me to sit. He'd be right with me.

Beside him there was a one-legged skeleton hanging from a stand. On the wall were photographs of celebrities and a portrait of Belli himself. The place was crammed with antiques and furnished in tasteless red velvet. Two small dogs scampered about the place and I noticed the stain of dog shit on the carpet.

Belli gave the secretary an affectionate pat on the rump, heaved a deep sigh, and struggled up from his chair. I was amused to notice he had a large bulge in his trousers as he extended his hand. "Wanna drink?" he bellowed.

We settled down for what turned into an extended Belli monologue.

There was no way the Stones were going to play in Golden Gate Park or anywhere else in the city of San Francisco, Belli told me, his voice steadily rising in volume. "Bill Graham and Ralph Gleason saw to that. I talked to the fucking mayor and he's afraid of what the kids will do to the park. We've got another site at the Sears Point Raceway but those sons of bitches are out to screw the Stones on the film rights!"

Belli continued as if he were addressing a courtroom: "We gotta have an alternative site, in case Sears Point falls through, and I've got you one. It's just over the Golden Gate Bridge and it's perfect."

I looked at Belli — a short, plump man with the puffy face of a libertine, neatly framed by a mane of silver-gray hair. His gut made him look six months pregnant. How could this bullshit artist possibly know what the Stones needed?

Belli leaned toward me, speaking in a dramatic stage whisper. "People I am associated with have property in Marin County just off Highway 101. They are prepared to host the concert. My assistant will take you out to see it immediately. I've fixed a meeting on site with the owner's representatives." He smiled and punched a button on his desk, whereupon Miss Long Legs cruised into the room. Belli drew himself up and started yelling again: "Take Mr. Cutler over to Corte Madera for a meeting with the Knights at one o'clock. Take him to his hotel and make sure he's comfortable. Bring him back here after the meeting."

The girl smiled as Belli grabbed my shoulder, pumped my hand, repeated three times that it was good to meet me, and virtually pushed me out of the door.

We clambered into a bright red Corvette and the secretary roared away from the curb, ignoring the parking ticket flapping under the windshield wiper. Her skirt was so short I could see her panties. We rumbled across the Golden Gate Bridge and she brought the car to a halt beside a quiet service road that ran parallel to the freeway.

There were no buildings and not a soul in sight and the green hills of Marin looked singularly inviting. Miss Long Legs suggested we walk to where a locked gate stood across a small overgrown path. We stopped and smoked a cigarette, waiting for the owners to arrive.

A white Lincoln Continental pulled up and out stepped two middle-aged men. "You're the guy Mel told us about; welcome to California," one of them said. "This property would be ideal for your purposes and our clients are happy to make it available. Mel will handle the details."

These two guys didn't look like they'd ever been to a rock concert. I walked along the overgrown track with them. It was barely wide enough for a car and ran around the base of a large hill before petering out in a small valley. Hills stretched in all directions and I looked at the long grass and wondered idly about snakes. There wasn't a tree in sight.

The real-estate man rambled on, picking his way uncomfortably through the grass and telling me that his clients owned several thousand acres of land here. It could accommodate as many people as wanted to attend.

"Who owns this land?" I asked.

"The Knights of Columbus." I didn't have a clue who the Knights were. I figured they were some kind of sporting franchise.

It was hot and there was little point in going on an extended tour of a bunch of overgrown hills, so we made our way back to the car and I promised that Mel and I would discuss the site. They shook hands and departed and I rejoined Belli's assistant. We drove in complete silence with the wind in our hair and me thinking naughty thoughts. If this woman was prepared to put out for Mel Belli, I reasoned, I might have a chance.

Back in the city, we found Belli in the bar next door to his office, surrounded by sycophantic associates. He was also attended by the obligatory beautiful women. Everyone was drinking heavily and Belli was holding forth and yelling. As soon as he saw me he demanded to know what I thought of the "perfect" site.

"Mel," I told him evenly, "it may be a beautiful site but it's absolutely useless for what we want."

"Three thousand fucking acres of fucking prime real estate; what more do you want?"

"Mel, we need access roads for a start," I replied.

He continued yelling. "We can get access roads built, we can do anything you want. The Knights are clients of mine. If we want to build a fucking helicopter landing site we can. We can do whatever we want."

Patiently I tried to explain. The free concert was going to be in two or three weeks; there was no way this site could be prepared in time. "And anyway," I said, "the site just isn't suitable. American cars don't take kindly to being parked on the sides of country hills at an angle of forty-five degrees," I continued. "Last I checked they need flat land and asphalt."

Belli motioned for me to follow him to an empty booth. He was not amused.

"Listen," he hissed. "I've put a lot of time and effort into this on behalf of the Rolling Stones." He grabbed my arm. "This is a great fucking site; the owners are powerful people. I don't wanna hear no, I wanna hear something positive. Don't give me that 'it's not suitable' bullshit. We'll make it fucking suitable."

One of the secretaries brought him another drink. "What do you do for the Rolling Stones?" he demanded.

I considered telling him I cleaned Mick's arse with a toothbrush.

"I'm their personal tour manager," I said, "and I'm telling you that the site you are proposing simply cannot be used. It's impossible."

Belli took a deep breath. "When you get back to Los Angeles you tell Ronnie Schneider to fucking call me, understand?"

I didn't bother to argue. Mel Belli may have been the greatest tort lawyer in the United States, but he knew nothing whatsoever about what it took to organize a rock'n'roll show.

On my flight back to Los Angeles the next day, I began to think of what I would report to Mick. The situation in San Francisco was a mess. The Rolling Stones would have to cut a deal with the owners of Sears Point Raceway because the alternative site offered by Belli was not an option. The Grateful Dead were a cool bunch of dreamers, though, and seemed keen to act as the local liaison for the gig. Rock and Grogan were old hands, and they were in touch with Jefferson Airplane, Santana, Crosby and those guys; they would be crucial in getting the support of the local community. The Dead themselves were the Hells Angels' favorite band, so their involvement was critical to the ultimate success of the project. With the Dead centrally involved in the organization of the event, the Angels should be cool. The shortage of time worried me, but the thought of the Stones playing for free with the cream of the San Francisco bands was hugely attractive.

What a fantastic show it could be.

CHAPTER 20

The makings of a dumb idea

At the Oriole Drive house the first person I ran into was John Jaymes.

"How was the Corte Madera site?" he demanded.

I was flabbergasted that Jaymes would know of the site and that I had been to see it. He was obviously in direct contact with Mel Belli.

"It was terrible," I replied. "A complete joke and totally unsuitable."

Jaymes looked crestfallen.

"We have to go with Sears Point," I said. "There's no alternative. Oh, and by the way, that Mel Belli is a complete wanker."

"He's the best fucking lawyer in San Francisco," Jaymes shot back. "He knows everybody, and is very well connected. Belli can make this thing work."

I looked at Jaymes calmly. "Mel Belli knows nothing about putting on music shows and neither do you."

"We put together the Beatles show at Shea Stadium," Jaymes protested, referring to the Fab Four's legendary New York show in 1965, where they played to 55,000 fans, the largest ever gathering at a pop concert.

With a sigh, I walked away. "Talk to Ronnie," I mumbled, "I'm tired."

Jaymes called after me. "We should take the Corte Madera site, it'd be perfect."

I shook my head in disbelief. What on earth was this man doing around the Rolling Stones? More to the point, what was the connection between Mel Belli, John Jaymes, and the Knights of Columbus?

Mick and I settled down for a talk. I described the Sears Point site in great detail and tried to impress upon him that we really had no alternative if the gig was to come together in time for us to complete the tour in Florida on November 30 and then do the free concert. Mick said there was no way he was going to give in to the extortionate demands of the people who owned the site. Ronnie and John Jaymes would be negotiating with those people. I looked at Mick.

"Who the fuck is John Jaymes and how come he's so involved with this?"

"Apparently he's very well connected; he can help. Ask Ronnie," Mick replied.

"D'you feel comfortable with John Jaymes? I thought he was here to do the rental cars and he's already taken over security on the tour. What's he doing trying to get us to play on a piece of land owned by the Knights of Columbus?"

With that, my beloved leader gave me one of his "this is boring" looks. When it suited him, Mick had the attention span of a flea.

I pressed on. "Did you know he promised the Sears Point people and Belli a hundred cops from back east?"

"Yeah, yeah, that's just promotional bullshit. Belli will sort out all the crap," Mick yawned.

"Belli and John Jaymes are trying to get us to put on this show at a site which is owned by the fucking Knights of Columbus. D'you know who they are, Mick?"

"Some Italian religious group," he replied, fiddling with his shirt and looking at his reflection in a mirror. By now I had found out for myself that they were an Italian-American

Catholic organization of immense influence and power.

I returned to the attack.

"The site they offered is rubbish, Mick, and there's no way in hell we'd ever be able to use it."

Mick smiled indulgently at me. "It's all right, Sam. Ronnie and Belli will sort out the Sears Point thing, the owners are just playing at last-minute brinkmanship. A deal will be cut, I'm sure." He was getting fidgety.

"Mick," I continued, "I'm concerned about John Jaymes. I'm concerned about the cops he has working for him. There's some creepy shit going on."

I received another one of Mick's indulgent little pouts. "Sam, stick to what you have to do. Ronnie and the lawyers will sort all this business shit out. We're back on the road the day after tomorrow. Don't worry about John Jaymes. Ronnie will keep a close eye on him."

Mick was a strange and inconsistent man. One minute he could be wildly enthusiastic about something and then inexplicably lose interest. He loved to keep people on their toes by being unpredictable. At least with Keith there was no such bullshit. Keith only knew how to be consistently Keith; Mick found consistency a bore.

"Leave it to Ronnie and the lawyers," Mick said, and I decided to take him at his word. It wasn't my free concert, it wasn't even the Stones' free concert; it belonged to the West Coast bands that were involved. My job was to look after the Stones.

"They send me to San Francisco to scope things out," I sulkily thought, "and then they don't bother to really listen to what I have to tell them." I persuaded myself that I didn't give a shit.

I left him and went into the kitchen to get something to eat. One of the girls who looked after us was there and as I sat munching away she asked me about the security. Apparently the cops kept coming in the kitchen and hassling her for food, and she didn't like the fact that John Jaymes used the telephone in the kitchen for his discreet phone calls.

"They've all got guns and cop badges," she said, "but they don't behave like cops. They behave like Mafia guys."

"What do you know about the Mafia?"

She laughed at me. "Sam, even I can tell you these guys are not what they seem."

"What makes you say that?" I asked.

The girl began to whisper. "They call New York all the time, and I've heard Jaymes on the phone asking for someone called Big Pauli. Then he talks to this guy about what's happening with the Stones tour and the free concert. Something heavy is going on, Sam. You're from England and you don't understand what America is like. These people are not cool; you should be very careful. So should the Stones."

I told her not to worry, and made a mental note to talk to Mick again. He soon wandered in and the girl left the two of us alone.

"Mick, why is John Jaymes so centrally involved in our tour, man? What the fuck has he got to do with the Rolling Stones?"

Mick gave me a sunny smile and replied airily, "Fucked if I know. I didn't hire 'im and as long as he doesn't talk to me I don't really care." Mick stared hard at me. "Sam, let me give you a word of advice. You need to learn how to relax." And with that he wandered out again, leaving me to wonder how a control freak couldn't give a damn about a bunch of armed thugs who were slowly taking control of his American tour.

CHAPTER 21

The Big Apple

We flew first class to New York the following day and checked into the Plaza Hotel under false names, with at least a hundred girls of all shapes and sizes eyeing us lasciviously in the lobby. Finally I was in the Big Apple, with the greatest rock'n'roll band in the world. I felt like I had reached the top of some lofty mountain.

After I had everyone settled in, I went upstairs to check on Keith and make sure that he was cool, and he decided he wanted to go to Manny's music shop. I called Stu and the three of us jumped in a limo.

Manny's was a treasure trove. Keith happily sat himself on a Fender twin amplifier and Stu and I would bring him various axes that he'd look at, either accept or reject, and then have a play. If he liked it, he bought it. Keith purchased maybe a dozen guitars and he seemed as happy as can be.

I found a small Gibson acoustic with a cut-away body and showed it to Keith. He wasn't interested, so while Keith mucked about elsewhere I sat doing my Big Bill Broonzy impression on the Gibson.

Keith noticed me playing. "You really like that one?"

I told him I loved it and Keith promptly bought it for me. It was the first Gibson I had ever owned and I thanked him profusely.

Keith sighed good-naturedly. "Sam, it's just a guitar."

"Not to me, Keef," I said. "I love it, and thanks for buying it for me, man."

"Yeah, well, that's okay, don't go on about it, I might change me mind," he said. "Where can I get a fucking drink?" I literally ran to the bar next door for my main man. (It's forty years later and I still have the guitar.)

God knows there have been some awful things said about Keith, but he always treated me with kindness and a generosity of spirit that never wavered. I loved the man. He was one cool motherfucker.

Back at the Plaza Hotel, Stones fans were everywhere and the hotel security were having endless hassles trying to keep sexy young things from riding the elevators and wandering the hotel corridors looking for the band. In my room I met with a rude surprise: most of my clothes had been taken and the only thing left was a TWA flight bag the thieves had not bothered to steal. I would have to go shopping. I decided to buy underwear and socks, a couple of T-shirts, and a razor; the whole lot would fit in the flight bag. I could keep it with me at all times and not have to bother with a suitcase.

From then on I bought jeans when I needed them and when they were dirty I just threw them away.

In the morning we were due to leave for Detroit and there was an evening to kill. I really wanted to talk to someone about the tour situation. All of the Mafia types were beginning to depress me and I was over trying to tell Mick about the unsavory characters surrounding him. Mick didn't give a toss about this traveling circus of misfits, miscreants, and lollipop-sucking sycophants.

I checked in with the troops. Mick was going out to dinner and wanted me to get him some cash from Ronnie. Keith was holed up in his room and didn't need anything or anyone, just a call fifteen minutes before we had to go anywhere. Charlie was off with the writer Stanley Booth to a jazz club and Bill was playing with his lady Astrid. Mick Taylor was nowhere to be seen. There was nothing for me to do, so my friend Chesley Millikin and I arranged to meet in the Plaza bar.

Chesley had a wise head on relatively young shoulders. We met in the bar and then made our way to my room, where we could talk in private. We started off with a couple of beers and some uninviting sandwiches. The beers disappeared in short order and we called for more. We rolled a spliff and I explained my dilemma.

"John Jaymes is slowly but surely taking over this tour. D'you know anything about him?" Chesley looked blank.

"I know nothing about the man," he replied, "except I can tell you he's a nasty piece of work."

"Chesley," I said, "I think he's some kind of front for the Mafia and is trying to take over the whole bloody tour."

Chesley gave me his take on the situation. "There's competing forces at work here, boyo. Klein's stuck in New York and has nothing to do with the tour, but he is still legally their manager. Ronnie's just looking after the money like he's always done. Mick thinks he's in charge, but if you want my opinion, the man has got his head in the clouds and his brain in his underpants. Mick's the pope and while he's busy dealing with what heaven wants, down here on earth the natives are doing what the natives always do."

"What's that?" I asked.

"They're squabbling about power and glory, Sam, power and glory."

I tried another tack. "Chesley, d'you know that John Jaymes says he was involved with the Beatles' gig at Shea Stadium?"

Chesley sighed. "Sam, what you call the Mafia is everywhere in America."

I toked on the joint and tried to pay close attention.

"Organized crime controls the Teamsters. If you want to go into any large facility in the States, your equipment has to be delivered by a Teamster truck. You can't fight it, and if you take my advice you'd do well to stay out of it. I mean, why would you bother? John Jaymes is a joke, just another flim-flam artist trying to pull some bullshit on the Rolling Stones. John Jaymes is not the Mafia, though he may well be working on their behalf. Ronnie Schneider's no mug; he's got the money and there's no way Jaymes or any of those sleazebags will get anywhere near anything really important."

I wasn't convinced and told Chesley about Belli, the piece of land, and the Knights of Columbus.

He smiled in a weary way. "Sam, the Knights of Columbus are powerful and are all over America just like the Teamsters. Take my advice, don't get involved. Look after the boys and stay out of all the other bullshit. These people are dangerous, Sam. If Mick can't be bothered about it all, then why should you? Fuck it, the tour will be over in a fortnight, who gives a toss about all of this? I don't want to see you getting hurt."

With a silly show of bravado I showed Chesley my boot gun. He was shocked.

"What on earth are you doing with a peashooter? This tour's got far too much cocaine going on, it's not healthy. Everyone's getting paranoid and you with a gun is downright ridiculous. Do you really think you could shoot someone?"

"I could only shoot someone that was trying to shoot me," I said, not too convincingly.

He shook his head sadly and I ordered more beers, feeling a trifle silly about the gun. "Chesley, what do you think about this free concert idea? Are the Grateful Dead and Scully capable of organizing this or are we getting ourselves into a huge mess?"

Chesley grinned. "Rock's a lovely man to be sure, but he doesn't understand what'll happen. If the Stones play for free there'll be a million people there; it'll be chaos. I don't think there's a chance in hell that the concert can be pulled off. There's not enough time to do it properly, you know that. Do you think this is a good idea?"

"No one seems to care," I moaned.

"Do your work, Sam, and stay out of it. Let Ronnie and John Jaymes and those guys take care of it. If it all goes wrong they can have the blame. Now let's get something to eat."

We hit the street and headed for supper, but I felt like I was eating the last meal of a condemned man. I would be damned by the Stones if I criticized the free concert idea, and condemned to having to work on the bloody thing if they decided to go ahead. After a couple more beers, though, I decided to just get on with things, telling myself not very convincingly: such is life.

CHAPTER 22

Bringing home the bacon

The following morning we just managed to make the flight to Detroit, and I had a chance to think things over. With each passing day, the free concert was assuming wider public relations significance. At a chaotic press conference we had held in New York, all the questions had been about the free concert and the price of tickets. You might say the Stones were stuck between a rock and a hard place; if they refused to play now, their unwarranted reputation for greed would merely be enhanced. Mick had foolishly and prematurely announced that the free concert would be held on December 6. There was, as yet, no site available, but there was no turning back.

We walked through the Detroit airport and a photographer took a picture of Mick and me. His name, I subsequently found out, was Andrew Sacks. It was a pretty standard shot, but when Sacks developed the photo, he stripped in a shot of the widely disliked President Nixon, which made it look as if he was standing in the airport watching Mick walk by. Nixon had his hands in the air as though he was saluting Mick as some conquering hero.

The subtext was plain: the Rolling Stones' "greed" over their ticket prices was equated with the worst elements of Nixon and his administration.

It was published in *Rolling Stone*. Incredibly, no one at the magazine seemed to realize what the photo actually implied and no reference was ever made in the accompanying text to Nixon and Mick.

To us it seemed like another snide dig at the Stones, subtly trying to undermine their position with the fans. Mick, ever the diplomat, decided to ignore it. As for me, I thought I looked cute carrying my TWA flight bag and made a mental note to ask the photographer for a copy, even if it was a savage put-down of the band I loved.

The Detroit show was fantastic. Motor City seemed to suit the Stones. The audience was racially mixed and the brothers were out in force with their dazzling girls, looking like a million dollars. The Stones picked up on the elevated vibe and delivered a show of powerful intensity.

I must have seen a thousand Tina Turner look-alikes that night, all of them in wigs and wearing some truly impressive bling on breasts that floated like lifejackets tantalizingly out of touch for us white boys drowning in testosterone.

Mick was in his element, surrounded by so much brown sugar, and he showed those ladies he could dance. The ladies loved him, while their men sucked on golden toothpicks, tried to stay cool and promised themselves they'd shoot his scrawny arse if he so much as said a word to their women. It was the best music of the tour. I noted that Mr. Booth, our resident tour writer, didn't make it to Detroit. He missed a great show, the sucker!

We returned to New York briefly and then we were off to Philadelphia. Now that the band were playing at their best, Philly felt like little more than a slightly extended trip to the grocery store. It must have felt to the Stones a bit like the old days, when gigs blurred into one another, and they'd slept in the back of a van that roared the length and breadth of England.

We returned to the Plaza Hotel around midnight and the band walked through the lobby to be greeted by a sight that I'll never forget. A distinguished-looking doorman in full uniform was wheeling a large blue tank of nitrous oxide (laughing gas) across the lobby, while close behind a bellboy struggled with various pieces of luggage. Directing operations was a man with a shock of bright red hair, a freckled face, and only one hand.

Goldfinger had made it to New York.

He passed me in the lobby and told me quietly: "Mr. Wilson." He had thoughtfully booked himself in under the name of the British prime minister. Nice touch.

It was just after midnight, and in a fleet of limousines the band and some friends went to Reuben's, the famous delicatessen, which served just about the worst corn beef on rye sandwiches you've ever tasted. Keith and I thought that the owners should be forced to go to the Stamford Hill Salt Beef Bar in London; there they'd learn what a real Jewish sandwich tasted like.

Keith and I made our excuses and left early. I escorted him back to the hotel, where I called Goldfinger. He said to come on up.

Three sleepy girls in the lobby were ecstatic when I invited them upstairs to party. Keith asked me to have Goldfinger call him and he went to his room while I steered the girls to where the nitrous oxide tank resided.

The ladies were a little unsure of Goldfinger, but were suitably mollified when I told them he was the president of the Rolling Stones' record company, a very powerful man. He was accompanied by a gloriously ethereal hippie chick who ogled the trio of groupies, no doubt anticipating what was to come. Some lines and a couple of spliffs did the rest and within minutes everyone was hard at play. The three girls who had hoped to experience a scene with Keith were now being expertly introduced to the pleasures of Sappho.

In a tangle of arms and legs, Goldfinger's lady was sucking and probing and tickling, accompanied by much giggling from the trio. Goldfinger left on some errand or other for Keith, which discretion demanded I know nothing about, so I found myself in a hotel suite with three hotties, Goldfinger's main squeeze, and the biggest tank of nitrous one could imagine.

CHAPTER 23

More foolish plans

A Learjet was organized to take us on the flight south to Baltimore. Somewhere on the journey another jet was visible flying in the same direction and we asked our pilot to fly as close as aviation regulations would allow. We attempted to wave to our fellow travelers through the small windows, but it was difficult to see whether our efforts had been successful, so we decided to moon one another, aircraft to aircraft.

We pressed our arses to the windows and strained to see whether the other people reciprocated. Whether we received a moon in return, or if it was merely a fat face pressed to a window, I do not know, but I'm pretty sure that if it happened it was an historic first and well worthy of inclusion in the Guinness Book of World Records.

Baltimore held nothing memorable as a gig, other than the transport that got us there, but the band took care of business and delivered a screamer of a show.

Madison Square Garden was next. The Stones would be playing three shows in two days to almost 50,000 paying customers. Back-to-back gigs all over the eastern seaboard were hugely demanding on both band and crew, so by the time we returned for the Garden shows everyone's nerves were as taut as a ballerina's buttocks.

Mick had to carry more than his fair share of the load. As well as fronting the band, he constantly had to talk with people, and fatigue is the enemy of the human voice. It was agreed that Mick should, if it were feasible, spend the time on the east coast with a scarf wrapped around his neck and saying as little as possible.

Mick's self-imposed period of vocal restraint coincided with the most frenetic stretch of the tour, with shows in Detroit, Philly, Baltimore, New York, and Boston in just nine days. This was when serious decisions were made about the free concert and they were made in an atmosphere of chronic fatigue, rampant cocaine consumption and near exhaustion. No wonder we didn't cancel the bloody thing; no one had either the wisdom or the strength to say no!

The Madison Square Garden shows were to be recorded as part of the film being made of the tour by "the Measles," better known as David and Albert Maysles. The filming of live music shows is problematic, as the requirements of film can sometimes override the requirements of the show. This can lead to a situation where everyone ends up playing to the camera rather than to the audience. Martin Scorsese's film of The Band's final show, *The Last Waltz*, felt very much like this to me.

The Stones were insistent that this would not happen at Madison Square Garden and the Maysles were told that no cinematic concessions would be made. They would have to capture the action as it happened and Mick insisted that he didn't want camera crew crawling about on stage and letting the audience feel that they were merely extras in a film.

Gimme Shelter, the Maysles' film, captures the shows perfectly. Mick was shattered, the band was exhausted, and Keith was several years past his best-before date, yet the Stones come across as one of the most high-powered rock bands one could ever wish for.

In a line of limousines we left for the Garden, and Goldfinger added his own car to the procession. We swept into the venue fueled by coke and optimism, and decamped into what felt like a police convention. In attendance was, seemingly, every off-duty drug squad officer available. I scuttled the band into the dressing-rooms and headed off to meet Jaymes and find out why there were so many cops backstage.

Jaymes was having an apoplectic fit about Goldfinger, whom his efficient security force had allowed to drive straight into the backstage area. Jaymes saw me approaching and began to talk like a man on speed.

"Sam, we can't have that man backstage, he's a liability, it's not good for the Stones." Jaymes drew himself up to his full self-righteous height. "He's a smuggler, he's known to the cops all over America, he's being followed by federal agents."

I looked around. Goldfinger was standing with his lady, minding his own business, and his limousine had exited the building. No one had followed him as far as I could tell. "He's a friend of Keith's," I lied. "It's not a problem. I'll get him a room to hang out in."

When I'd taken care of Goldfinger, I headed back to sort out the security. Jaymes was busy handing out backstage passes to his cronies. It was time to give him my official voice. "Now, John, see all these people? Get 'em out front of house where they can do some good. Leave half-a-dozen here and get rid of the rest."

Jaymes looked at me. "I'll get rid of my people, but some of them have invited their family to the show. They all want to see the Stones."

I went ballistic. "Since when did you have the right to decide who can be backstage at a Stones concert? Go fuck yourself. Put two security men at the stage door, two backstage by the stairs, and two by the dressing-rooms, and get everyone else out of here. And get this straight: no one can authorize anyone backstage except me, Ronnie, and Chip Monk. We'll decide who comes in here and that's the end of it."

Jaymes looked glum — he was going to have to explain to

his men that they weren't going to get the royal treatment. I told him I wanted a private word.

He followed me to a small dressing-room next to where I had stashed Goldfinger. I asked him to sit down and listen carefully to what I had to say, and not interrupt.

"John, what's the name of your company?"

"Young America Enterprises," he replied.

"Has your company been negotiating with the people who own Sears Point?"

"No," Jaymes replied. It was a barefaced lie.

"Has your company been negotiating with Mel Belli or the Knights of Columbus?"

"No," he lied again.

"John, I know that you offered Sears Point up to a hundred off-duty police officers. How can someone like you, the man from Chrysler, get one hundred police officers from the East to the West Coast? I also know that you offered them insurance. Please don't bother to deny it, John, I know this happened. I have to tell you this. My job is to look after the Rolling Stones. I don't give a fuck if this free show happens or not, but I do care about who we're going to be working with. If you're going to be involved, John, here's a word of advice: you better let people know what you're up to. As far as I know, you have no right to talk on behalf of the Rolling Stones."

Jaymes spoke with the intensity of a rattlesnake about to strike. "Ronnie and Mel Belli know everything there is to know about what I'm doing, Sam. Might I suggest you're a little bit out of your depth. I have Mel Belli's full cooperation and we're going to come up with an alternative site for the free concert. The people at Sears Point can go fuck themselves, the show's never going to happen there. Don't get involved in stuff that's not your responsibility."

I wished Mick could have heard what he'd just said and witnessed his arrogance and pride.

"John, we'll talk some more. I have work to do right now.

There's shit happening that we don't like and we're going to have to get to the bottom of it."

I had to go and rescue the band from the idiots that Jaymes's security people had let enter the dressing-rooms.

Jaymes called out to me as I left: "See you in San Francisco!"

There must have been fifty people in the dressing-rooms, including Jimi Hendrix and a very drunk Janis Joplin. In the corner, a politician from the mayor's office was talking to a reporter, and various girls were on the prowl. Charlie Watts and Bill Wyman were sitting forlornly by themselves, and Keith and Mick Taylor were playing their unplugged electric guitars.

I went to cheer Charlie up and he gave me a wan smile. "Isn't this great," he sighed. "It's a bloody circus. I'll be glad when this is over and I can go home."

He was due on stage in thirty minutes to play one of the most important shows of the tour, and was not in the best of moods. I decided to clear the dressing-room of all but the musicians. It was time for the amiable Tony Funches to do his thing.

Tony, a huge cat with rippling muscles, never raised his voice, but he took shit from no one. People reluctantly cooperated, and even Jimi Hendrix kindly offered to leave if it would help cool things out. He was a sweetheart. I winked at him and let him know he was okay while I maneuvered the other people toward the door. Jimi sat chatting quietly to Mick. Only Janis made a fuss.

I smiled at her, introduced myself, and explained that the band liked to have fifteen minutes alone prior to going on stage. Janis wobbled unsteadily on her feet and breathed fumes of Southern Comfort into my face. "You know who I am, man?" she mumbled.

I gave her another smile. "Yeah, you're Janis Joplin and we love having you drop in to visit but now it's time to clear the dressing-room."

Janis seemed confused and took a swig out of the bottle she was carrying. "D'you know who I am?" she demanded again.

"Janis," I said sweetly, "please don't be difficult. The band wants the dressing-room cleared of people."

Janis swiveled around to face Keith, who was sitting behind her. "Hey, man," she whined, "your dude is trying to throw me out of your dressing-room."

Keith smiled indulgently. "Yeah, baby, them's the rules. We gotta have a little peace and quiet before the gig begins. How else we gonna get in tune?" he chuckled.

Janis sat down with a bump on the seat beside Keith. She wasn't going anywhere. Keith shrugged at me and grinned, as if to say, Over to you, Sam. This was obviously a job for the Stones' diplomatic corps.

I sidled up to Janis and sat down beside her. "Hey, Janis," I whispered in her ear, "would you like a couple of lines of the finest Peruvian flake?"

"Chop 'em out, big boy," she answered in her distinctive Texan drawl.

"Not here, Janis, not in front of all these people. There's press in here. I have a room next door."

Janis rose unsteadily to her feet and addressed the Stones: "Well, I guess I'll see you boys later, I gotta see a man about a dog." I wheeled her to the room where I had stashed Goldfinger and his lady. Needs must when the devil drives.

We knocked and entered to find the couple hastily adjusting their clothing. Janis let out a high-pitched squeal. "Kenny, you ol' bastard! What are you doing on the East Coast?" She collapsed into his arms with laughter all round.

What a blessing. They were old friends from the San Francisco scene. Janis forgot all about the Stones and focused instead on the bag of drugs hanging from Goldfinger's shoulder. Goldfinger promised to look after her as I headed out the door.

When I ran into Ronnie, I asked for an update on the free concert. He was against us doing the show but Mick was committed to going ahead. I pointed out to Ronnie that we had actually announced the date of the show. People all over

America would now be making plans to attend. The fact that no one knew where the concert was going to be held didn't matter.

"Sam, you have to go to California and get this sorted," he sighed. "It looks like we're going to have to find another site."

I knew this was coming and asked Ronnie when he expected me to leave for the coast.

"After the Florida gig," he replied. "The Stones are going to Muscle Shoals and there's nothing for you to do there. We need you in San Francisco. Mick wants the concert to go ahead. Discussion over. It's up to us to get this together and make it happen." Ronnie assured me that I had his and Mick's total support, and then, at last, it was showtime.

As usual, we were running late, and when the Stones hit the stage to a deafening roar, the building felt like it was trembling.

Goldfinger supported a drunken Janis to the side of the stage and everybody was more or less happy. All I had to do was to make sure that she didn't try to get on stage to sing with Mick. Fortunately she was so drunk that if Goldfinger hadn't found her a chair to sit in she would have fallen over. Even Janis didn't have the balls to actually crawl on stage to reach the microphone.

Now that I knew I was going out to California again my attitude to the project subtly changed. I did not want to be in charge of the whole thing; no way. Let it be Rock Scully, Emmett Grogan, or Michael Laing, the producer of the Woodstock festival, who had suddenly turned up on the West Coast. I had already heard that they were talking to West Coast radio stations. I really did not want to be in charge; not at all.

I was equally sure that we should not present the free concert as a Rolling Stones project, but rather a cooperative effort on the part of all the bands involved. In this way we could spread the glory and the risk. I had previously made this suggestion but it had been received with stony silence by Mick, who was not in the business of sharing top billing with anyone.

"Sam," he had told me, "whoever else we have on the bill,

this will always be the Rolling Stones' free concert. It's our baby whether we like it or not."

Back at the Plaza I cornered Ronnie and talked about money. Ronnie promised that he would be in San Francisco and liaising with Belli and everyone else and that he would be holding the purse strings. Without the authority to spend money, I pointed out to Ronnie, there was little point in my being in San Francisco. Who was going to pay the Angels the money for beer, for starters? Ronnie thought all the bands should chip in, but I thought this impractical. What was I to do — pass round a collection plate?

The problem of the money for the Angels' beer never did get sorted out in a satisfactory manner. In the end I paid for it with my own money, thinking that the Stones would reimburse me.

None of the other bands that played on the day managed to get it together to make a contribution. The Stones never repaid me and all I got for my trouble was forty years of bullshit about how the Stones had hired the Hells Angels for $500 worth of beer.

CHAPTER 24

Welcome to California

I arrived in San Francisco on December 2 with $1,000 in my pocket — an advance on my wages. It was the last money I ever received from the often-parsimonious Rolling Stones. I didn't have a budget and I didn't even have a hotel room and nobody had bothered to meet me at the airport.

Welcome to California!

I put in a call to the Grateful Dead's office and soon got a wildly enthusiastic Rock Scully on the phone. The energy levels were cookin'. I should come over, he said. Michael Laing, the producer of Woodstock, was in town.

I rented a car and made for Marin County. Somehow or other I was to coordinate the rock dreams of the Rolling Stones and the Grateful Dead, Jefferson Airplane and Santana, the Flying Burrito Brothers and Crosby, Stills, and Nash, and some half a million kids who were rumored to be heading in our direction — "like lemmings," as one of Belli's lawyers put it.

John Jaymes and several of his associates were already on the West Coast. Chip Monk was weaving his magic at Sears Point, building the stage, working on the assumption that a deal would be brokered between the site's owners and the Stones.

I arrived at the Grateful Dead's offices to be greeted by what can best be described as pandemonium. There was Rock Scully, talking earnestly to someone from a Los Angeles radio station on the office phone. The place was packed with people, none of whom I knew, running around like chickens with their heads cut off. Music was pumping in the background, joints were being rolled and smoked, and everyone was high on organizing a concert that as yet didn't even have a location.

I was introduced to Michael Laing, who seemed a nice enough guy, though I couldn't for the life of me understand why he was there. What did he have to do with a free concert in San Francisco? As soon as I could get everyone's attention, I demanded that we have a meeting without any of the press. We retreated to Lenny Hart's office and the first thing I did was put in a call to Craig Murray, the president of the Sears Point Raceway.

Murray was pissed off. He complained that he had been telephoned by many people claiming to represent the Rolling Stones and I was just the latest. He said he had talked to "Chipmunk," Mel Belli, and Ronnie Schneider, and had long conversations with a guy called John Jaymes, who also claimed to represent the Stones. I asked him to speak to Belli's office to confirm my bona fides and get back to me. I then called Belli's office and was staggered to hear that John Jaymes was there coordinating things on the Stones' behalf.

I got through to Ronnie Schneider at Muscle Shoals. What the hell was Jaymes doing in San Francisco? Ronnie didn't have an answer to my question. When I told him that Jaymes had promised Murray a hundred cops, Ronnie snorted with disdain. He'd be there within twenty-four hours, he said, and I shouldn't worry. It looked like John Jaymes and "Young America Enterprises" were effectively in the driving seat, though they had still to come up with a site.

I decided to take a look at the preparations at Sears Point. The offer of a helicopter to fly out there came as something of a surprise. It had been made available by a local company for "the Rolling Stones' free concert" and was being paid for by a San

Francisco radio station. With a reporter asking me questions, we flew to Sears Point, where it was clear that little was happening. A road grader stood idly; it had obviously been used to carve out a patch approximately twenty meters square upon which a stage was being constructed. Things did not look promising.

The stage construction was perhaps a third complete and there wasn't a soul in sight. Two bored security guys came up to the helicopter as we landed and demanded that we leave, telling the radio journalist that there wasn't a chance in hell there was going to be a concert at this facility, "if the fucking Rolling Stones won't pay," as they put it.

I put in a call to Mick at Muscle Shoals and told him in no uncertain terms that everything on the West Coast was fucked. Once again he told me that Belli would take charge and things would work out. When I mentioned John Jaymes, Mick screamed that Jaymes had nothing whatsoever to do with anything. The best I could get out of him was a sigh and a "talk to Ronnie" and then he simply hung up the phone. With the benefit of hindsight I don't know why I didn't quit then and there. We didn't even have a site. Come to think of it, I didn't even have a bed, so I went out to the Dead's ranch, where I slept for a few hours in the barn. I was beginning to feel very alone.

On Wednesday I went to Mel Belli's office and found John Jaymes confidently talking to the press about the Stones. I asked to see Belli and was fobbed off with one of his juniors, who explained to me that I was a negative influence and Mr. Jaymes didn't want me talking to the press. While Ronnie Schneider was in transit John Jaymes was establishing himself as a spokesman for the Stones.

A camera crew from the Maysles team took shots of Jaymes as he talked on the telephone and confidently predicted that half a million kids would be at the concert. I left Belli's office in disgust and headed back to the Grateful Dead headquarters. Belli and Jaymes were taking over the whole project and the hippies out in Marin County were not going to be involved if this pair had their way. If they controlled the concert site they could ultimately control the film, which was where the money lay. I wondered what Jaymes was telling "Big Pauli" back in New York now that he was so close to running everything.

Back at the Dead's office I went into yet another meeting. Jerry Garcia was a bit like Jagger — if the concert was "free," he refused to believe that there was anything that could ultimately be controlled by any kind of criminal interests. He felt confident that if the Stones allied themselves with the West Coast musicians, all would be well. I tried to explain about the film, about Mel Belli and the lawyers, John Jaymes and the off-duty narcs, and none of this seemed to faze Garcia or the other people at the meeting. "Just keep the concert free" was their insistent mantra, as if that would keep it out of trouble.

We needed an alternative desperately; did anyone know of a site that could accommodate half a million people? The hippies thoughtfully smoked their joints and not one of them came up with a suggestion. They were lovely people, but as much use as the proverbial chocolate teapot.

On Thursday morning we finally had a breakthrough. Belli's office informed me that we were being offered a site at Altamont in the East Bay and that I had to get someone to approve of it as soon as possible. The suits knew that they couldn't go ahead without the okay of someone from the Stones. No one at the Dead's offices knew where this proposed concert site was, except for one of the office girls, who said it was high desert country and the last place anyone would want to go for a concert, free or otherwise. I asked Rock and Michael Laing to jump in a helicopter and check it.

Again, with the benefit of hindsight, this was a mistake. I should have gone and checked out the site myself, but decided it was better that I stay at headquarters. If I had gone to see the site I could have at least refused to sanction it as suitable. So while Scully and Laing roared off in the helicopter I went into the Dead's office looking at maps of California to find

Altamont. It wasn't even on the map, though there was a place worryingly called "Altamont Pass."

Within half an hour I was on the telephone to Dick Carter, the owner of the place, who told me that the site was a car racetrack and it was a go as far as he was concerned. I talked to Scully and Laing and, while they had reservations about the site, they reckoned that it could be done. It was a qualified yes, but a yes nonetheless. I relayed my approval to Belli and one more piece in the diabolical jigsaw puzzle was firmly put in place.

Unbelievably, Carter then told me that he didn't want any money for the show, just insurance. He'd take the publicity as payment. He told me that he'd already talked to Jaymes and Belli and that he was going to Belli's office to sign a contract. Ominously, he also told me that he had no idea who Ronnie Schneider was.

Thirty minutes later I was listening to the news being broadcast triumphantly upon the local radio stations: Altamont was to be the site of the Stones' free concert. No one with any authority from the band had given their approval for an announcement to be made. None of the Stones' management had even seen the site yet. I was in Marin County and I wasn't to see the location for the concert until the Friday evening, the day before the show.

CHAPTER 25

The construction of nightmares

In less than forty-eight hours the Rolling Stones were due to play a free concert that was being gleefully confirmed on every radio station on the West Coast of America from San Diego to Seattle. Tens of thousands of kids were frantically consulting maps to find out where Altamont was and jumping on every available form of transport in order to get there as quickly as possible.

The original Sears Point site had a half-constructed stage and perhaps ten portable toilets and a pile of scaffolding. All of this would need to be moved across the San Francisco Bay to Altamont, a distance of some ninety-odd miles.

The Grateful Dead family and friends, in conjunction with Chip Monk, decided that it was possible to get the show together in the time, and reluctantly, I agreed to do my bit. I went on the local radio stations asking for volunteers with trucks and pick-ups to go to Sears Point to help move everything to the new location. In an outpouring of generosity, several hundred people made the journey and helped out.

Owsley Stanley (aka The Bear, the Dead's long-time sound-man) and the Dead's other equipment people sorted speakers and amplifiers and arranged for them to be shipped to Altamont by truck and helicopter. Giant spotlights were maneuvered into position, scaffolding towers were built, and the many other concert necessities were put in place by a willing and positive work force of Bay Area volunteers. It was a staggering effort, and one that received little recognition from the press, who were obsessed by the Stones and cared little for the ordinary people whose herculean efforts had made the concert possible at such short notice.

I finally met up with Keith at Altamont on Friday afternoon and I was appalled by what I saw. The place was an absolute shithole, the worst possible spot for a concert one could imagine. There were already more than 100,000 people at the site and their numbers were increasing by the hour.

The sight of Keith Richards spurred the workers on. Keith was absolutely blown away by the general good vibes and the sheer effort people were putting in. He happily walked around, sharing a joint and thanking people for their heroic devotion. We retreated to the proposed backstage area, where someone had thoughtfully parked a tiny caravan-cum-dressing-room. I reviewed arrangements with an ad hoc committee of Bay Area volunteers.

The stage was impossibly low, less than a meter in height, and this was a primary concern. It was located at the foot of a hill in the neck of a valley. We decided to build a barricade of trucks at the back of the stage so that at least we would have some protection from the crowds. I noted with concern that a lot of people now at Altamont already seemed drunk.

I went to the offices of the racetrack and met the owner, Dick Carter. He seemed a nice enough guy but completely out of his depth. He told me that he had a contract for the concert and I asked to see it, but it suddenly became unavailable. He said that it had been signed by John Jaymes on behalf of Young America Enterprises. The Rolling Stones hadn't actually signed the contract themselves. I smiled inwardly, feeling reasonably certain that there was no way anyone from the Stones would sign a contract for a site that was inherently unsuitable for the purpose.

Carter said he had insurance and that John Jaymes had promised that he would be indemnified from all liabilities. Jaymes now controlled the site and, in effect, the whole show. I wondered if Mick had a clue about any of this, and then decided it was perhaps all part of a fiendishly cunning master plan of Ronnie Schneider's to protect the Rolling Stones from any legal liability should things go wrong. I went off in search of Jaymes to talk about police and security.

Jaymes was speaking with a high-ranking officer from the California Highway Patrol. The police were decidedly unhappy about the number of cars approaching the site; there was already gridlock on the main north-south highway. Thousands of cars were being abandoned some five miles away and people were wandering all over the neighboring ranches. There was a distinct possibility that kids could be shot by hostile ranchers.

The Highway Patrol was finding it almost impossible to keep any of the roads open for emergency vehicles. The police had hired every tow truck from miles around and as fast as cars blocked the roads, the cops towed them away.

Two deputies arrived from the Alameda Sheriff's department and talked about getting a court order banning the concert. I laughed in their faces. What did they think the people who were already here would do in that event — simply disappear? The sheriffs told me that every available man was on duty. They had asked the Governor's office for extra police.

When I asked how many men the Alameda Sheriff's department had on duty, I was told "around twenty." The Highway Patrol said that every available car and officer in the East Bay had been diverted for duties at or near Altamont. They estimated this was around thirty cars. They also had a helicopter.

It looked like there were going to be roughly fifty cops to control a crowd of half a million people. It was becoming increasingly clear that we were going to have to use our own people for personal security.

I asked Jaymes how many men we had. Twenty, he told me.

"Are they all armed?" I asked.

"Certainly," said Jaymes.

"What the fuck happened to the hundred guys you promised at Sears Point, then?"

Jaymes shrugged and said he didn't think they were necessary.

I told Jaymes that I wanted every one of our police officers on the stage and directly answerable to me. Jaymes agreed and then told me that he would be in the racetrack offices with Dick Carter, close to the phones in case of any emergencies. I dismissed this as Jaymes simply opting for the superior comfort and safety of the office, and demanded that he get all of his men to the site early in the morning.

The music was due to begin in something like fourteen hours and I wanted to be sure that our security was present from the get-go. I wanted Jaymes there with me to instruct his men on the chain of command. Jaymes assured me that this would not be a problem. I went off to find Keith.

It was now getting dark and in the dusk there were people spread across the site as far as you could see. There were at least a couple of hundred thousand people present already.

There was nowhere for helicopters to land in darkness, and I told Keith that if we didn't leave soon we were here for the night. He was having such a good time he decided he wanted to stay on site until the show. I left him in the trailer, having made him promise he wouldn't wander off on his own. A couple of Hells Angels were in the backstage area and they seemed chilled out. I left them chatting with Keith and a group of others who were sitting in the caravan rolling spliffs and having a good time. I needed to check out what was happening on the hillsides surrounding the stage.

From the stage itself, the view was unsettling. Hundreds of campfires had been lit and people could be seen partying. A huge crane was lifting massive spotlights onto the top of a scaffold tower, with crowds of people immediately below. If one of the lights had been accidentally dropped, many people would have been killed. Equipment guys could be seen swarming over the PA towers.

Slowly the whole stage area was coming together. Everyone was going to work right through the night. More than fifty equipment guys from the Bay Area's most prominent bands struggled to make it happen: the crews from the Grateful Dead, New Riders of the Purple Sage, Jefferson Airplane, Big Brother, Santana, Quicksilver Messenger Service, plus guys from venues including the Family Dog and the Fillmore West and Bill Graham's outfits. These guys built the sound, the back-line, and the whole show at Altamont in less than thirty hours! I did my best to at least let everyone I met know that the Rolling Stones appreciated their efforts. I watched the underground community at their cooperative best. It was very inspiring and strangely moving.

I was proud that Keith had decided to stay. He sat in the caravan surrounded by admirers with literally hundreds more waiting outside to see him, and was as sociable as could be. I popped my head in the door and checked on my main man. "Everything sweet?" Keith made me a virtually imperceptible sign and I knew that I had to get him somewhere private where no one could see what he was up to, including me.

I had a word with Jackson, one of the Grateful Dead's crew, and we took Keith from the caravan to the truck, which Jackson had parked against the back of the stage. We put Keith in the rear of the truck and pulled down the roller door, allowing him to do whatever it was he had to do. I had to reassure Jackson that he wasn't going to shit in the back of his truck, which was all that Jackson cared about. Keith banged on the roller door and walked out of the truck with a grin on his face and powder on his nose. I got him back to the caravan and all was well.

I decided to go with Jackson and take a stroll around the concert site to see what was going on and gauge the mood. It was after midnight, and there were fires blazing for miles. We picked our way through the crowd and the further we walked the more concerned I became.

Many of the punters were drunk and in places it looked like some bacchanalian orgy was underway. People were having sex quite openly around some of the fires, children were wandering about, and I couldn't believe how many dogs strolled through the crowd hopefully looking for their owners.

Everywhere I looked, I saw people with crazed expressions on their faces, suffering from some form of bum trip. Jackson said bad acid was no doubt responsible, but we were shocked at the numbers of people who seemed to be affected. They were in their hundreds, if not thousands, and Jackson muttered to me, "Man, this is an ugly scene, real ugly."

People were offering us acid for free, and I asked someone where he got it. He grinned like a maniac and said, "They're giving it away, man, giving it away." I never did find out who "they" were, but I certainly wasn't going to take any street acid.

The further we got from the stage, the weirder it became. It was absolutely freezing. People were not dressed to deal with the low temperatures and thousands went on the hunt for fuel to throw on the fires. There wasn't a fencepost left within miles of Altamont, and several derelict barns were pushed over by the crowd and demolished to feed the hungry flames. For the cattle farmers whose properties adjoined the concert site it was an absolute disaster. Traumatized cattle were wandering all over the county and thousands of people were trespassing.

I saw abandoned cars burning and people with madness in their eyes dancing in the firelight. I became very afraid.

"These ain't San Francisco people, man," Jackson told me. "These people are from the Peninsula, nothing to do with San Francisco." We headed back to the stage.

I wanted tomorrow to come as fast as possible so that we could do what we had to do and get the hell out of there.

CHAPTER 26

One way or another

Back at the caravan, Keith was in full swing, with a lady seated on either side of him to keep him warm and at least twenty people stuffed into the small space, hanging on his every word. I decided to get bossy and announced that we would have to take a break. I wanted Keith to see what was happening outside. Keith refused. "I ain't going anywhere, man. This is where I'm staying."

And that was that.

He should have witnessed the chaos that was happening outside. But what could he have done? Made a phone call and canceled the whole thing? The sad truth was that there was no way to go back.

Dawn broke at Altamont on December 6, 1969, and from the stage it looked like I was observing the camp of some dreadful invading army. In the gray light, a thousand fires sent smoke straight up into the still and bitterly cold dawn air. Tens of thousands of people stood around the remains of the fires. Whenever anybody spoke, clouds of steamy breath punctuated the freezing air.

Amazingly, the concert was more or less ready to go.

We had a PA system that worked, and all the bands' equipment had arrived and was in place. A helicopter site had been laid out; medical facilities had been established. The stage was the size of a small handkerchief, surrounded by a quarter of a million people.

Keith had run out of cigarettes and was wide awake and needed a drink. What to do? I found Jaymes drinking coffee with Dick Carter in the speedway offices, looking very pleased with himself. I asked for one of his men to go on a supplies run, which meant getting on a helicopter and going to the Huntington Hotel. We needed cartons of Marlboros, bottles of Southern Comfort and two, no, three film canisters of coke. It was now forty-eight hours since I'd had any sleep.

Our compliant cop got on board the first available chopper. As he was about to depart, I gave him an urgent message for Ronnie Schneider.

"Tell Ronnie," I said, "to get the band out here early. We should play as soon as possible in the afternoon and get the fuck out of here while it's still daylight. The Grateful Dead should play last."

I made the man repeat the message and off he went, giving me a self-important wave. I returned to deal with John Jaymes.

We reviewed the situation concerning the local police. The Highway Patrol now had eighty officers on duty, Jaymes said, and every available man from the Alameda Sheriff's department was working. There would be half-a-dozen plainclothes cops from the Sheriff's department around the stage, and the San Francisco office of the FBI had been asking various questions about the organization of the event. They were, said Jaymes, intending that their own observers would be present. People were coming down from the Governor's office in Sacramento. There was going to be plenty of security, Jaymes assured me.

"How many men do we have?" I asked.

Jaymes said he had five remaining at the Huntington who'd travel with the band to the concert site and the rest would be on site at 11 a.m. All would be armed and carrying their police ID. We'd have fifteen officers in all. I reminded Jaymes about my desire to meet with our guys at 11 sharp, and departed for the stage area. There was a lot still to be done.

It was about 10 a.m. when I saw the first fight near the stage.

A young guy with a pool cue savagely beat the crap out of someone. The victim was led away, bleeding profusely from the scalp. No one had lifted a finger to intervene. The Hells Angels were at their bus, which had been parked in front of the stage and diagonally off to the left.

The general vibe seemed okay, but every once in a while there was an outbreak of violence. There didn't seem to be any clear reason for the fighting, at least from where I was on the stage.

I noted that more young men armed with pool cues had turned up. Some of them had the mini-patch that showed they were Hells Angels "prospects," people who were on probation and could become full members of the club. Most of them were dressed in street clothes.

Two Hells Angels who'd been there all night were sitting on the side of the stage and getting completely fucked up, slugging from a large flagon of wine. They weren't bothering anyone, though, so I went off in search of coffee for Keith.

By the time our own police arrived, it was clear to me that we were in for a tough day. Fights had been increasing and more Angels were congregating around the stage. The Angels themselves were pretty cool, hanging out and drinking beer. The problem was the people who wanted to hang out with them. There seemed to be scores of aggressive young guys with pool cues who waded into people at the mere hint of any argument.

These young guys seemed intent upon impressing the Angels with their savagery, as if they were auditioning for parts in some violent movie. They beat people indiscriminately, while the Angels basically didn't give a shit.

It should be noted that not once did I see a man with a pool cue attack a Hells Angel. They weren't that suicidal.

Who invited those guys? I was never able to get a satisfactory answer to that question. It certainly wasn't the musicians, so I guess the word had originated in biker circles.

Things were getting heavier by the minute, so I took the Stones' security guys and went to Dick Carter's offices.

This is what I told them: "You're not the only cops here. There's police from the Sheriff's department and from the Highway Patrol. Even the FBI's going to be here. I want each of you to link up with one of the local cops and stay with them as much as you can. If it gets really heavy, I don't want any of our guys pulling guns. Let the local cops deal with whatever's going down, you guys act as backups. Okay?"

One of the New York cops spoke for everyone.

"Sam, we ain't here to deal with those crazy biker dudes; they're not our problem. We were hired to look after the Stones, not to protect a half a million kids from a bunch of fuckin' psychos."

I explained it to everyone as simply as I could: "We gave the Angels five hundred bucks' worth of beer and told them we would take care of our own security. All they gotta do is drink beer and stay cool. They won't be involved in security; that's why we've got you."

The cops didn't look too convinced. I continued: "I want you to do as I say. Get involved with the local cops. They've got backup if it's needed and they've got radios. It's important we maintain relations with them and keep them on side. We need to get back to the stage and I'll sort out who goes where. Only use a gun if your own life is directly threatened."

"What about other people's lives?" asked one of the cops.

"If it's not your life, or the Stones' lives, then fuck it, it's none of your business. Don't get involved. Let the local cops handle that stuff."

I noticed that several of the cops were arguing with John Jaymes in confidential whispers as I headed out the door.

I checked in at the medical facilities beside the stage and was shocked to see scores of people looking totally bewildered and crazy. One of the medics told me that they had been overrun by people having bad trips. Small yellow pills had been given out on the Friday evening in the thousands and lots of people were having adverse reactions. The acid was either of very poor quality or had been adulterated with some other drug.

The medics were injecting people with Thorazine, the standard drug for anyone having psychotic reactions to LSD. But in many cases it wasn't having its usual effect. One of the doctors told me they were beginning to think that the LSD was laced with something else — perhaps strychnine or arsenic. Whatever they were, the little yellow pills were causing havoc.

It was midday on Saturday December 6, not a note of music had been played, and already the medicos were running out of Thorazine. A guy from the Haight-Ashbury Free Clinic told me that in all his years he'd never seen so many bad trips and that we should warn people over the microphone to be very careful.

The doctor said we needed to have a medical evacuation helicopter on standby. The bad acid was so toxic that someone who took a lot of it could be poisoned and could die. I left the medical tent feeling decidedly strange.

Jackson and I had been repeatedly offered free acid on the Friday evening. A girl had a glass jar filled with the small yellow pills. I had the impression that someone had been deliberately distributing bad drugs, presumably to sabotage the entire free concert. It just seemed too bizarre for words.

Santana played first, and they played well, but the crowd didn't seem interested. The music was just aural wallpaper for the petty squabbles near the front of the stage that often erupted into full-on savagery. The guys with the pool cues were dealing out a massively disproportionate response to any challenge to their authority. A small argument, which in normal circumstances should have been easily settled, would escalate to head-busting, split-scalp thuds. I spoke to several of the "full" Hells Angels and they just shrugged. They were used to levels of violence far worse than they were witnessing today.

I decided early on that appeals to people not to fight would probably lead to even more violence. I also decided to limit the number of personal announcements made from the stage so that there wouldn't be an endless litany of bad news. Even so, I regularly found myself taking the mic throughout the day to appeal for doctors to attend to the wounded and for people to help get the injured to the medical facilities.

As Santana played, I looked out from the stage over the freezing cold high chaparral surrounding the speedway. A naked 300-pound man wandered past, battered and bewildered, hands held out in passive supplication as blood, snot, and tears poured down his face. Not a soul in that seething mass of humanity would lift a finger to help him. People shrank from him as if he were a ghastly vision. One of his lips had been cut and there was a gaping hole in his mouth. His head had been split open and his hair was matted with glistening blood.

Twice I saw him beaten senseless, smashed to the ground with pool cues, and twice I watched as the pathetic and blubbering wreck of a man somehow regained his feet.

I debated whether I should leave the stage and go to help him, but in consternation I realized that I could be of more practical use to everyone if I stayed at my post on the stage and attempted, however feebly, to cool things down.

I looked on in disgust and horror as he stumbled aimlessly, the packed masses of people parting in front of him. I was mortified. I wanted to vomit. How could people treat one another like this?

The "peace and love" my generation had so assiduously promulgated as the antidote to the violence and hypocrisy of "straight" society was a hollow miasma. This was not a community intent on caring for and loving one another. Before me was the ugly truth of what we had collectively wrought, manifested in greed, blood, drug overdoses, spilled guts, and hatred. The peace and love generation was busy smashing itself to bits.

Then I witnessed a lone expression of compassion. A mere slip of a girl bravely took hold of her fellow human being's hand

and gently began to lead him toward the overstretched medical personnel. Her one small gesture helped me reconnect with my own violated sense of human decency.

Santana left the stage mystified by the flat response. It was as if no one knew or even cared about their music. People from the Dead family were bewildered by the violent vibe and repeatedly told me that this was like nothing they had experienced before.

I looked around the stage and saw several uniformed police officers as well as our own guys, looking conspicuous and uncomfortable, unsure of what to do. With each wave of pool cue bashing, the cops would whisper to one another in urgent consultation, but no one did a thing to actually stop the violence.

I spoke to a uniformed cop who was standing on the back of the stage and looking very anxious. I asked him why nothing was being done about the fighting.

He showed me his radio. "I been callin' for backup for an hour now and they just keep giving me the run-around. They're more interested in keeping the roads clear so we can get emergency vehicles into the site if we need to. We don't have enough manpower to deal with these punks. These guys are psychos. They're not from Oakland or Richmond. We're not equipped to deal with this. They should send the riot squad over from San Francisco. This is completely outta hand."

He looked around and whispered in my ear: "You know what, buddy? I got a family. I don't give a shit about Mick Jagger and the Rolling Stones or these fucked-up people here. I don't have to put up with this shit." It was the last I was to see of him.

A quick head-count of our own cops proved that they were not on the stage where I had asked them to be. I found John Jaymes in a heated argument with some of his men, who said that while they didn't mind looking after the Stones, they weren't going to be involved with crowd control. "We're outnumbered by the Angels and there's at least a hundred of 'em," I heard one cop tell Jaymes.

Jaymes then noticed me. "Sam, we ain't doing this. This ain't what we signed on for. We got families to think of. People wanna bust one another's heads, it ain't our problem."

He turned back to his men: "We gotta look after the cameramen. I need six men for the cameramen. We gotta protect the film, if nothing else."

"Yeah," I thought to myself, "protect the film, 'cos that's where the money is." I wandered away in disgust.

Now I understood: it didn't matter where the police came from, New York or the Bay Area. None of them wanted to tangle with the Hells Angels. Not one police officer in the place (and they were all armed) was prepared to confront a patch-wearing member of the Hells Angels. Quite simply, the police were afraid.

By the time Jefferson Airplane was playing, I couldn't see anyone I recognized on stage. It was as if the "organizers" of Altamont had decided it was a bummer and gone home. Then the Airplane's Marty Balin chose to play hero and get involved in someone else's fight. He screamed some unintelligible words at one of the Hells Angels and jumped from the stage into the crowd. He was effortlessly smashed to the ground with one punch.

Marty lay on the ground unconscious as singer Grace Slick announced, "The Hells Angels just knocked out my lead singer." It was what could be described as a delicate moment. The Angel who felled Marty with one punch was a short and stocky guy with broad shoulders and thick upper arms, wearing a raccoon-skin hat.

I approached him warily with my hands open in front of me in a traditionally pacific and calming posture.

"Brother," I said, "I don't know what happened there, I really don't, but if the musicians get knocked out, then we sure as shit ain't going to have any music." I smiled at him while he considered what I'd just said.

"That motherfucker insulted my people. He talks like that about my people, he's going to get it."

I shrugged and gave my best impression of sympathetic understanding. "Fair enough," I said, "it was a dumb thing for Marty to do. Let's see if we can get this straightened out."

To my surprise the Hells Angel, who told me his name was Animal, agreed to square things away with Marty. We approached the singer, who was rubbing his jaw and looking very groggy.

Animal extended his hand but Marty, seeing the man who'd just knocked him out, screamed, "Fuck you!"

Two seconds later, Marty was unconscious again. Animal looked at me, shrugged and said, "I tried."

I accompanied Animal to the edge of the stage where we could speak privately. He seemed friendly enough and told me to call him by his nickname, "Mule." I guessed he was around thirty-five years old. I quickly checked him out. He had scar tissue around his eyebrows and a nose that had been broken several times. Each of his fingers was loaded with large silver rings, what we used to call a knuckleduster. I noticed that even the guys with pool cues kept out of his way.

I smiled disarmingly at Mule, and asked him in my gentlest voice if I could get some advice. He nodded.

"Mule, we gotta problem here. Not with you guys," I said, pointing to the Hells Angels, "but with these other guys, the guys with pool cues." Mule looked around and remained silent, so I had no way of knowing whether he agreed or not. "Mule, it ain't necessary what these people are doing."

Mule looked vaguely interested in what I had to say, but not that interested. While I was speaking to him, he kept a close eye on what was happening down in front of the stage, where scuffles were continuing.

"Mule, what have I got to do to get them to stop this shit and just cool it?"

Mule looked at me and shook his head. "Man, I came here for a good time. A man's my friend, he's my friend, no problem. He's my enemy, he's got a problem, a fuckin' big problem."

He looked at the pool cue boys. With a sigh, shaking his head, he told me: "These people are fucked up, man. They've been taking too many reds and wine and there ain't no stopping 'em." He explained that the people behaving like demented psychos were not actually "made" members of the legendary motorcycle club, and thus were not subject to the club's direct control. Some of them were "prospects" and some of them were simply good ol' American boys who enjoyed cracking other people's heads. Mule told me that there was nothing he could do, or wanted to do, to influence anyone's behavior. Then he wandered away in search of a beer, as unconcerned as someone attending a vicarage tea party.

I watched as he walked toward the Angels' bus. Some guy with a pool cue bumped into him on the fringe of yet another fight. Mule took the cue and busted it over the guy's back and then continued on his journey.

I sent one of the cops to see John Jaymes. Things were getting so serious that I didn't want to leave the stage area.

"Tell Jaymes," I instructed, "to call the hotel and get the Stones here as quickly as possible. Tell Ronnie and Mick that I said if we're going to play this thing we have to play it during daylight hours."

The cop ambled off and I went to check up on Keith. What the fuck was I going to tell my main man?

Various people had told him about the hassles and he was concerned, but I made light of the problems. "Just a few fights, Keef, nothing too serious. Still, I want us to play this afternoon, not tonight. We need to get out of here while it's daylight. I don't know how secure this place is going to be tonight — there are a lot of fucked-up people out there and they're going to be totally off their heads come nighttime."

Keith nodded and told me that Tony Funches, our bodyguard, had gone off to hospital. Apparently he'd broken his wrist in an altercation with someone or other. Yet another of our security team was now on the missing list.

I went to check on the cop situation and was horrified to see we had only two men left on the stage. They told me the others had gone back to the hotel and didn't want to know about the concert. The place was wall-to-wall Hells Angels, prospects, and hangers-on.

CHAPTER 27

When the going gets tough

I found Jackson at the back of the stage, standing by the door to the Dead's equipment truck. He had a very conspicuous black eye. He didn't want to talk about it, but apparently he'd had a run-in with one of the bikers. Mercifully, Jackson had decided not to retaliate, realizing that if you punch one Hells Angel, effectively you've punched all of them.

We retreated into the back of the truck and helped ourselves to two monster lines of Peruvian marching powder. I noticed Mule outside the truck and offered him a suitably generous line. He smiled and snorted it with practiced élan, then left the truck, not saying a word.

Jackson pointed at his own eye and said: "That's the guy that gave me this."

I sighed. "Well, he's obviously forgotten about it, and so should you. What a god-awful day. Where the fuck is Scully? Have you seen Rock? I haven't seen him for hours."

Jackson hadn't seen Rock or Michael Laing.

"When are the Grateful Dead coming?" I asked.

Jackson shrugged. "Man, I don't reckon they will come, this is bullshit. They won't wanna play."

I couldn't believe what he was saying. The one band who could chill the whole thing out would be the Dead.

Crosby, Stills, and Nash had been hopeless, too fey for words. It was bizarre hearing their gentle lyricism accompanied by the screams and moans of the injured. The only act that received a vaguely positive response was the Flying Burrito Brothers, Gram Parsons' band, who had just finished. While the Burritos played, there had been no fights.

Now Jackson was telling me the Dead would probably not play!

It was time to get on the telephone and find out where the hell the Rolling Stones were.

On the way to the office, I saw Mick and Charlie walking down through the crowd and felt hugely relieved. Mick was a bit unhappy; some madman had slapped his face. Other than that, he was in one piece.

To his credit, Mick had demanded that no one hurt the man. Mick Taylor, meanwhile, looked as white as a ghost and Charlie appeared shell-shocked. There was no sign of Bill Wyman.

"Where's Bill?" I asked, as I led the Stones to the caravan at the back of the stage.

"We couldn't find him," said Ronnie. "He went shopping." Tony was back, despite his broken wrist, and I got him to stand at the door as we emptied the caravan of all but the band.

"We have to go on," I told them. "This has turned into a nightmare, people are getting hurt, it's going to get worse, and I don't want us here playing when it's dark. There's no guarantee I'll be able to get you out of here."

Mick sighed. "We'll go on when Bill gets here. What's happening with the Angels?"

"Basically they're beating the crap out of people, but it's not the Angels, it's the prospects and hangers-on. People are really getting hurt."

Outraged as I was, I knew there was no turning back, no way that anyone from the Rolling Stones could avoid what we had come here to do. Even if we had wanted to split, there would have been no conceivable way we could have escaped from the center of so many people. We had to play.

Mick asked me to tell Chip Monk that as soon as Bill arrived, the band would play. I rushed to ensure that the helicopter landing site was rigged with lights so that we could make our getaway if it was dark.

We waited another two hours for Bill to arrive. Various bands had played and, as each of the artists had completed their set, the violence increased exponentially. Fifty people or more had been beaten so badly that they needed serious medical attention. Hundreds of others were freaking out. The doctors had run out of Thorazine twice; the medical tent resembled a war zone. The Grateful Dead, unbeknownst to me at the time, had arrived by helicopter and been told by Santana's drummer what was happening. They left without wanting to play.

All of the Rolling Stones, except Bill Wyman, were ensconced in a small caravan backstage, effectively marooned in a sea of some 300,000 people. With darkness rapidly approaching, and no sign of Bill, for the umpteenth time I made my way from the trailer to survey the scene and report back to my very worried band.

Looking around, I saw that all the people I had got to know as volunteers in the previous forty-eight hours had split. The only ones I knew from the original crew were Owsley, who was manning the sound, and Dan Healy from Quicksilver Messenger Service. Jackson and a few of the crew were keeping an eye on the equipment.

Every single person who had originally told the Rolling Stones to come to San Francisco and play a free concert had deserted them.

Where were the people who only four days before the event had been so keen to talk to the television cameras and the reporters?

Where were the people who had confidently said that a free concert by the Rolling Stones was possible and who had actively encouraged thousands of fans to descend on a totally inappropriate site?

Some of the same people who had organized the era-defining Woodstock festival had taken a lead role in organizing Altamont. Where were they when the going got tough?

Where were the people who had actually chosen the site and reported back to me that it was a suitable venue for a free concert with an expected attendance of tens of thousands?

Which of all the "organizers" had shown either the decency or the courage to step forward and speak on the microphone, to call for calm? Which of them had even bothered to speak to me or offer help as I endeavored to stop events from spiraling out of control?

Not one of the people who had played central roles in the planning of the event had said a word or offered any assistance — as soon as things got out of hand, they had returned to the shadows from which they had previously so confidently emerged. The man who had first suggested that the concert was a good idea had simply vanished. Where were the cops? The lawyers? Where was Jerry Garcia, or for that matter any other member of the Grateful Dead? What had they done to try to cool things out? They had arrived at the concert site, seen what was happening, and simply turned around and split!

What kind of a response was that to the challenge that all of their fans now faced?

Bill Wyman arrived and ten minutes later I got the band on stage. It was now dark, and the vibe was worse than it had been all day.

I told everyone what we were going to do: the minute they finished, they were to follow me and I would lead them to the helicopter that was being guarded by the Angels. It was ready for immediate take-off.

Several of the Angels made a point of telling me not to worry: "Nothing's gonna happen to your band, get 'em to play and it'll all be cool." With a dry mouth, I thanked them and felt truly nervous. Everyone could pick up on the threat in the air.

I begged Mick not to stop once the set had started, regardless of what was happening in the crowd. Get through the numbers as fast as possible, and let's get the fuck outta here. Mick seemed to agree, but was very worried. It was an act of absolute bravery for him to go on stage.

Mick Taylor looked scared out of his wits.

Charlie and Bill stared impassively ahead.

Keith was not happy and I could tell he was praying that the music would save us.

The Stones lumbered into their first song and the violence erupted immediately.

CHAPTER 28

The death of Meredith Hunter

The Stones played the opening bars of "Under My Thumb" as the first fights broke out in front of the stage. The small group of men with pool cues attacked the audience, lashing out indiscriminately at anyone who got in their way.

The music stopped and Mick appealed for people to be cool. The band started playing again, but each new song brought a fresh outbreak of violence. It was almost as if the beatings had become natural components of the music itself. Young psychopaths would charge into the crowd with their pool cues flailing, the crowd would part, the injured would be removed, and the concert would continue. It was surreal.

By that time I was accustomed to all sense of outrage at the thuggery I was witnessing, but Keith was becoming more and more agitated as he watched the scene unfold in front of him. When they were forced to stop again he was incandescent with anger, screaming into the microphone that the band would not play if the violence continued. I begged him to cool it. We had no choice but to play if we were to get out of there alive. I began to think of how we were to escape this madness.

Mick peered from the floodlit stage into the dark mass of the audience and made an absurd plea for calm: "If we are as one, then let us be as one."

I feared for his safety as I watched several very stoned people looking at him with murderous intent.

The band began to play again as if their lives depended on it. The music momentarily stilled the crowd and I hovered at the side of the stage, afraid of where all this might end.

Then there was a commotion and perhaps ten Hells Angels ran toward the stage, away from a man in a luminescent green suit, yelling, "He's got a gun!"

The man lurched forward and an Angel rushed toward him, through his retreating brothers. The Angel grabbed at the man's wrist, and, holding his gun hand up in the air, began to stab at him. I saw the long-barreled silver gun shining in the stage lights, and so did others near me.

People on the stage apron actually threw themselves down onto the floor so as not to present a viable target. The man with the gun collapsed under a mountain of Angels as they rushed in for the kill.

I stood there looking at it all, totally dumbfounded.

The band's music ground to a halt and Keith started shouting at the Angels. "If you guys don't stop it right now, we're gonna quit!"

I ran across to Keith and spoke into his ear. "A guy's got a gun Keith, he's got a gun! Please cool it, man, someone's been hurt real bad."

I turned back to Mick. "There's a guy with a gun. Give me a minute; I'll check on what's happening. Fuckin' cool it — somebody may have been killed." Mick went deathly pale as I rushed down into the thick of it.

As soon as I saw Meredith Hunter, I knew he was dying. Lying on the ground, with medics in attendance, he had blood pouring from his body. He was on his stomach and the doctors were lifting his jacket so they could get at his back. A hysterical woman was screaming, "Don't let him die, don't let him die!"

As I turned away, holding back tears, one of the Angels spoke to me in an insistent voice: "Tell Mick he had a gun! The guy had a gun! He got two shots off! He had a gun!"

I forced my way back through the crowd and regained the stage. The band stood staring into the dark mass of the audience, unsure what to do. Once again Mick appealed forlornly for calm.

I wanted to get the Stones off stage, then and there, but Mick would not be moved. I whispered in his ear, "Let's get this over with," but Mick insisted that he would finish the show.

I stood as close as I could to Mick and Keith while they restarted the music, nervously eyeing the people on stage, wondering who would be next to launch an attack.

In the pocket of my jacket I had the derringer, and wondered if I'd have the balls to shoot someone if they tried to hurt Mick. I have never ever wanted a policeman around more than I did at that moment. Not that it mattered; there wasn't one of the cowards in sight.

The band played and I stood on the side of the stage, a couple of yards from Mick and Keith, and I think I would have defended them with my life. I was numb from lack of sleep and exposure to the worst violence I had ever seen. I could only think: *I have to get my band out of here. I have to get them on the helicopter.*

There was a walk of some 200 yards from the backstage area to where the chopper would take off and speed us to safety and there was no way that we would be able to make that journey unescorted. None of Jaymes's big bad cops had bothered to stay; they'd flown out on the helicopters with the other acts, saying that they were their security. I had to talk to the Hells Angels and ask them to help us. Surprisingly, they agreed.

As the last notes of the performance died we rushed from the stage, frightened and distraught. Behind a phalanx of Hells Angels, the Rolling Stones reached the helicopter and made their escape. None of the musicians from the other bands had bothered to stay for the Stones' set. Everyone had fled the dreadful scene.

As the rotors created an ungodly racket above us, no one spoke and I had some time to think. What the hell was a young guy doing bringing a gun to a concert? You don't bring a loaded revolver to a rock'n'roll show for purely innocent reasons.

He'd drawn the gun, fired two bullets, and been stabbed to death.

The realization that I too had a gun weighed heavily upon my mind, and I hated myself for it, while saying a silent prayer of thanks that no one had actually attacked the band. What would I have done then?

Hundreds of local, state, and federal laws had been broken and not one police officer chose to act. There was no police inquiry following Altamont, no public inquiry.

Why?

For the simple reason that such an inquiry would have exposed the fact that the police had done nothing in the face of serious violent crime.

Nothing, that is, other than bravely towing away hundreds of cars that had been parked illegally.

CHAPTER 29

Aftermath

Upon reaching the hotel after a very dangerous flight in an over-loaded helicopter, I had my last meeting with Mick.

In a large hotel suite strewn with empty bottles, I sat half-asleep in a chair, barely able to focus on what had happened, desperate just to close my eyes and nod off. I hadn't slept for days.

Mick was pale and very frightened that some form of legal action against the Stones was imminent. He wanted to leave the country as quickly as possible and had already packed his bags.

He had only a few minutes to talk. Any questions seemed irrelevant when we both knew there was a body in the morgue, some furious Hells Angels to be dealt with, and hundreds of journalists eager to delve into the story of the free concert that turned into a nightmare. I thought that I was the obvious choice to stay and represent the interests of the Rolling Stones. Mick absolutely hated the idea and suggested forcefully that I leave America straight away, simply split. Disappear. We argued briefly; wouldn't this look like cowardice?

I stood my ground. Someone had to represent the group. No one would understand their splitting, and furthermore, the way in which this disaster was handled could well impact upon their future visits to the States. Mick agreed and promised that the band would pay my legal expenses and "cover my arse." Within the hour, everyone but me had left for Europe. It would be years before I would see any of them again.

The general atmosphere was thick with malevolent hostility toward the Rolling Stones. The press was in hysterics, radio and TV stations were baying for retribution, and at the highest levels of law enforcement the search was on for those who were being described in the media as murderers. I was yet to know any of this, and fell asleep on the floor. I must have slid directly from the chair to the carpet. There I slept, unaware of the gathering storm.

The following morning, I turned on the TV and every channel was full of the Altamont concert: that fact that four people had been killed and many others injured, the damage to the farmers' livestock and the missing miles of fences, the wrecked and abandoned cars littering the highways, the missing, the injured.

The Rolling Stones had gone from heroes to zeroes in the space of twenty-four hours.

Already my name was being mentioned and I knew I was in serious trouble. I had 300 bucks in my pocket, what turned out to be a worthless promise from Mick that the Stones would pay my expenses, Mel Belli's law firm to theoretically protect my interests, nowhere to live, and no one to turn to.

My first decision was to sneak out of the hotel without paying.

With just the clothes I stood up in, which were beginning to stink, I departed by the fire escape to the basement, where I had a white Lincoln Continental rental, courtesy of the band. In the glove box were my pistol and my stash.

I turned the radio on to hear a KSAN announcer analyzing the cause of the disaster. I decided to head for Marin County and check out Mickey Hart's ranch.

Mickey wasn't home and I was greeted by his lady at the time, Cookie, who looked very worried. She had never spoken to me before, but knew who I was, and she kindly invited me into the house. Over coffee she explained what was happening.

The Dead were being careful to distance themselves from the media: no one was talking. The Angels were pissed off. I listened in gloomy silence.

Mickey came home and we walked outside the low ranch house, surrounded by the hills of Marin. It was a pretty spot. I told Mickey that I could have gone home, just stuck 'em with the shit and split, but I felt that would have been dishonorable. I wanted to stay and clear up the mess, whatever the personal cost. Mickey stared strangely at me and then generously told me I could stay in the barn.

Things were looking up! I had a car, a place to stay, and as far as I knew, no one knew where I was. I began to feel a bit better.

Mickey and Cookie were beautiful to me, very special. They knew I was completely out of my depth and had no real understanding of the Bay Area and the alternative culture. I think they felt sorry for me. At least they knew I wasn't going to run away, unlike my employers. I headed for the barn and decided to change all of my clothes. One of the girls on the farm lent me a T-shirt, and a quick trip into Novato saw me decked out in jeans and a pair of boots. Now I looked like a local. I returned to the ranch and was invited into the house.

Mickey and Cookie looked even more serious, if such a thing were possible. The Hells Angels had been on the telephone and wanted to see me. *Now.*

I was stunned and frightened. It was the very last thing I wanted to do, but I knew that one day, sooner or later, it would have to happen. Without the presence of the Angels, it might be Mick's body lying in the morgue.

I knew someone from the Stones owed them at the very least a meeting. Cookie told me that Sweet William, a San Francisco Angel, was on his way over to talk to me. This initial meeting would be cool; while I was at their ranch nothing would happen. I was safe.

I didn't feel safe, I felt afraid, but sometimes things have to be done regardless of what one is feeling, and this was one of those moments. I didn't want to play hero, dead hero especially. With Cookie's assurances ringing somewhat hollow in my ear, I prepared myself.

The low putt-putt sound of Sweet William's Harley coming up the road reminded me horribly of the events at the concert. Without anything but the nod of a head, we retired to the barn.

William told me that I would have to attend a meeting with the Angels. Representatives would be there from all the Californian chapters. He gave me his word that no harm would come to me, though I had the impression that he would have been happy to wipe me out on the spot. He was pissed off and the way he stared at me left me in no doubt that the meeting was non-negotiable. There was no way out. The meeting would be in San Francisco and in due course I would be told a specific location.

I was to be absolutely sure to come alone.

We didn't speak of the events at the concert. Again, he assured me that I would come to no physical harm, and with a handshake he departed in a cloud of dust. My legs felt weak.

In a matter of hours we received a phone call telling me that the meeting was to be held in a house in the city. I departed the ranch with Cookie assuring me that I would be all right; the Angels only wanted to talk.

The drive from Novato to San Francisco takes about half an hour and it was one of the worst of my life. As I crossed the Golden Gate Bridge toward the city the Bay had never seemed more beautiful, but it occurred to me that pretty soon I might well be feeding the fishes down there. Alcatraz looked positively homey and I felt miserably sorry for myself. With that sinking feeling I arrived in a very upmarket area of San Francisco and parked the Lincoln outside a multi-storey house. I checked that I had the correct address and nervously knocked on the front door. There wasn't a Harley in sight.

A slim man in expensive clothes opened the door slightly and told me that the meeting was to be in the basement. I followed him and we entered into what I expected would be an empty room.

Approximately a dozen Angels, all deathly silent, were seated at a large table.

A man asked me to join them and I tried to introduce myself and shake hands. He said he didn't want to touch "a piece of shit." I think that I had given them a bit of a surprise, with few of the people present thinking I would have the balls or the stupidity (take your pick!) to actually turn up. As I looked around the room I recognized William, who nodded for me to sit down. The "civilian" who had first greeted me left us in the basement with a warning to one and all not to bust the place up. I felt sick to my stomach.

The meeting was businesslike. I asked if I could say something and was told no. I would be told what they wanted and then I could speak. A very large biker explained things to me in a low and even voice, without any apparent hint of malice. I already knew it could be the most serious thing I would ever have to deal with in my life, and before departing the ranch I had wondered whether I should take my piece. I thought better of it; I was sick of guns.

The spokesman continued talking directly to me: in the course of a fight at Altamont a man had died. His body was in the morgue. The Rolling Stones were, in his opinion, directly responsible for the whole mess.

It was not a comfortable position.

We were here to talk peace, he said, but if people wanted a war then so be it. The Stones had filmed the concert at Altamont, they owned the film, and it was obvious that right now various law enforcement agencies would be looking for the film to see what evidence it contained.

I was told that a copy of the film had to be produced immediately. I swallowed hard and did my best to speak without appearing nervous.

I didn't have the film, and didn't know exactly where it was. It belonged, as far as I knew, to the Maysles brothers. My guess was that it was being processed as we spoke, in New York somewhere. Some forty-eight hours had now elapsed since the concert and I was absolutely sure that on the plane back east, the cameramen would have discussed who had actually captured the footage of the deadly fight. The film from that camera would have been first to the lab.

"Can you get us a copy of the film?" I was asked.

Everyone in the room stared hard at me, as my mind went back to the events of the concert. I only had a few moments, at most, in which to make a decision.

It wasn't hard.

With sweaty palms I gave my word that I would do my best to get them the film. I would not run away from what I saw as the Rolling Stones' responsibilities. For once I was on the side of the Angels.

CHAPTER 30

Shelter from the storm

I drove away feeling drained and unsure of myself, but pleased that certain things had been established. Somehow or other I had managed to get on top of my fear. I had tried to speak on behalf of my band, the musicians I loved, and attempted to get across that I didn't feel the Rolling Stones were at fault.

I didn't blame the Angels for behaving in the way that they did, because one can no more complain about the Angels being violent than one can complain about polar bears being white. It's simply the nature of the beast, most of the time, to be the way that it is. Fuck with a polar bear — or the Angels — and you'll see what I mean.

I was pleased to have gained a modicum of respect from the Angels and to have survived the experience. Now I had to somehow deliver on what I had promised.

Mick would be hostile to any kind of cooperation with the Angels, but as he was in Switzerland and the film was in New York it was really not Mick's call. Keith would be in London and almost certainly lost in the pleasures of his reunion with Anita. The Rolling Stones office was already refusing to accept my telephone calls. It was as if everyone had gone into hiding.

This was, I decided, a peculiarly American problem and the solution was to be found here, though I told myself not to count on anyone involved with the band to help me.

I called one of the Maysles brothers and told them exactly what was happening. The film was undoubtedly primary evidence as far as the death of Meredith Hunter was concerned.

My words could not have been clearer.

If we all wanted to stay alive, then the film footage that showed the death of Meredith Hunter had to be located double-quick. Not only that; someone had better jump on a plane and get it to the West Coast. My demands were met with a stony silence.

I closed the conversation with the promise I had received from the Angels: that no one would be hurt if they arrived with the film. No film, and the shit was going to hit the fan big time.

The fact that I had been to see the Angels served to reassure the filmmakers that they would not be in immediate danger if they got the film to the Angels. There must have been some debate, though, because it took the relevant footage nearly seventy-two hours to make its way to San Francisco. I heard nothing from the filmmakers or the Angels during that time.

Apparently when the film finally arrived for the Angels to see, the person who delivered it got a slap for his tardiness. It could have been significantly worse than that, so he got off lightly.

It was delivered directly to the club. I didn't want to see the footage. I was sick of the whole business and relieved that my part of the bargain had been taken care of. It was in nobody's interest, I felt, for the Rolling Stones and the Angels to be at loggerheads, so I'd done my bit for peace and harmony.

After my meeting with the Angels, things were out of my hands, and I foolishly thought that would be the end of the nightmare. I returned to Mickey's ranch where I had been sleeping in the barn, and was surprised to see a concerned Jerry Garcia. I had never really spoken to the man, except at a couple of meetings with the Dead, and he had barely said a word. He had struck me as a somewhat cautious cat, so I was interested to see him there. We nodded to one another, Garcia rolled a spliff, and it became clear to me that he wanted to hang out and have a chat. We put the kettle on for coffee and retired to the barn.

Garcia was an odd-looking guy. He was wearing a poncho and old cowboy boots and had his hair in two bangs. He hadn't shaved in a couple of weeks. His hands were soft and pudgy and he looked as if he hadn't done any exercise since he was a child. He chain-smoked cigarettes with a manic intensity. He had arrived in a battered old Volvo, and was the very antithesis of what one would think a leading musician would look like.

Known as "Captain Trips," he looked more like Private Trips to me, but what the hell — I was thrilled to meet the man properly, and truth be told, I knew nothing about the real Grateful Dead. All I knew was what Rock Scully had told me, which meant my head was filled with silly fantasies.

Garcia surprised me by asking at the outset to describe the set-up in the Stones' London office. He was particularly interested in how they organized themselves as a band and who was in charge of what. Garcia seemed bemused by the fact that Mick made most of the decisions. This struck Garcia as wildly impractical; he just couldn't get his head around the idea that one guy could make decisions on everyone's behalf.

I soon discovered that behind Garcia's somewhat battered exterior there was a keen and lively intelligence at work. Garcia was interested in the Stones' set-up because he was dissatisfied with the Grateful Dead's current arrangement. We talked about Allen Klein and then the conversation veered toward the Dead's own management issues.

I asked Garcia point blank about Lenny Hart: was it really true that he was a minister? Garcia sighed and described his first meeting with Lenny: the reverend had shown up with a Bible under his arm and swore that he would never rip them off. All of the somewhat naive hippies present had given Lenny their vote of confidence — with some notable abstentions. Garcia admitted that he had gone for the reverend because he was sick to death of their previous managers. I gently probed and Garcia told me an involved story about the film *Zabriskie Point*.

The famous Italian film director Antonioni had used Pink Floyd for the soundtrack, with mixed results. The director rejected most of what they had recorded, and when the action of the film had moved from Europe to the States, Antonioni decided that he wanted American musicians for that part of the film. Enter Jerry.

Garcia had done the work, but was having a hell of a time getting paid for his contribution. His manager was telling him that he hadn't been paid, but the film people were saying the money had been given to the Dead's management. Garcia didn't know whom to believe. He was broke, and, on top of everything, getting hell from his old lady at the time, Mountain Girl.

We laughed bitterly at the similarities between the Dead and the Stones and Allen Klein. It seemed simple to me, I said, that you should use an accountant to handle the money and take its control away from anyone involved in managerial decisions. My suggestion must have made an impression, for it was something he incorporated into the Dead's own business structure further down the road.

The conversation moved to Altamont and Garcia was obviously unhappy with many aspects of the concert. The violence appalled him and he pointed out that none of the San Francisco Angels who were known to the Dead had been involved. The worst of the violence was from people who had no connection with San Francisco or the Bay Area, people who saw the concert as a chance to beat the crap out of the hippies they despised. The people who were responsible came from places like San Jose, San Bernardino, and Fresno, Garcia reckoned.

It began to dawn on me that large parts of California were filled with country rednecks who hated hippies. The people who had been violent at Altamont were rural Californians, not people from the "alternative community."

I told Garcia about the meeting with the Angels, and my promise to get them the film, and he asked what would happen if I could not get the film. The thought had never occurred to me! I laughed and said I'd go and live in Mexico. Looking around at the barn, Garcia told me, "You can't stay here."

I had no real plans, other than to remain on the West Coast long enough to sort out the mess of Altamont, and then to go on an extended holiday.

Garcia made me a proposition. I could stay at his house in Larkspur, we could continue our conversations, and we'd review the situation as and when necessary. It would be best, Garcia reckoned, if I kept as low a profile as possible, and didn't go anywhere near the Grateful Dead's offices or the ranch. After all, as he pointed out, there was a body in the morgue and lawsuits would soon be flying.

I gratefully accepted his generous, though surprising, offer of accommodation. In hindsight, I think he felt somewhat responsible for my predicament. The free concert idea, after all, had originated with his people.

With no other real alternative and no funds to speak of, I threw my stuff into my rental car and followed Garcia's battered Volvo to Larkspur, where he lived on Madrone Canyon Road.

A new chapter in my life was about to begin, and I didn't have a clue what was going to happen. It didn't worry me; my life had been a constant series of changes and I was inured to fear of the future.

Meanwhile, according to the press, various law enforcement officers were eager to interview me and others who had been involved in planning the free concert, and they were busy searching the site at Altamont for evidence. Arrests were going to be made.

CHAPTER 31

Jerry & Janis

I was surprised when we arrived at Garcia's place to find that he lived in a perfectly normal house in a perfectly normal street intertwined with massive redwood trees. Perhaps I expected him to dwell in some strange version of Gandalf 's Garden, or a peculiar Hobbit's cave? His house was set back from the road and had a driveway beside a front lawn that needed mowing. There was no front fence; the garden was open to the road.

It was a three-bedroom house that I guessed had been built in the early 1950s. The back garden, which could be seen through the kitchen window, had a bit of a vegetable patch and a kid's swing. It was a perfectly domestic home in a perfectly American street. It was cool.

Garcia introduced me to Mountain Girl in the kitchen and she peered at me with evident disapproval. "Wanna coffee?" she boomed.

I sat in a chair as Garcia disappeared. A blond-haired little girl asked me my name. This was Mountain Girl's daughter and we shyly spoke. She asked me, "You a musician like Jerry?" I told her that I looked after musicians, and she nodded sagely. The coffee arrived. "If you're looking for Garcia he'll be in the front room," Mountain Girl said. I retreated to find Jerry.

He was seated at an elaborate pedal-steel guitar of the type featured on a million country songs. At his feet were an array of different pedals and he was wearing headphones. In front of him, perched on a small coffee table, was a TV. The volume was off, but a cartoon flickered on the screen.

Garcia remained preoccupied with what he was doing, his back to me. His hands were moving across the strings of the pedal steel and his feet were moving about; even his knees were pushing against various levers, but there was absolutely no sound. He was deeply engrossed in a silent symphony.

I wandered back to the kitchen, where Mountain Girl informed me in her strangely masculine voice, "Garcia's learning pedal steel. He sits in that room for hours; been in there for weeks, every minute he gets."

Garcia had been playing for barely a couple of months, but he'd already advanced considerably and had recorded an overdub for Crosby, Stills, and Nash's "Teach Your Children."

He was clearly immersed in a blessed and private dance, so I didn't interrupt the man. I smiled at Mountain Girl, she smiled back, and I decided to go for a walk.

Most of the dwellings in this idyllic Marin County street were made of redwood with shingle roofs. I wandered down the road and maybe a dozen houses along from Garcia's I came across an expensive-looking place. Parked in the driveway was a Porsche painted in the most extravagant psychedelic colors. I knew immediately that the car belonged to Janis Joplin; photos of it had been in the newspapers and magazines. It was a famous car, like John Lennon's psychedelic Rolls-Royce. I walked up the drive and banged on the front door.

Lo and behold, a sober Janis opened the door, looked at me, and yelled, "Fuggin' Sam Cutler! What you doing here, man?"

I explained I was staying with Jerry. With a smile and a hug from Janis, I went inside.

Garcia's house had barely any furniture in it, whereas Janis's house was stacked with the stuff. Styles and periods were mixed together in a mad psychedelic mélange of colors, expensive but overwrought, gaudy and visually incoherent. In some ways it was the perfect mirror for its owner.

We picked our way to a corner of the large living room where Janis liked to hang out, and she asked if I'd like a drink. We sat on a luxurious spread of cushions and caught up. The first topic of conversation was Altamont. Janis took a swig of her drink and held forth on a subject on which everyone on the West Coast had an opinion.

"You dumb Brits!" she started. "What the hell were you doing working with Scully and Emmett? I knew them in the Haight and I've known them through all kinds of trips and while they're great guys, they couldn't organize shit. Hell, even the Grateful Dead don't want 'em. They been partying too long, they're shot. They're as much use as a bull's ass in fly season." Janis then hit me with a belligerent question: "How come you decided to play in the fuggin' desert? Who told you that was a good idea. Rock?" She cackled wickedly. "You didn't really think they'd let you play in the city, did ya? You guys musta been dreamin'." She paused for breath. Sitting there, in a multi-colored caftan and pink boa, Janis looked like a benevolent psychedelic witch. "Yeah, man, it was a complete fuck-up, and I didn't hear from nobody — nobody asked me."

I shrugged my shoulders. "Well, consider yourself lucky; it was a fuckin' nightmare and you were blessed to have missed it. You'd have hated it anyway."

I asked Janis what she was doing now, and she completely ignored my question. "Anyway, man, Albert didn't want me to do the gig, and you know what, man? He was right. He knew it would be shit; everybody did." (Albert Grossman was her manager.)

I sighed and went to the kitchen in search of another beer.

Janis was a curious lady, radically different from any woman I'd known. While I stayed with Garcia, she and I became friends. I'd pop in and see her, we got drunk a few times, we talked, and I listened to the demo tracks she was recording in the garage with her new band.

I stayed out of her bed and we stayed friends, though whenever we got drunk she'd be sure to remind me of Madison Square Garden and my "throwing her out" of the Rolling Stones' dressing-room, as she described it.

Janis hid her insecurities behind an act — what the Italians call menefreghismo. A menefreghista is basically someone who doesn't give a fuck. Janis cared so deeply and passionately about so many things, but found it incredibly painful. To protect herself from her own feelings and vulnerabilities, she wore a shield when she was in public, a "fuck you" attitude that was macho and vulgar — and, at heart, totally false.

Sing the blues, dress outrageously, and have a big mouth. Most men loved her for it, but I couldn't stand that phony act. Thankfully, in private she was usually a whole other person, and because I'd worked with the Stones she rarely laid that shit on me. Relieved of the pressure that comes with having to be the life and soul of the party, the private Janis could hang out and be herself. The rough-as-guts bravado was replaced by a sensitive soulfulness. She spoke quietly and with emotion.

When you were alone with Janis you got the feeling you were being given all of her. She could be intense, and she could be what I'd call emotionally demanding, but when you were with her she made you feel special.

On several different occasions, over spliffs and drinks, she would describe her latest perfect lover, some guy she had met in the previous few days. She always seemed to have a new man in her life and yet she remained chronically insecure. I really wasn't that keen to hear her intimate stories, but I grew fond of Janis. She was the kind of woman who made it easy for you to feel that you were close to her. She was very Texan like that.

Janis would have made a wonderful mother. All of the men in the San Francisco music scene worshiped her for the generosity of spirit she possessed. The lady really knew how to party, too.

When Janis got down, though, it was downright depressing.

We'd sit around and she'd tell me her romantic tales of lasting love and some wonderful man, and I'd do my best to sound interested and be supportive. Then she'd turn round and announce that "the bastard" had left her asleep in bed and gone off without saying goodbye. Finally, after even more drinks, she'd be practically sobbing and I'd find myself giving her a sympathetic cuddle, stroking her hair, and agreeing that most men were absolute bastards. If we had another drink or two Janis would probably nod off with the glass in her hand. I'd then recover what was left of the drink, pull a cover over her, close the door behind me, and make my way back to Garcia's. I have always thought that a man can get sex anywhere in this world, but friendship's harder to find.

A couple of times, Janis and I talked about me being her tour manager, but it never came to anything. The problem was Albert Grossman; while I knew that he adored Janis, he was very much in charge of her career and all that she did. He kept a room just for Janis at his home in Woodstock, as he'd done for Bob Dylan. I knew that in essence I would be working for Albert Grossman and answerable to him, not to Janis. Albert was managing Peter, Paul & Mary, Paul Butterfield, Bob Dylan, and The Band, and had an industry reputation for being one tough cookie. I didn't need the hassle of having to deal with such a man, and in any case Janis was (I knew) a handful on the road. She was into all kinds of heavy drugs and I was over that scene. I'd just done a chaotic tour with the Stones, and I was looking for something a bit more fun. And I wanted to have a holiday!

So while we remained friends, I never got to work directly for Janis, though we were subsequently together in Canada on tour. In less than a year, Janis was to die tragically on the road, of an overdose.

Janis was no typical beauty, though she had a smile as wide as the Golden Gate Bridge and just as beautiful. When she smiled she was radiant, genuine, and open. I sometimes used to think Janis would have been happiest on the back of some big ol' biker's hog, with her hair blowing in the wind, and with nothing to do but keep a funky man happy. Freewheelin' Franklin from *The Fabulous Furry Freak Brothers* would have been perfect for Janis — unfortunately, he was a character in a cartoon book.

There was a strain of trailer-trash vulgarity in her that I never wished to encourage, and I always felt that she was letting herself down when she retreated into crude and belligerent fantasies. Janis would look for an argument, especially if she was bored and there was no boy around to take her fancy, to allow her to forget about herself.

I used to think, who the hell would want to be Janis Joplin, or for that matter, any famous artist? Must be a total drag, and how could you trust people to ignore your fame and the dumb baggage that came with it, and only want you for yourself?

At the height of her renown, Janis was smothering the ever-present loneliness with alcohol and drugs. Every day, it is said, the reasonable person begins the hunt for happiness. Janis searched like all of us, and unfortunately, in the end, that elusive human joy seemed to escape her. As the rabbis say, there is nothing more whole than a broken heart.

CHAPTER 32

Garcia

Garcia was always busy. Most evenings he'd be off at a local club in Marin or across the bay in Berkeley, playing with one of his bar bands. Garcia simply loved to play. His days were spent in mastering the pedal steel, and once in a while he would talk with me.

From what Garcia was saying, it appeared that the Grateful Dead were in the midst of a conundrum. He hinted at musical issues that he was having with other members of the band and talked a little about his old friend Ron "Pigpen" McKernan, the band's harmonica player and keyboardist, but it was all very elliptical. He told me how arriving at unexpected places was something of a specialty for the people in the Dead. We had something in common there.

Jerry was not one to talk too much on a deeply personal level, but once early on we had a revealing conversation about our backgrounds. We sat in his back garden, rolled a spliff, and reminisced about our childhoods, filling in pieces of the jigsaw puzzle that made us who we were. We shared a fascination with how people arrived at who they were.

He asked me what it was like to be raised in a city that had been bombed. He wanted to know where I played when I was child, what kind of toys I had, what my relationship with my adoptive mother was like. I told him about a friend of mine at school who'd lost his hand playing at a bombsite and Garcia told me about losing the tip of his right middle finger as a kid in a wood-chopping accident. I taught him a skipping song kids used to sing when I was in school:

> Little Johnny's got two stumps
> Got 'em at the ammo dump
> When he went out there to play
> The ammo blew his legs away.

He found that very droll and admitted that he had been ribbed at school about his missing fingertip; it was something that had stuck deep in his psyche. We talked about how children made light of the horrors of war, and how music was used by the common people to answer and embrace every aspect of the human condition.

I wanted to know what it was like to be raised in San Francisco, home to the Beats whom I so admired. What was it like to be a musician on the West Coast? As far as I could tell they were treated with an almost unseemly reverence. "What is it like," I asked Garcia, "to have so many fans hang upon your every word?" It sounded like a nightmare to me and I sensed the man's frustration at having to endlessly point out that he was "just" a musician.

We discovered that our grandmothers had essentially raised us both. Jerry's mother had struggled to get by when her husband had gone; my own mother had faced the same lonely struggle of widowhood. Jerry's mom had gone on to have relationships with men whom Jerry didn't like, just as my own mother had married a man I couldn't stand. We were both sons who had carried some serious scars from childhood to adulthood.

Strong and radical women had been involved in both our childhoods; my mother was a trade union organizer and Jerry's grandmother had been an organizer for the Laundry Workers Union. Even more incredibly, his maternal grandmother's name was also Tillie! We were both truly amazed at the coincidence. The similarities in our childhoods were spooky.

Garcia was what I would describe as a political progressive. He'd been raised in a union household, and was familiar with the history of the epic strikes on the San Francisco waterfront. He had a basic respect for the values of ordinary Americans and his attitudes were those of a good solid San Francisco Democrat.

A couple of hours spent sharing some California homegrown and discussing the formative experiences of a couple of lives and we were in tune. We had both shared where we came from, and we had common childhood disappointments. We had transcended those childhoods and were now involved in other realities. That pleasant afternoon conversation formed the basis of my personal loyalty to Garcia. It was the only conversation about our respective childhoods we were to have, and it has remained with me ever since.

Garcia was very hip like that. You could talk to him about something and he would ask questions and thereafter that particular area of interest would never be directly addressed again. Once he had received the information, he never forgot it. As soon as he understood how the Rolling Stones structured their arrangements as a band, he didn't bother to revisit that subject. When we talked about the early history of psychedelics in England it was the same.

He was vaguely curious about Pink Floyd, but once he'd heard the story of London in the '60s, that was enough. Tales of Blind Faith, Eric Clapton, and Fleetwood Mac would only interest him insofar as their bearing on his own experience with the Grateful Dead. His total focus when I first knew him was how his band could survive, pay its bills, and keep body and soul together. Other than that, I'm not sure that Garcia was interested in anything else to do with the wider music business.

On a drive together to the East Bay, where Jerry was to play a gig with Merl Saunders, we talked about records and recording. Garcia gave me a potted history of the Dead's way of making records.

In essence, he said, the Dead had constantly been experimenting, trying to make a record that somehow sounded "like them," and had failed. Even their live recordings hadn't captured their magic. The new *Live Dead* album had come close, but Warner Brothers had spent a fortune on supporting the band's efforts and they owed the label a lot of money. Thus far, not one of the records the Dead had released had actually made any real profit. In a word, they were broke, and had been since they began making records. The pressure to come up with a successful album was increasing. The band had to make a commercial record or, at the very least, a record that would recoup what it cost to make. The secret to this was slowly dawning on Garcia: don't be profligate with studio time and keep recording costs as low as possible.

Could the problem be not so much the recording of the various albums but their marketing? I asked. How were the albums being sold? What kind of promotional co-ordination was going on between the album being released and the band's live appearances? Could it be something as simple as ensuring their albums were available in the record stores in a town where the Grateful Dead played?

In the late '60s in San Francisco very few people in the music scene were aware of this type of thing. The bands were concerned about album artwork and test-pressings — their interest in sales rarely strayed beyond the size of the advance they were to receive. The actual selling of records was something that was left to the record companies; it had the uncomfortable stench of "commerce" about it.

Most of the people in control of the San Francisco bands were friends who'd been made tour managers, equipment managers, and promo people. A certain type of inspired amateurism seemed to be the order of the day. Somehow the San Francisco bands felt more comfortable with friends as their managers, and as far as I could tell the only ones who were managed in a strictly professional way were Creedence Clearwater Revival and Janis.

Garcia was a big-hearted man. He had taken me into his own house and I was humbled by his generosity of spirit. He constantly thought of the welfare of others and naturally put the interests of the collective before his own. The Grateful Dead, I sensed, weighed heavily upon him; he felt responsible for the problems they were having and was eager to develop a way forward.

Sitting in his garden and listening to him talk about his music and how much he cared for his wider family took me back to my own upbringing. It reminded me in some ways of the commitment and passion of the people who had raised me; people who had seen the disaster of war and poverty firsthand and who knew that conflict and greed were no solutions to the problems of the world. Garcia had gone through the experience of the Haight-Ashbury and he had retained a core commitment to the values that had been developed there. Now he was struggling to reconcile those values with the demands of the wider world. It all boiled down to the same old question. How was the band to survive?

CHAPTER 33

Trust me –
I'm a Christian!

Rock Scully, one of the Dead's original managers, had fought hard to get the band to realize that close cooperation with Warner Brothers was imperative to their long-term success, but the relationship with the label had always been somewhat troubled. As Garcia explained it to me, it appeared that money was unaccounted for. Suspicion and negative feelings were running high and it seemed as if the Reverend Lenny Hart was central to some of the accounting "issues." It seemed that the man of God might well be ripping them off.

At the end of the 1960s, the time of Altamont, the Dead's management had morphed into a peculiar beast. At its apex was the reverend and then there was John McIntyre as assistant manager. He'd been a family member for a few years, and was obviously an erudite and well-educated cat, but no one could ever quite describe what his specific role was. Mind you, in fairness to McIntyre, and most of the weird and wonderful people I was being introduced to, specifics were not (and never had been) the order of the day.

Only a rank fool would meet with someone from the Dead's family and ask, "What do you do?" Such a ridiculous question would probably be answered with "as little as possible." Where the band began and the family ended no one could really say.

There were people who got taken on the road merely because they'd make a welcome addition. They were titled the "Pleasure Crew" and had no discernible responsibility other than to have a good time. Specifics were really not applicable to the Grateful Dead. People just got on with things.

So the manager was (probably) ripping off the band, but there was no point in asking Garcia about it. The man could make a million decisions when he played music, but when it came to making a decision in life, he could beat around the bush with more obstinacy than an Oriental sage. Garcia could think up more reasons why something should not be done than anyone I have ever met. It wasn't that he was opposed to action per se. He was perfectly happy to go along with what was decided; he just didn't want to be the responsible party. Perhaps music was the only place or space on the planet where he found it easy to make decisions.

I didn't have any problems with making decisions, or living with the consequences. So I volunteered to find out what was happening with the money, and to discreetly let Garcia know. I thought I'd start with a chat with John McIntyre. A spliff and a drink soon confirmed what I had guessed: the Dead had a big problem with what could be described as the "conventional approach" to organizing any kind of collective endeavor.

John was a sincere guy. He told me that he had found bags of receipts from the days when Rock Scully and Danny Rifkin managed the band, but that the Dead had never kept books in a "square" sense, and that Lenny was secretive and behaved bizarrely. Virtually everything John told me about the reverend had the characteristic markings of a rip-off, if only by omission and good old-fashioned confusion.

I had to be careful about jumping to conclusions. The Grateful Dead was a strange beast, so I needed to be cautious.

While I was looking for sophisticated swindles, though, it transpired that the reverend was simply helping himself, because he assumed that was what the Grateful Dead's managers had always done. In some respects this was true!

The reverend had fallen by the wayside and given in to temptation. Mammon in all its sordid glory had appeared to him in the shape of a pile of money and a pretty girl — and soon he took the money, grabbed the girl, and ran. But Lenny Hart only ran as far as San Diego; he didn't even bother to leave California.

He made no attempt to cover his tracks and moved into a motel by the beach with his sweetheart, who happened to have worked at the bank where the Dead's money had been deposited. What did he think he was going to do? Live there for the rest of his days? What amazed me was the reaction of the people in the Grateful Dead's family — they were very far out.

Firstly, everyone's thoughts were with Mickey the drummer, betrayed by his father. Not one voice was raised in criticism, and everybody lent Mickey their support. There was an extended discussion of whether it was even appropriate that Lenny be prosecuted by the authorities.

No one got too cut up about being ripped off for more than $100,000, except for Billy Kreutzmann, who was the most pugilistic of the band. Even Kreutzmann thought it would probably be sufficient to thump Lenny.

Garcia was more than happy to leave it up to karma. To Jerry, the reverend's betrayal was but a little stone on the path upon which the band had trod. It had made them feel a little pain, but it was not life-threatening. He was all for doing nothing. I stressed to him that if he did nothing, he really couldn't complain if other people came along and thought it okay to do the same thing. (Which several years later, they did!)

Jerry didn't really care about money and I tried to demonstrate to him that it was this attitude that made Lenny feel comfortable with the prospect of taking large lumps of the stuff, but he simply refused to be too concerned. In the end, he came up with a typically Garcian solution: instead of one manager, he persuaded the band they should have three!

He wanted me to be a member of the troika and act as the

Dead's tour manager. Each of the three members of the management team, he explained, would look out for the interests of the band, making sure that none of their fellow managers was ripping them off ! I tried to explain that this was a paranoid solution to what was inherently an accounting, structural, and organizational problem, but Garcia was adamant.

The Grateful Dead had tried one manager and they'd tried two, Garcia explained to me. Now it was time to try three. I asked Garcia (following his own logic) if, when he was a fifty-year-old guitar player, whether he expected to be cared for by, let's say, ten managers? He didn't dignify my sarcastic comment with a reply. Three men in the Grateful Dead boat it was going to be. Who was I to argue? I was living in the man's house, without a job and broke. I persuaded myself that it all sounded cool!

For the record, the good reverend was eventually arrested, as reported by *Rolling Stone* in 1971, and did a short stint in the Marin County Jail, but the band never got their money back.

Altamont, meanwhile, had faded somewhat into the background, but it wasn't going to go away. In the middle of my getting to know the Grateful Dead, it came back to haunt me.

CHAPTER 34

Witness for the defense

Through intermediaries I received a message from the Angels asking me to contact an attorney-at-law named George Walker. He was the criminal defense lawyer representing Alan Passaro, the Angel who'd been arrested and charged with the first-degree murder of Meredith Hunter.

I arrived at a nondescript office building and sat down to talk to Walker, who seemed pleasant enough, if all business. He questioned me about my position in relation to the incident, my sightlines, and my having seen the gun in Hunter's hand. Could I be absolutely clear about such things? The lawyer believed that he was defending a man innocent of first-degree murder. His take was that no American jury would convict a man of murder if the man was defending himself with a knife against someone wielding a gun and reasonably considered his life to be in danger.

The lawyer's questions continued: Had I ever met the defendant before? Could I recognize him in court? What was my relationship to the Angels?

I was somewhat shocked when the lawyer told me he was thinking about calling me as a witness for the defense, but I reluctantly agreed if he thought it was absolutely necessary. In my estimation, Passaro had been acting in self-defense, so I could hardly refuse. I considered him innocent of the crime with which he was being charged. He was undoubtedly a violent man, but to my mind not a murderer.

I didn't enjoy the few hours I spent being grilled by the defense attorney. It rekindled memories of that horrible day in the desert, and it prompted all kinds of speculative thoughts about the whole mess of Altamont. In the weeks following the concert I had gleaned details about who the principals were in the murder case. These were some nasty people.

Alan Passaro was twenty-one when he was accused of the murder. He was a comparatively recent member of the Hells Angels, having previously been a member of the Gypsy Jokers in San Jose, a club that had been absorbed into the Angels. That was how Passaro had come to be in Frisco colors and at Altamont. He was being held in jail on other charges at the time he was charged with the murder of Hunter.

Meredith Hunter was the third of four children born to an African-American woman named Altha May Anderson and her Native American partner Curley Hunter. His legal name was Meredith Curley Hunter, but his girlfriend Patti called him by his street name, "Murdock Supreme." She can be seen in the film *Gimme Shelter*, crying over his corpse. Hunter was a tough guy from the East Bay and was known to carry a weapon. He had a short fuse and law enforcement authorities knew him as a methamphetamine user and dealer.

Meredith Hunter was, like the man who killed him, a gang member, belonging to a black crew called the East Bay Executioners. The Executioners were deeply involved in the sale of marijuana and methamphetamines and had well-established markets in East Bay's black community. It was an absolute condition of membership that they remain armed at all times. Most of them used methamphetamines and the pathologist's examination of Hunter's corpse revealed track marks on his arms.

Both men, the accused and the victim, fitted the description "armed and dangerous." One speed dealer got killed by another at a concert and somehow the Rolling Stones were responsible?

This was the muck that was being peddled by the American press at the time: a poor black fellow had been ruthlessly murdered by the Hells Angels, virtually at the behest of the Stones. Nothing was said about Hunter's past or the fact that he was armed at the concert. Apparently it was quite acceptable in America to attend an outdoor gig carrying a revolver.

None of Altamont's central characters seemed to have shared the "peace and love" ethos that the naive Rolling Stones thought still held sway on the West Coast. Later, when I got the chance, I hit Garcia hard with my doubts and asked how any of this violent bullshit could be blamed upon the Rolling Stones.

Garcia said nothing and shifted uncomfortably in his chair. I said that the whole business of Altamont was essentially the fault (if fault was the right word) of the Grateful Dead, not the Stones.

"You guys suggested this in the first place," I told him. "Your office was used to organize it, and your people went on radio to encourage people to attend the concert. So how come the Dead's shit doesn't stink?" We were sitting out the back of his house in Larkspur. The conversation was part of a wider rap we were having about legal representation for the band, which played out a few weeks later when Hal Kant was appointed as their legal adviser.

Hal Kant was an expert on music business and entertainment law, an urbane and sophisticated man, and has the distinction of being the only man I ever knew who won a million dollars in a poker game. He would later represent my touring company, until the Dead and I parted ways. I still have a great deal of respect for him. My only regret is I never had the time to get the man to show me how to play poker . . . but I digress.

Garcia grudgingly agreed that there was some responsibility on the Dead's part. He had thought the concert was a great idea, as had most of the family and many people in San Francisco.

"It just all got fucked up," he said, "when it got bigger than the local people could handle and involved people from out of state who had no idea about the whole San Francisco thing."

"Jerry," I told him, "the people from out of state were kids and they didn't drive to Altamont with pool cues in their micro buses. The violent minority came from the San Jose Peninsula and from the West Coast itself."

Garcia was intensely uncomfortable with what had happened and I could sense his embarrassment about his own family's role in what had gone down.

I suggested that the real reason for the horrible events of that day perhaps lay within America itself. It wasn't anything to do with the "Satanic" influence of the Rolling Stones. People here carried guns, even to a concert. Didn't that have to do with an absurd misreading of the American constitution? It had been framed to allow individuals to carry and possess arms because of the need for a well-regulated militia, not so that every inadequate little man could pack a piece.

Garcia peered at me and shrugged. "The Grateful Dead," he said, "don't really take positions; we're musicians, not politicians." The Dead, Jerry said, had started out in the Haight wanting something very different to what was currently going on in American society. They were essentially communards, people who were into communal living, who believed in the values that were inherent in sharing. But none of them shared a specific vision of how things should be done, or at least they didn't share a vision that anyone had successfully articulated.

In any case, the Grateful Dead meant hugely different things to different people. They defied classification because they wanted things to remain loose and unstructured. If anything, they specifically wanted to be beyond description. Essentially, the Dead could only use words to reliably describe what it was they did not approve of, Jerry told me, and the one thing they did not approve of was people killing one another at free concerts.

In due course, Passaro went on trial, and I attended the Alameda County courthouse where he was arraigned. I spent several uncomfortable days sitting in a room with windows set high in the walls so that one could not see out or in.

As I sat there, I wondered whether I should alert the press that a former member of the Stones' management was attending the trial of a Hells Angel as a witness for the defense. They would have had a field day, especially if they knew that representatives of the Stones were offering Meredith Hunter's mother money to compensate for her son's death and to head off the possibility of a lawsuit.

I had plenty of time to consider the whole mess of Altamont and specifically to think about my relationship with the Stones. I had been proud to work for them, but now they seemed happy for me to accept a large portion of the blame for Altamont.

But I was not vindictive. I still held on to the idea that loyalty was a noble and desirable virtue.

I decided to drop the whole sorry business. I no longer worked for them. In fact, today they still owe me wages from when I did work for them! But there's more to life, I decided, than working for the Rolling Stones. I consoled myself with the thought that, unlike Meredith Hunter, at least I had a life to move on with.

I never got to see the actual trial, as I was a potential witness, and in the end I wasn't called, such was the strength of Passaro's defense. Just as the lawyer had predicted, the Hells Angel was found not guilty. Passaro went back to jail on other charges and was eventually to drown in highly suspicious circumstances with a large amount of cash in his pockets. Like Meredith Hunter, he met his end in a violent and unpleasant manner.

The Stones regrouped in Europe and we went our separate ways. We were not to meet again for many years.

CHAPTER 35

Yin and yang

After months of vulgar rock'n'roll predictability with the Rolling Stones I was ready for something different and refreshing. Working for the Stones could be a challenge but there's no way that it could really be described as fun. I decided to take up Jerry Garcia's offer and become one of the Grateful Dead's managers.

Late in 1969, the Grateful Dead were Jerry Garcia and Bob Weir (guitars), Phil Lesh (bass), Ron "Pigpen" McKernan (organ, harmonica), and Billy Kreutzmann and Mickey Hart (both on drums). After Lenny absconded with the band's money, Mickey went on an extended sabbatical, but eventually returned. In 1970, Keith Godchaux would join on keyboards, and his wife Donna on vocals. I wouldn't just be managing the band, though — the Dead had a large "family."

As I got to find out more about the Dead and their family, I became increasingly intrigued. How did you join this group? Where did all these people come from? Neither Garcia nor Robert Hunter, the Dead's lyricist, could really explain the process coherently. Apparently, one was either on the bus or off the bus and that was pretty much it.

I loved the mystery of it all. Life for the Grateful Dead seemed like such a pleasant and surreal dance, conducted with a sunny grin and an amused detachment from the tedious realities of straight existence. Being a member of the Dead family had none of that feeling of heavy responsibility that weighed upon a member of the Rolling Stones' entourage. You couldn't have found two more different bands.

Throughout my life people I have met have been fascinated by the differences and similarities between the two groups. I've had many a pleasant conversation discussing the finer points of these musicians' contributions to rock'n'roll, their personal strengths and weaknesses, and the iron-clad connection that both bands have managed to maintain with their devoted fans.

The Rolling Stones have been variously described as aggressive, arrogant, and self-important, belligerent, obsessed with being number one, highly competitive, and "the greatest rock 'n'roll band in the world." Initially guided by their savagely anarchic and brilliant manager Andrew Loog Oldham, the Stones affected a disdain for all things promotional while managing to garner more column inches than any other band this side of the Beatles. Mick Jagger and Keith Richards were supremely gifted media manipulators. These two ostensibly unlikely promo-tarts were experts at self-promotion and publicity, masters at dealing with and manipulating the straight world. In some respects, the straight world had made them.

The Dead adamantly refused to believe that they actually needed the straight world and its media to make their whole trip a success. They resolutely aimed themselves at a minority and were unfazed by mass-market tastes or opinions. The Haight-Ashbury district from which the Dead had evolved had been an attempt to create an alternative to straight society.

The Rolling Stones were interested in exploiting straight society, not in coming up with a viable alternative. They were a show band whose onstage delivery had all the razzmatazz and glamour the world expects from its superstars. Like most of the superstars I have known they were basically interested in producing a spectacular performance, being as successful as possible, loved by one and all, making tons of money, and putting the cash in a Swiss bank where they shared it with no one. Can't say I ever blamed them for that.

The Grateful Dead were the polar opposite — despising the music industry and all that it represented. They were cooperative, sharing and caring, directly supporting an extended family of more than forty people and dedicated to getting high at their concerts with an audience of like-minded souls. Promotional stickers of the time used to claim that "there is nothing like a Grateful Dead concert" and they were right. Nothing I've ever seen has even come remotely close. A Grateful Dead concert was decidedly not a show in the classical sense, more of an ethereal experience to be shared. Where the band began and the audience ended were profound questions and nobody cared how long it took to learn the answer.

With the Dead there could often be long pauses between songs as the band and the audience took time out to re-establish what the hell was going on. Like, where are we? The Rolling Stones have always, it seemed to me, hated the space between songs.

A Grateful Dead concert could take many hours, and who knows where the musical journey might meander and which little mysterious forest glades of beauty might be revealed and enjoyed in the process. The Stones went from one number to the next with the velocity of an express train.

A Stones concert rattled along without brakes, bashing down the track and determined to reach a specific destination without much of a pause. Get on board, hold tight, enjoy the journey, job done, collect the money, and split. That's the Stones, with Keith at the musical helm, proud to describe himself as "five strings, two fingers, and one arsehole."

Unlike the Stones, the Dead have never had a hit album (though they've had some big-selling ones) and only once has one of their songs, 1987's "Touch of Grey," ever made the top ten. They have millions of fans in the U.S., but are not very well known elsewhere. When the Dead were finally given a gold record, Jerry Garcia took out his lighter and tried to burn the disc to see if it would melt! On another occasion they played a gold record they had received on a turntable and fell about laughing when the music that came out of the speakers was of some other band. They positively strove to ensure that their image was of a bunch of good ol'-fashioned fuck-ups who had no more clue about what was happening than you or I — maybe even less.

The Grateful Dead would only reluctantly agree to be photographed and refused to wear anything but their everyday clothes for a shoot. Down home and funky, the antithesis of flash, there was little to distinguish the members of the band from the people who adored their music and attended their concerts — everyone looked pretty much the same. People in the Dead dressed like they had just walked in off the street, or more accurately, just got out of bed, thrown on yesterday's clothes, and headed straight out the door without bothering even to think about looking in a mirror. No one in the Dead gave a shit about their image and any suggestions about such things would be greeted with dubious scorn.

The press and all the associated giddiness of fame left the Grateful Dead feeling very uncomfortable and several members of the band refused to give interviews. Jerry Garcia reluctantly became spokesman, as he was the only one who'd talk to journalists, but he was uncomfortable with the press trying to cast him as spokesman for his generation. Garcia didn't want to be a spokesman for anything, except perhaps a new paradigm where people looked at the world with unclouded eyes and a fresh consciousness. In the several years I was with the Grateful Dead, they never held a press conference that I can remember, whereas the Stones have done so many that no one can keep count. The Stones always loved the media hoopla. As long as the focus was on them, be the story good or bad, they enjoyed the exposure.

Another interesting difference between the bands was in their attitude toward each other. The Grateful Dead simply adored the early songs of the Stones and incorporated them into their live music performances from their earliest days as the Warlocks until the band ceased playing when Garcia died on August 9, 1995. The Rolling Stones, on the other hand, viewed the Dead's freewheeling music and funky West Coast Californian thing as a bit of a joke. One thing's for sure, no one ever heard the Rolling Stones play a Grateful Dead tune. It stretches the limits of musical credulity to consider what they would make of many of the songs in the Dead's vast catalog.

I doubt that the Rolling Stones (other than their guitarist and co-founder Brian Jones) even knew much about the Grateful Dead or the whole San Francisco scene until that fateful day when a member of the Dead's family came to London and suggested to Keith Richards that the two bands should play together at a free concert in San Francisco. When the Stones thought of California, they thought Hollywood and Los Angeles were where it was at, and were deeply suspicious of the San Francisco scene that had given birth to the Grateful Dead. Mick would make snide jokes about the "Grateful Airplane" and the "Jefferson Dead" and viewed the whole hippie trip with some distaste.

The Stones and the Dead were the yin and the yang of bands, as unlike one another as they could possibly be — and yet they both loved the early blues artists. They simply took two very different approaches to what constituted "being in a band."

When I was first hanging out with Garcia, immediately following the debacle at Altamont, I asked him to describe what the Grateful Dead was all about. Garcia looked at me thoughtfully and replied, "In the great forest of music, you, the listener, explore and wander between the trees, until by happy accident you stumble upon a forest glade. There in a beautiful clearing in the woods spread with verdant grass in the sunlight, you stand in awe as the birds sing. Walking carefully toward the center of the clearing you notice an isolated group of delicate small flowers radiant in their perfection and perfect in their radiance. Those flowers, so fragile and insubstantial, so manifest and yet so vulnerable, are the Grateful Dead."

I cannot imagine Mick or Keith ever talking about the Rolling Stones like that.

CHAPTER 36

Cool conundrums

Getting to know the Grateful Dead showed me that their psyche-delic scene was fundamentally different to that in England. In England, those who wanted to live communally generally moved to rural areas, because living in the major cities was expensive and accommodation hard to find. Most of the people who took acid in London were "weekend hippies." Full-timers were rare. The English had no experience in the sixties that equated to the Haight-Ashbury, where a large number of freaks lived in an inner-city community. There was no Golden Gate Park in which to frolic.

England also never experienced anything like the "acid tests" — where people took acid and were bombarded with crazy stimuli in a chaotic environment. Even though a band like Pink Floyd might play with a light show illuminating the scene, there was a more gentle and introspective approach to the acid expe-rience. Acid remained a somewhat solitary pleasure, with the English retaining their deeply ingrained insularity. Even on acid, the English stiff upper lip more or less held firm, though it some-times trembled with psychedelic uncertainty.

In England I saw very few people having bad trips, whereas in America it seemed like an everyday occurrence. When I became the Dead's tour manager, I often saw people freaking out at their gigs, and frequently had to intervene to save them from the police, who were poorly equipped to deal with the "crazies." At an English gig in the '60s one would be hard pressed to tell those who were tripping from those who were just "being there."

People in England tended to go quietly mad; in fact, the quietly mad had long been a feature of English society. The acid casualty often slipped beneath the radar of day-to-day existence and became hard to distinguish from his fellow countrymen, whereas in America only a certain level of crazy was acceptable. Get too crazy and the Americans would reject you; get too crazy in England, like Syd Barrett, and everyone would start calling you a genius, while discreetly abandoning you to your fate.

Leaving the Haight-Ashbury had, in a sense, cast the Grateful Dead adrift in the world. Now, instead of living collectively, they lived in their own homes and led somewhat more distant lives. This change in their immediate environment would give rise to the great albums *Workingman's Dead* and *American Beauty*. Nonetheless, it was a stressful time and the move from urban to rural definitely changed the zeitgeist, just as it changed the music.

The Dead had been prescient enough to see the impending "death of the hippie." The Haight-Ashbury scene had only been beautiful for a very short period of time; after that it had become unsustainable and rapidly degenerated into an ugly trip. The fortunate ones, like the Dead, got out while the going was good. Now they had to rediscover and redefine how they wanted to live, in a different and less supportive environment.

I thought of the Grateful Dead as the psychedelic equivalent of those early Christian sects who had been forced to leave their ancestral homes in Europe and to wander to a new place where they could live in peace. I saw the Dead as immigrants to straight America, involved in a process that obliged them to redefine who they were. Then I realized that for the Dead family, redefinition was a constant process. How anybody joined or left this evolving group of people I didn't have a clue, though after a few years I was to find out. As it transpired, you were always free to step off the bus, even if it was hurtling down the highway at top speed.

Now that I was on board, the Dead forged ahead with the latest evolution of their management model. I joined John McIntyre and David Parker in a management triumvirate. David set up Dead HQ in an old house in San Rafael.

David Parker was an old friend of Garcia's and had an accountancy background. He and his wife Bonnie had shared a house in Palo Alto with Garcia, Hunter, and David Nelson, the guitarist from the New Riders of the Purple Sage. They had tripped, played, and hung out together. Garcia and Hunter trusted the Parkers, and after the debacle with Lenny Hart, trust was a much-needed commodity.

David and I immediately set about pursuing the two things necessary to our working relationship: we got high together and talked a lot.

I was thrilled that the Parkers were going to be handling the financials, as I have never found anything more boring in this world than money and wanted as little to do with it as possible, though this was to change as I became more involved with the Dead's financial predicament.

Parker, as everyone called him, was there to deal with the money, assisted by Bonnie, and they received a lot of flak for being necessarily parsimonious on the band's behalf. He was good at saying no and people resented that.

But fiscal responsibility had to be established or all was lost. In the old days, people who wanted money from the common pool simply went to the managers and made their pitch: the better the rap, the more money they got! The Parkers now held the keys to an admittedly empty vault with grim determination.

Parker struck me as a shy guy, but he came from the right space. I admired him and Bonnie for their stoicism; Parker and I soon established common ground as we analyzed the Dead's massive debts. We both knew that the band could not expect any kind of real income from the sales of their records, so we would have to look elsewhere.

The only way the Grateful Dead were going to make any serious money was by doing gigs. It was that simple. They just had to be prepared to spend the next three or four years on the road. To do that, they needed a tour manager — me — who would (among other things) help them bring home as much of their tour income as possible. They also needed to re-evaluate the way in which they toured so that it was both financially viable and fun. That job would also fall to me.

I concentrated on what we needed first to survive, and then to thrive. The Parkers and I drew up a master plan that outlined the necessary income we'd need to generate to get through. Based on what the band was earning when I first started with them, there was a huge amount of work ahead. The question was, could we do the work, bring home the bacon, and still have fun? Everyone agreed that we'd go for it, or die trying.

Even at the height of their financial crisis, fun was still a vital consideration in all things Grateful Dead. There was no way the band was going to approach this as if they were going to work like straight people. Being in the Grateful Dead was not a job! The question soon arose (from me): Who was going to decide what was fun? And it was answered for me in an inimitable Grateful Dead way.

Prior to my arrival, decisions about gigs were made very haphazardly. Whether a gig was to be played could often be the subject of a day-long meeting, which would be attended by those who considered themselves members of the family and therefore entitled to a say. The ladies of the band, the girlfriends of the equipment guys, old friends from Haight-Ashbury days — sometimes fifty people would sit in and give their opinion.

I pointed out in one of my first such meetings that no one made suggestions about how the music should be played when the Dead was on stage, so why should they have input when tours were being planned? This produced howls of protest.

People simply refused to believe that "the community" should not have some input. This way of doing things, the emphasis on consultation and community, was new to me. The Stones worked entirely differently. It's well known that Bill Wyman didn't even talk to Keith Richards for ten years 'cos he thought Keith didn't like him. Perhaps this lack of communication was the secret of their longevity. Who knows? It sounds chronically dysfunctional, but somehow it worked.

At one of my early meetings with the Dead I pointed to someone in attendance and no one present knew who this person was. It turned out he was a curious freak who'd walked in off the street. Everyone decided it was cool for him to stay.

This way of arranging business was clearly unsustainable.

We needed to perform over a hundred gigs a year and the old decision-making methods meant we could be trapped in one virtually endless meeting debating what we were going to be doing on these tours. I invited the band to suggest a better way. In one of our backyard raps, Garcia proffered a solution.

Of all the band members, Jerry said that Phil Lesh was most reluctant to go on tour. It frequently came down to everyone having to persuade Phil before a gig could happen. So the obvious solution was to give Phil, the hardest bugger to please, the ultimate decision-making authority on behalf of all the band members. Phil's natural resistance became the path of least resistance for the band overall. It was ordained that it was Phil I had to work with. I figured I had better get to know the man. We met at his house and I suggested to him that we should make our meetings as pleasant as possible. We needed to work out a way of operating that was hip, efficient, and not time-consuming. Phil agreed with this basic approach and then we got down to the nitty-gritty.

I first briefed Phil on the number of gigs we had to do to enable everyone to survive and to pay off debts. Phil now knew that if the band were to make it through, most of his natural tendency to object would need to be curbed. We needed a lot of money, which meant a lot of gigs. Once we had agreed on that, we could progress to discussing what kind of gigs we needed.

Phil took his new responsibilities very seriously and was interested in how the whole plan for the gigs was going to pan out. I explained to him how I saw the Grateful Dead making money from touring. For one, we had to have a sufficient number of gigs within specific areas of the U.S. for touring to be financially worthwhile. To do a single gig in Florida followed by a show in New York was plainly absurd, as the costs of transportation alone would be prohibitive. Following from that, then, we had to do gigs in a coherent series, so the travel between shows was economically viable. To play Pittsburgh, then Boston, followed by Philadelphia and then Bangor, Maine — with New York somewhere in the middle — was not the way to play the East Coast.

If we went on the road with twenty people, airfares became an important consideration. We obviously needed to generate sufficient income on the East Coast to warrant the expenditure. Historically, I reckoned the Dead were lucky to return home with five per cent of their gross tour earnings.

We also had to increase the number of people who wanted to see the band. We were going to have to promote the Grateful Dead, a proposal unlikely to receive the band's support.

Rock Scully was a valuable ally when it came to "flogging" the Grateful Dead. He had issues with the band that went back a long way, but he was a founding member of the tribe. He looked after the promotion and sales of the band's records once they had been delivered to Warner Brothers, and he was probably the only member of the Dead family who had any real idea as to what was involved in promotion. Rock and I agreed to put the Altamont debacle behind us, and work together for the common good.

My friend Chesley Millikin would also become an indispensable ally to the group of people who cared for the Dead. He knew Rock well. Chesley was a real professional, and there was no question that he loved the Dead and also loved to get high. He hung around with the Dead's family for years and yet was never to be directly hired for his wisdom and business skills. (Chesley found his niche as the manager of the New Riders of the Purple Sage, but there he languished, with his specialized skills barely utilized.)

Sometimes the Dead were brilliant and as profound as any group of human beings could possibly be, and at other times they were so damned stupid it made one want to scream with frustration. They had a simple survival technique (one of many they employed) when it came to their own fallibilities — they were unfailingly cheerful about being "fuck-ups." It didn't seem to worry them at all.

When they made collective decisions, they could sometimes be hopelessly awry, but the possibility of getting things spectacularly wrong didn't inhibit them. They'd steam ahead with reckless abandon, giggle like kids, and jump feet-first into whatever mad scrape appealed to them. The levity inherent in the band's approach allowed them to not get too depressed when things went wrong.

This was one of the reasons why Woodstock, where they played poorly, and Monterey Pop, where they also sucked, never had much of a long-term effect on them. Best to accept some things for the absolute bummers they were, and then move on. The Dead's approach was not to analyze their failures, but to absorb them and carry on down the road. "Forward" was very much their company motto. Sometimes I used to think that they loved being reckless and it annoyed me. But I mellowed and began to realize at times, don't we all love irresponsibility and recklessness?

When Garcia asked me if I'd like to go to Hawaii as my introduction to being their tour manager, the crafty old thing knew that he'd answered two of my needs in one hit. I needed a vacation and a job. His timing was impeccable. With that, I was "on the bus," so to speak, and became a member of the Grateful Dead family.

I consumed rather large amounts of acid on the Hawaiian sojourn, so that the whole experience felt like it melted into a series of barely connected vignettes. Sonny Heard, one of the Dead's equipment guys, was my constant companion. He'd probably been deputized to ensure that I didn't go off the rails, and see whether I could pass the "acid test."

Clifford "Sonny" Heard certainly knew how to "get high and get by" and had an uncanny ability to keep things in perspective even though we were tripping off our tits.

We all stayed in an amazing house, set back a little from the beach, and there beneath the coconut palms we'd lounge about and play and have a wonderfully relaxing time, smoking some of the best grass known to man. I remember sitting on the beach late at night with Heard, looking up at the sky, which was dripping in sparkling jewels. The waves were bigger than I had ever seen and I wanted to go swimming. Sonny was an Oregon farm boy, definitely not beach material, and as soon as I suggested a dip he dragged my arse off that beach. No way was this wise old bird going to allow me to drown in the monstrous Pacific on his watch.

The Dead played a show in Hawaii and Heard came with me to collect the money. Together, tripping along nicely, we counted the many bills and made sure the "take" was correct. One of the first things I learned to do with the Grateful Dead was to count money while on acid, and believe me, it can be done. I never got it wrong, and Sonny Heard was frequently my backup.

We had an infallible system for counting the money. I'd sort it into $1,000 piles, and Heard would check it. Assuming it was right he'd put an elastic band around the cash. No problem. Anyway, we collected the money at the Hawaii gig, stashed it in my briefcase and then went backstage to join the band.

For some reason, along the way, while walking through the

crowd, we decided to place the briefcase in the middle of the dance floor while we sat and watched what would happen to it. A couple of thousand freaks danced high as kites around several thousand dollars and no one went near the thing.

Heard and I watched in silent amazement. The polished aluminum briefcase sat there like an alien spacecraft and yet no one took a blind bit of notice. Eventually we got bored and rescued the case and headed back to the stage, which I remember was higher than our heads, about eight feet off the ground.

We stood at ground level beside the stage, smoking a joint and waiting for the set to finish. When they were done, Bob Weir unplugged his guitar and walked off the side of the stage, stepping smoothly through the air in an arc, passing literally over our heads, not breaking his stride as he hit the ground and continued on to the dressing-room. I suspected that Weir could walk on water, but to see him walk on air impressed me no end.

Here was a man, I thought to myself, who I could follow across a few rivers.

*Three years old with my parents
Dora and Ernie in the back garden
of 22 Kings Avenue Buckhurst Hill
— on my new trike!*

*...c years old and wearing a
...mper my gran knitted —
...e nervous forced smile of
a frightened schoolboy
having his "official"
photograph taken.*

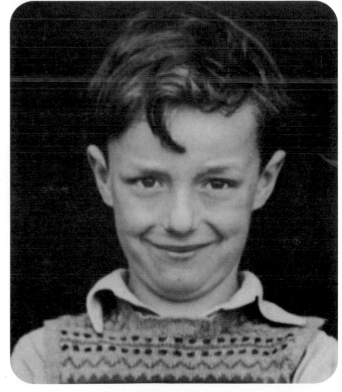

Mick reading a passage from Percy Bysshe Shelley's "Adonaïs" in memory of Brian Jones, who had been found dead three days earlier. Half a million people attended this concert in Hyde Park in London on July 6, 1969. Notice the boxes of butterflies sitting against the speakers. (© REG BURKETT/HULTON ARCHIVE/GETTY IMAGES)

At the airport in Dallas, Texas, waiting for a plane and explaining to Mick and Keith that not all Texans like rock'n'roll — and yes, some of them are weirder than Martians.

ambling in Vegas, doing my bit and watching Keith's back.

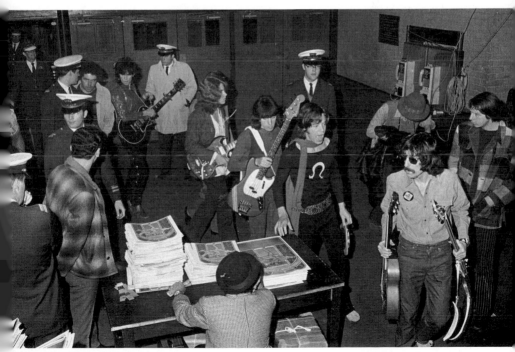

...ading the Rolling Stones on stage — those with a keen eye will note that we've ...gotten to bring Charlie Watts. I'm carrying the guitars.

The boys used Stephen Stills' house as their home base during the U.S. leg of the 1969 tour. Here is one of the rare moments when they were actually rehearsing.

sun was still up at Altamont, and the concert was already turning into a
ster. I tried to calm the crowd (with Michael Laing standing beside me), but
acid casualty lying on the ground in front of the stage speaks volumes. Note
height of the stage, which was a major factor in the chaos that was Altamont.
BERT ALTMAN)

Violence at Altamont. Above: The camera sits on my shoulder, showing what I saw from my position at the side of the stage. People run across in front of the band to where a fight has started. Below: Me (bending over in leather jacket) doing my best to defuse the situation and stop the fighting while Mick looks on, very concerned. (© AP PHOTO)

Before the tragedy of Altamont we were all smiles during the press conference at the Beverly Wilshire Hotel. (© ROBERT ALTMAN)

western union **telegram**

SPB240 (28)SYE548 PRA337
PR SFA226 KJ PDF SANFRANCISCO CALIF 9 524P PST   DEC 10 AM 5 07
RONNIE SCHNEIDER DLY 75
   4601 HENRY HUDSON PARKWAY APT A8 RIVERDALE-ON-HUDSON NY
AM STILL IN FRISCO THERE IS A WARRANT OUT FOR MY ARREST I DESPERATELY
 NEED MONEY AND HELP PLEASE WIRE WAGES AND BONUS IN CARE OF
BILL THOMPSON 2400 FULTON ST SAN FRANCISCO CALF DO NOT KNOW
THE CHARGES AS YET IT'S ALL VERY WORRYING I'LL CALL
   SAM
644).

SF-1201 (R5-69)

After the show, the Rolling Stones returned to the UK, leaving me behind to clean up the mess. You can feel the desperation in the telegram I sent to Ronnie Schneider, which went unanswered. The Stones never paid me a cent back then and they haven't paid me to this day. (COURTESY RON SCHNEIDER)

After Altamont, I became the touring manager of the Grateful Dead.
(© ROBERT ALTMAN)

e Festival Express tour in summer 1970 featured the Dead, Janis Joplin, The
nd, and many others traveling across Canada and making select stops. This is
ry with his wife, Mountain Girl (left) and Delaney Bramlett of Delaney &
nnie (right) enjoying the show in Calgary, Alberta.

Despite their reputation, the Grateful Dead weren't all about peace and love. Here's Jerry at target practice with me (far right) and Ray Slade, the president of the Pleasure Crew. The man with his back to the camera is actor Peter Coyote. (COURTESY RAY SLADE)

Ray Slade with one of my dearest friends, Chesley Millikin. Chesley has been a friend of mine since the days of the Stones, and he tried to warn me about going ahead with Altamont. He became an indispensible part of the Grateful Dead "family" and I even named my son after him. (COURTESY RAY SLADE)

One day I accompanied Keith Richards into a guitar store and found a Gibson acoustic I particularly liked. When he realized I liked it, he bought it for me. Forty years later, Keef's guitar is still one of my most treasured possessions. (PHOTO BY ELLA HOWARD; FROM THE COLLECTION OF THE AUTHOR)

What a long, strange trip it's been! This is me in Melbourne, 2008, wearing my prized Grateful Dead ring. (© DUKE DINH)

CHAPTER 37

Only whisper
and you'll be heard

In between the moments of psychedelic confusion in Hawaii I had managed to have a good look at the Grateful Dead and their trip. Back on the mainland, I decided that one of the first things I needed to do was to establish a working relationship with the equipment guys. They were absolutely central to making the whole touring thing work — as tough and ornery a bunch as you could wish for, but also, as it happened, the greatest brothers on the planet.

The Stones had only had one full-time equipment guy: Ian "Stu" Stewart. When they toured Stu would get others to help carry the load, but basically he was a one-man band. The Grateful Dead's set-up was a little different. Their crew would swell dependent upon each tour's needs.

In the hierarchy of the Dead family, equipment guys had far more influence and say than mere managers. A good equipment guy could take at least a few weeks to train, if not months, and they were hard to find. While the band knew how to use their gear, very few of them actually knew how to set up the equipment without assistance. Consequently, equipment guys were well looked after and their opinions noted and acted upon. (Most of the time.)

When I first arrived, the band's crew was comprised of just

Ramrod, Jackson, and Heard: three men from the rodeo town of Pendleton, Oregon. Ramrod was the number one equipment guy, the man upon whom the whole band relied. Whether it was in the midst of some psychedelic maelstrom or in band meetings, Ramrod, in his quiet way, sat at the very epicenter of the Dead's world.

Ramrod had an impeccable underground pedigree. He had been named by Kesey, hung out with the Pranksters, and had known Neal Cassady well. Kesey, in his wisdom, had sent Ramrod to the Grateful Dead secure in the knowledge that he would be a great asset to the band. Ramrod had gone from Oregon to the wilds of Wyoming via the Merry Pranksters to the Grateful Dead. Talk about one strange trip.

Ramrod was totally devoted to the music and to the musicians. The intensity and depth of his unswerving dedication was without parallel; everyone else in the family measured themselves and their own contribution to the trip by Ramrod. Being a man of few words gave his input a weight and finality that only Garcia could match. There would be a long discussion, everyone would have their say, and then they'd turn to Ramrod to ask for his opinion.

Ramrod would have his say and that was that. Somehow his words would be a perfect summation of what lay dormant in each of our hearts.

On top of his underground experience, Ramrod had worked for Bill Graham on the Rolling Stones tour and had been at Altamont, so we knew each other before I began hanging out with Garcia. Ramrod definitely had his views on tour managers; he'd been "experimented on" by several of them. I sensed he was reluctant to let it happen again, but it was imperative that he and I have as close a working relationship as was humanly possible, so there was plenty of communicating for us to do. In our several years together we never disagreed, and I've lost count of the number of times we got higher than Jack in the story of the beanstalk. He became a brother to me.

Ramrod had an unusual way of talking to people. He spoke very quietly, in what can best be described as a conspiratorial whisper, regardless of how mundane the topic being discussed. When I first knew the man and we were talking, I could never understand why he was whispering. I mistakenly thought he didn't wish anyone to overhear what we were saying.

I asked Ramrod about his strange habit and he told me something interesting. It came, he said, from being around really loud music. Instead of shouting to make himself heard above the music, he had discovered that if he talked at a substantially lower volume than the ambient noise and pitched his voice under the music he could be both heard and understood. Now he talked softly all the time and consequently he was always heard. Even Bill Graham, who loved to rant and rave at deafening volume when we argued at gigs, was forced to admit that this low-volume approach was more successful.

Check it out for yourself when you're next at a gig. It'll save you a lot of unnecessary yelling and you'll avoid getting a sore throat. People will also listen much more closely to what it is you have to say if you whisper instead of yelling to make yourself heard.

Rex Jackson was second in the pecking order of the equipment guys. He and I got along well, though people with more different backgrounds would be hard to imagine. Rex was a skilled ranch hand; he'd grown up around horses and cattle. He was a tall, good-looking man with fine features and hair down past his shoulders — and an eye for the ladies. The ladies, it seemed, loved him right back, and it soon became clear that Rex had made out with just about every available woman in Marin County, if not the entire West Coast. Jackson had the strange distinction of being more handsome than any of the musicians he worked for; ladies were often drawn to him before the band.

Like Ramrod, Rex had worked on several Rolling Stones shows for Bill Graham. He had been at Altamont and stayed until the bitter, bloody end, so we'd shared times in the rock 'n'roll trenches. We would eventually become housemates, and like Ramrod, Rex became a brother to me.

Although he never said it out loud, I'm pretty sure that Rex decided he would knock me into shape for work with the Dead. He sure as hell gave me a lot of advice, and most of it was pretty solid. Just like Ramrod, Rex had his own theories about tour managers and touring, and he was eager to share them. Each of the tours we undertook became an extended conversation about the art of moving a number of people and their equipment across long distances.

The goal of the tour manager, I explained, was to ensure that the constituent parts of the enterprise found themselves in the same place at the same time — easier said than done when one is looking after a bunch of anarchic freaks. Rex lapped up everything I had to tell him, as he wanted to be a tour manager one day, though sometimes I doubted if he had the personal skills necessary to the task. Rex could be "country belligerent" and not very diplomatic. Knocking someone out because you fundamentally disagree with them is not one of the skills that a tour manager necessarily needs to develop.

Sadly, Rex died in a car accident in 1976 before he could live out his tour manager dream.

Sonny Heard, the last of the original trio, decided that he would be my other "adviser," along with Rex, so I had to endure "stereo Oregon." Rex and Heard were both built like brick shithouses, and definitely not men to upset. To earn extra money in Pendleton they used to stack hay bales, one of the most tiring farming jobs. This work had to be done by hand and was exceptionally physically demanding.

Heard was amiable enough, but when he got riled he was to be feared. He had a fearsome straight right punch with which he "cold-cocked" those he decided offended him beyond endurance. A couple of times when we argued I made damned sure I was well out of range.

Rex and Heard had drifted down from Oregon to the Dead

via Kesey and his people and they were two of the greatest equipment guys I have ever known. At the end of a long night, when the music had finished, Heard and Jackson would lead the charge and load the twenty-odd tons of equipment without complaint. In the end we had the "load out" down to two hours. Mind you, that would demand that twelve equipment guys and one skinny tour manager worked like the slaves who built the pyramids.

At the end of a gig I would make sure that the entire band got home safely to the hotel. I would then rush to my room and change into some jeans and a sweatshirt and return to the concert hall. By now it would be well after midnight. The equipment guys would be busy dismantling the gear and rolling up literally thousands of feet of cables.

The truck would be backed up to the rear and everything would then be loaded; sweat poured from us as muscles we hadn't used before were asked to do work that surely no human body should. Some of the amps weighed almost 150 pounds when they were in their flight cases. I always got down in the trenches and sweated along with the crew like any good officer would.

As they say in London, I worked my bollocks off. In my whole life I have never asked a man to do what I wasn't prepared to do myself, and this has led me into a lot of trouble. But that's another story.

CHAPTER 38

The Bear

Augustus Owsley Stanley III, as he was originally named, was known to one and all as "The Bear" and was in charge of the technical aspects of the equipment scene when I arrived. But as with all things to do with the Grateful Dead, things were never quite what they seemed.

I had first met The Bear at the Stones concert in Oakland in 1969. He was the little man who offered me a pipe of DMT behind Keith Richards' amplifier, which I smoked before promptly falling over.

We had a couple of cursory get-togethers at the Grateful Dead's offices when we were involved in the frantic efforts to put together the Stones' free concert. He, along with Dan Healy, had coordinated the sound at Altamont, but we didn't really get to know one another well until I joined the Dead's outfit at the beginning of 1970.

I certainly knew The Bear by reputation, and had sampled some of the acid he had made. My first introduction to The Bear's alchemical wares came at a Blue Cheer concert in Porchester Halls in London. The American band had been named after a batch of acid that The Bear had made and were reputedly the loudest act in the world.

One of their crew gave me the trip. These were early days of rock'n'roll in England and I was amazed to see that Blue Cheer traveled with a sound system they had brought all the way from the States and that they had onstage monitors. Such sophisticated equipment was unknown in England at the time and a bit of a revelation. Blue Cheer's music was certainly loud enough to nail me to the walls of the theater. I had a high old time that night.

Before laws had been invoked making LSD illegal, Bear had been responsible for the manufacture and distribution of some legendary acid. Purple Haze, White Lightning, Sunshine, and Blue Cheer (the acid, not the band) were testament to The Bear's pharmacological skills. He made acid so pure and wonderful that people like Jimi Hendrix wrote hit songs about it and others named their bands in its honor. He had kept the Dead and a lot of others high for a long time.

He was the family's postmodern shamanic alchemist and guide, so I approached him with the reverence that was naturally his due. As soon as I arrived, The Bear took me under his psychedelic wing. I was soon a better man than the one who used to work for the Rolling Stones. The Bear's attentions, in a sense, rehumanized me. At least that's what I thought. (Others in the family will no doubt fall over laughing when they read these words.)

Bear loved the Grateful Dead, and had, since their earliest days, helped the band in every way that he could. But he could be an annoying genius, so there was considerable tension between The Bear and various musicians and equipment guys by the time I arrived.

When it came to technology, The Bear was one of the most far-out and interesting guys on the planet, but when it came to the demands of tours he suffered from one massive problem: he had no sense of time.

Bear and I would have some crazy discussions about what was necessary to the whole trip of the Dead, and we would come at the problem from two wildly different perspectives. The Bear was really only concerned with the music and how it could best be amplified, recorded, and reproduced. He aimed for the best: a far-out state of affairs he described as "boss." Boss meant the best equipment, the best instruments, the best stage set-up, the best PA. The best of everything was his primary concern.

I would listen respectfully to what he was telling me and then try to get him to see what I was on about. The music business, I insisted to him, is a time business. Everyone plays together in time. We get on trains, buses, and airplanes, and we expect them to run on time. If they don't, things rapidly get weird. Promoters advertise shows that are on specific days at specific times. The information in the advertisements is time critical. Once people get to the concert they want it to start (more or less) on time, and at the time that was advertised. They pay money for this.

None of these considerations seemed to matter that much to The Bear, and I don't think they mattered that much to the Dead either before I arrived. They thought I was being too straight when I raised such mundane matters. When the equipment arrived for a show many hours in advance of the doors opening and the public gaining admittance, I would be pleased. I would expect the show to open on time. With The Bear, unfortunately, this was virtually never the case. There was always something that had to be fixed or fiddled with and there was always a delay.

The Dead's shows were never on time. The Bear never let this worry him, though it used to drive me and other people nuts. He was only interested in ensuring that the music sounded as good as possible. His abiding philosophy was: Everything for the music. Never mind the clock!

It was absurd and unprofessional, but when I pointed this out I was told that it would be even more unprofessional for the band to go on stage when the sound wasn't perfect.

Then reality cruelly intervened. After a bust in New Orleans, The Bear could no longer go on the road, and the way we toured gradually changed. Slowly and surely, the Dead began to do things with due regard to the dreaded clock. But The Bear's influence on the Dead's trip didn't end just because he couldn't come along on tour. He was responsible for all of the technological innovations the band developed. He played a key part in their "wall of sound" and the constant efforts to improve their audio fidelity.

The first FM live simulcast could be, in part, attributed to his vision, as could the first quadraphonic simulcast on radio. The first sixteen-track recordings, phase-canceling microphones, and other electronic exotica way beyond my limited technical understanding must all be accredited, at least partially, to The Bear's unique vision.

With Ron Wickersham, Bear founded the instrument makers Alembic, who continue to produce some of the finest guitars on the planet.

His was the guiding hand that led me through the "transitive nightfall of diamonds" to gaze upon a different psychedelic dawn. He taught me perhaps the most important lesson of my life: the difference between getting high and getting fucked up. Understanding and remembering that particular distinction has kept me functioning and alive.

For me, The Bear was one of the most important influences on my life. He was a mentor and a brother, a man without peer and someone whom I grew to love deeply.

I owe The Bear a great deal.

CHAPTER 39

Loose in America

On the first Oregon gigs I was a member of the Pleasure Crew, and basically along for the ride. It was also where I met Ken Kesey for the first time, though he just looked at me strangely and said very little. He was checking me out from afar, but I had a couple of long chats with Ken Babbs, his main man, who seemed like a groovy guy.

My first working gig with the Grateful Dead was at the Family Dog on the Great Highway in San Francisco on February 4, 1970. There followed a succession of gigs where we worked as hard as was humanly possible in order to pay off their massive bills.

Once I'd joined the family, I decided that one of the first people I had to deal with in the Dead was Bob Weir.

Weir, their second guitar player, considered the whole business of being on the road an opportunity to try out every dumb practical joke he knew. He loved to wind me up and it annoyed me no end. Strictly speaking, he was one of my employers, but I wasn't prepared to be the focus of Weir's childish pranks for long. Things would have to change.

Weir, I quickly noticed, had problems in airports. In fact, Weir had problems in any kind of public space. I tried to think of a name for his condition and the best I could come up with was "anarchic agoraphobia." In other words, give the guy a wide open space, and you'd have complete chaos on your hands.

The later it was in the day, the more likely he was to indulge in all kinds of silly tricks. I only wished I could deliver him to every airport at 5:30 every morning.

My first task was to work on myself. Whatever Weir got up to, I decided I could not and would not overreact. Come what may, I would refuse to get angry — or even involved. I resolved to ignore the man, pretend he didn't exist. This way, I reasoned, I would not be encouraging him.

It was a great mistake, as my indifference to Weir made him even more determined to behave like a naughty child. At times I felt like I was stuck in a bizarre old Western, where I was the boss of a wagon train, and the families traveling west were headed up by people like Charlie Chaplin and Abbott and Costello and every other clown you can think of. As the Indians attacked us and we were about to be slaughtered, the settlers, who should have been circling the wagons and defending themselves, would be up to all kinds of comedy tricks and driving me frantic with worry about our imminent fate. Then, just when I thought disaster was sure to hit us all, the Indians would start laughing at the antics of the foolish men they were attacking — laughing so hard they would fall from their horses. Subsequently none of the Indians could aim straight, and we were saved. The film would end with the settler women showing the Indians how to put on makeup and do their hair and the Indians letting the comics play with their headdresses and everybody becoming good friends.

Traveling with the Grateful Dead, when I first joined them, felt just like that movie I had imagined. A disaster was always just about to happen, but somehow it never quite materialized, because, oddly enough, humor usually intervened.

To show up at an airline check-in desk with a bunch of stoned freaks could be an almost enlightening experience. People simply couldn't believe that people looked like us, let alone traveled on airplanes. I initially decided that my best move was to come on like a hard man, but it didn't always work, and the Dead would burst out laughing at me. The harder I tried to act, the more amusing the Americans seemed to find me.

I would be explaining to the startled woman behind the airline desk that the Grateful Dead was a rock band . . . no, they were not a convention of undertakers . . . I was the tour manager, which was why I had twenty-seven tickets . . . no, the people in the group were not with me as such because they were at the airport shops . . . and then all of a sudden, Weir would sidle up behind me, place his chin on my shoulder, and stare at the startled woman at the desk with his big brown bovine eyes.

The woman at the desk would shuffle nervously and ask Weir politely, "Can I help you, sir?" and Weir would say nothing and simply stare at her. She would get increasingly flustered, behaving as if she was confronted by a man with two heads. It made me feel like Long John Silver with his bloody parrot. I wondered if there was bird shit dripping down my back. With Weir, anything was possible.

"Can we call the rest of your party to check-in, sir?" she'd ask me. I'd say, "Certainly. Please page the Grateful Dead."

There would be a long pause, and the woman would say something like, "Oh, I'm sorry sir, I can't say that." That would be the signal for Weir to intervene.

With a lovely smile, Weir would berate her. "Why can't you say that? We're a band, that's our name, it's what we're called, the Grateful Dead. D-E-A-D."

The woman would reach beneath her desk and push a panic button, which summoned her supervisor. Things would get progressively more fraught, with me telling Weir to piss off while the supervisor and the check-in girl discussed the problem.

Meanwhile, behind us, a growing line of irate Americans would be mutinously mumbling. The supervisor would then demand that all of my party should be with me at the counter, and until that happened could I please stand aside and let the other people check in. I would have to round up all the people who were traveling with us before we could check in.

Weir operated best at those moments when his adversary was most vulnerable. On one of the earliest tours I did with the band I managed to get everybody on board the flight, and settled down for a sleep. I was shattered. I think we were flying home from New York to San Francisco, so the prospect of a lovely nap was very enticing. I got as comfortable as I could, bearing in mind it was an aircraft seat, and soon fell asleep.

A slight tickle at the end of my nose disturbed me and I scratched and went back to sleep. Soon the tickle reappeared and I brushed my nose. This happened several times before I finally dragged my poor old brain into some form of consciousness and opened my eyes to see Bob Weir leaning over the seat in front of me and wielding a long feather. Several people were watching and grinning, thinking it a great joke. I looked at Weir and told him in no uncertain terms that if he did it again the feather would end up where the sun didn't shine.

He did it again.

I snapped and whacked Weir on the end of his nose. This was greeted with howls of disapproval from all who were watching.

"Wow, man! Look, man, Bobby's nose is bleeding! Uncool, man!"

Garcia asked me incredulously, "Why did you do that?"

"Because it's not fair!" I spat out.

Five or six Americans looked amazed. I think it was Phil Lesh who said, "Fair? What the fuck is fair? What does that mean?"

Three or four experiences like this were enough for me. I sat down with the band and insisted that we thrash out an airports and airlines "policy." This is what we agreed.

When we got to an airport everyone had to follow me. Especially Weir, who had the disconcerting habit of walking across open spaces in airports and then suddenly stopping as everyone else continued on. Suddenly Weir would be lost and I would have to locate him. He seemed to be oblivious to the fact that all the people he was with were no longer around him. He probably didn't even realize he was in an airport; with Weir it was hard to tell. I would grab his arm and lead him back to the rest of the group like a stray.

I would check people in and give them their boarding passes. At that point, and not before then, everyone could go wherever they liked, and it was then their responsibility to get themselves to the gate for boarding.

It was further agreed that when I was checking the group in, everybody would pretend to act "normal" and stand in line and be quiet. This was so that we didn't scare the living daylights out of the airline's staff or our fellow passengers.

Even the Grateful Dead conceded that there were only a finite number of airlines flying domestically in the United States and if we were banned from one then it was highly likely we would be banned from them all.

I painted a picture for the band and crew of what could easily happen. We might be forced to drive from coast to coast instead of fly, and that would effectively be the end of the band, because no one would want to spend five days on a bus getting across America. With some reluctance, the Grateful Dead decided to fool everybody and pretend that they were "normal."

I had a special talk with Weir to make sure he understood.

"Bob, airports are not playgrounds," I told him.

He seemed a little surprised by this, but accepted what I had to say. I tried to get a little more serious. "The next time you creep up behind me at a check-in desk and interfere with what I'm doing, I'm going to slap you so fuckin' hard your teeth will rattle." I stared belligerently into his eyes. "I really mean it."

Weir, who is one of the world's most peaceable men, looked at me good-naturedly and I continued.

"Plus, when we're in the airport you have to stay with me, and I mean stay with me. I don't fuck around when you're on stage and doing your thing, so don't you fuck around when I'm doing mine. When I'm in an airport I'm on stage, so don't get in the way, Bob, and don't make my job harder than it is already or we're going to have to deal with some down-home serious shit. Okay?"

Weir looked thoughtful for a moment and we agreed to a truce.

To my surprise and gratitude, and to his credit, he never put me in the position where I had to slap him, and overnight he changed into a model rock'n'roller, at least when he was in airports and public spaces.

If the Grateful Dead were to earn enough money to clear their debts and survive, it wasn't all going to be fun. When we were traveling through America's public spaces we would have to behave almost exactly the same as everybody else. If we misbehaved and fucked around we would draw attention to ourselves, and this could be unhealthy, given that half the people in the group probably had illicit substances in their pockets. At the very least, it could mean we were banned from a flight. Stay cool, practice invisibility, and get on the plane without making a fuss — this was the new policy.

We also scrapped the previous rules that allowed the tour manager discretion as to how much money he gave to people when they were on tour. Everyone on tour was now to receive per diems. It was a novel concept for the band. To begin with, it was fixed at ten dollars per person per day and this is what everyone had to feed themselves with. In addition, it was agreed that I would arrange for people to be fed at the gigs, so that at least once a day people would get some real food.

Some of the Dead were good at arranging things to eat; others didn't have a clue. Pigpen would spend his per diems on booze, and would rarely eat anything but a hamburger. Garcia would smoke like a chimney and eat only when he remembered to, so I made a point of ensuring that he ate at the gigs. He always wanted to be at the gig as soon as the equipment was there, so this was easy to arrange.

As our tour arrangements evolved, things began to improve. During the first few gigs we began to professionalize our whole approach to touring. Everything, we collectively decided, was up for discussion; nothing was sacred, except the music. All of our efforts were made to support the music; nothing else mattered.

Weir became very much the sophisticated traveler, able to float effortlessly through airports; he became well versed in the art of near invisibility. He also became a dear friend to me (or, at least, he acted like a dear friend, so what's the difference?). At one stage I lived at his ranch on Lucas Valley Road in a teepee and had one of the best California summers of my life, thanks to his hospitality.

Bob Weir managed to work out musically where to sit between Phil Lesh on bass and Jerry Garcia on lead guitar, a feat that deserves accolades, but more than that, he was part of a musical trip that spoke to my head and my soul. The Grateful Dead's music took me to places I had never been, and for that I am forever beholden to him.

If he remembers me smacking him on the nose I'm sure that he's forgiven me by now; Weir was always the most generous of cats.

CHAPTER 40

Where's Jimi?

On May 16, 1970, the Grateful Dead played at Temple University in Philadelphia on a bill with Jimi Hendrix and Steve Miller. It was the last time I was to see Hendrix, who looked terrible, played in a desultory fashion, and seemed like he wasn't even on the same planet as us.

Jimi was to die several months later of a lethal combination of drugs and alcohol. He was in London; it was September 18. (The same deadly combination also claimed Janis's life less than a month later on October 4.)

The Temple University facility was a small sports stadium that seated around 20,000 people. A stage had been built at one end and an audience of about 7,000 people was gathered on the playing field in front of the stage. The promoters, who had rented the facility, had expected the show to sell out. They had lost lots of money and weren't happy. They were an unsavory lot, and wore the kind of clothing sported by John Jaymes and his gangsters on the Rolling Stones '69 tour. These guys were Philadelphia heavies. One of their main problems was that on top of all the other costs the artists somehow needed to be paid.

I went to say hello to Jimi and on the way to his dressing-room, which was a trailer parked some way from the stage, I was confronted by a crew guy from Steve Miller's band who I knew from San Francisco. He whispered to me that he'd heard there was not enough money for everyone to get paid, so they were going to pay only Hendrix, as he was top of the bill, and nobody else. I knew Jimi — I had often met him in London, even before I'd come to the States — so I thought I would go and talk to him about it before getting together with the other tour managers to sort things out together.

The door of Jimi's trailer was opened by a good-looking girl. I politely asked her to tell Jimi who I was, and that I was here to see him, to say hello and to talk about a problem that had come up.

Jimi was sitting on a chair, playing runs on his guitar and looking glassy-eyed. I smiled and introduced myself. "Hi Jimi, Sam Cutler, remember me from Tramps in London and with the Stones? Last time I saw you was at Madison Square Garden. I'm working with the Grateful Dead out of San Francisco now. It's good to see you."

Barely a flicker of recognition crossed Jimi's face, so I pressed on. "Man, there's a problem here at this gig."

"Problem?" he mumbled.

"Jimi, the promoters say they're not going to pay the artists. It's a big problem."

Jimi, a small and frail-looking man with huge, innocent eyes, looked at me. "Man, I do music, I don't do money." He returned to playing scales.

I tried another tack. "Wanna smoke a joint?"

Jimi nodded, and we sat in silence smoking some pleasant California grass. He finally opened up and recognized me. "Yeah, man," he said through clouds of smoke, "I remember you from London. You were a stage manager and had all that great Orange Sunshine." He leaned toward me. "What you got to get high on?"

I had a small eye drops bottle in my pocket containing the purest LSD known to man, and offered him a taste. I put a drop on the back of his hand, at the base of his thumb, and he contentedly licked it up. I had given him enough for just a little "tickle of light," nothing more.

I had a drop myself, grinned at Jimi, and decided to go back to talking about the problem. Jimi said nothing, though he at least stopped playing scales on his guitar.

"It can't be right that these people pay you and no one else, man. Surely you can see that?"

Jimi looked closely at me and sighed. "Man, my management don't let me have nothing to do with that shit, I don't know from nothin', baby. I handle the music, they handle the bread, you'll have to talk to them. Like I say, I play and I pray, that's me, man, a good Christian boy. The rest I leave to other people."

I looked into Jimi's eyes. "Do me a fucking favor, Jimi — don't play until I tell you we've been paid, okay?"

Jimi smiled and nodded, but I sensed there was not much chance that he would get involved. I smiled at him. "I'll be back in a bit, Jimi, it was nice to see you. Stay high, brother."

I never saw him again.

I stepped into the blinding sunlight of a very hot day and prepared to do battle.

Hendrix, being top of the bill, was going to be the last to play, so that gave me some leeway. Steve Miller Band was to open, with the Dead playing second. I went back and briefed the troops on what I was going to do.

"They're fucking around with the money. Remember what I always say: no pay, no play. I'm going to go and sort this out; there's no way you can play without hearing directly from me that it's cool. If someone comes and tells you, 'Sam says it's cool to play,' don't go for it. You have to hear this from my mouth with me standing in front of you!" Everyone nodded in agreement.

One thing you can say about the Grateful Dead at that stage of their collective lives — everybody knew how to be on the right bus and knew how to make sure it was going in the right direction. We were as one. I smiled happily at everybody, accepted a toke on a lovely joint, and told Sonny Heard, "Come with me, man, let's go sort this shit out." I wouldn't swear to it, but I'm pretty sure that as we made our way to the box office, Steve Miller Band was singing "Take the Money and Run," years before that song became a number one hit for them.

The box office was situated under the main stand and we approached the goon guarding the door. "Hello, mate. Please tell the promoters that the tour manager from the Grateful Dead is here." He opened the door and whispered to a man on the other side, and after a short interval we were admitted. In a long room seated around a massive table there were half a dozen burly men in shirtsleeves, all sweating profusely and counting piles of banknotes that were spread all over the table.

It was a scene I'd witnessed before: people compulsively counting money in the forlorn hope that somehow, through the very act of counting, the pile of cash would expand and magically grow larger. At a glance I reckoned there was fifty grand on the table and these guys needed at least double that — they were counting ferociously and looking very unhappy.

I made my play. "Who do I speak to about getting paid?" They looked at me as if I was nuts.

A smaller, bald man came forward and said, leading me by the arm to the back of the room, "Let's talk over here."

Heard followed close behind. The man whispered, "You see, we have a problem, we haven't got all the receipts back from the ticket outlets and we're waiting for those to come in. Until I get those I can't pay you."

I looked at him and put on my sweetest smile. "Mate, there's at least fifty grand on the table; fifteen of it's for my band. Gimme the money, we'll get our arses out there and play. The Steve Miller Band's playing right now; you must have paid them" — I didn't know this for sure, but it was a fair assumption — "and you're going to pay us."

The small man continued with his "let's be reasonable"

approach, wheedling on about ticket receipts and how he'd go back and check on the amount that had come in. Heard and I settled down to wait. The little bald man went and had an animated chat with one of the money-counters, who occasionally looked over his shoulder at the two hippies standing by the water cooler. I looked at Heard and decided I'd give it another five minutes. We chilled.

The small man returned and smiled hopefully and said, "I can give you five grand now. Tell your band to play and we'll have the balance by the time your set is finished."

This guy must think I'm a total fucking chump, I thought. I decided to whisper, whispering always being good for dramatic effect.

"Listen, buddy. I'm going back to my band and I'm going to tell them that you're fucking us around. Then I'm going to tell my equipment guys to pull our gear off the stage. Then I'm going to go on stage and tell the 10,000 kids out there who want to see the Grateful Dead that you guys haven't paid us. Then we're not going to play and Jimi Hendrix won't play either, and you'll have a huge fucking riot on your hands."

The little man looked crestfallen. I pressed on. "Not only that, you're still going to have to pay us 'cos we've got an A.F. of M. [American Federation of Musicians] contract for this gig. You know who the A.F. of M. are, don't you, brother? They're affiliated with the fucking Teamsters." (They have nothing to do with the Teamsters, but when I'm talking to promoters who don't want to pay my band, anything goes.)

The little man looked unhappy and knew a threat when he heard one, so I pressed home my advantage. "Listen, brother, nobody fucks with the Teamsters. Right? Let's be reasonable here. You got the money; all I need is fifteen grand, it's right there on the table. I'll tell you what I'll do." I smiled at him to put him at his ease. "We'll have the money and we'll play you a set that Philadelphia will be talking about for fucking years. I'll go and talk on the PA, man, and make sure the whole scene is cool. We know how to do these things. Steve Miller Band weren't even introduced, and that's very poor. Let us handle this, we'll be happy to do it, and you'll have a hell of a show on your hands."

He began, I thought, to look hopeful, so I pulled out my trump card. "I tell you what! I'll call the FM radio station that's co-sponsoring this gig and we'll put out stuff on the station inviting people to come down for reduced price tickets. You should let 'em in for half price, man; the show's been running for an hour. That way you'll get enough to pay the bands and cover your expenses. If we get enough people you could even make a profit."

He needed no more persuading. With images of paying off the gangsters dancing in his head, the little fella led us back to the counting table and said to the goons, "Count out their fifteen grand, it's going to be great, they're going on the radio."

They bowed their heads and got down to counting out our money. By this time the acid was coming on a bit strong. I began to think the water from the water cooler tasted stale in my mouth.

Making our excuses for a moment, we returned to the cooler and replaced the old bottle with a fresh one. Like a skilled and silent magician, Heard deftly squirted at least thirty or forty trips into the bottle before we put it back in place. We thoughtfully poured half a dozen paper cups of water for the nice gentlemen who were so kindly counting out the money for us, and approached the large table. Heard and I amiably checked the dough, found it to be correct, and with profuse smiles and grins all round we wandered back to the dressing-room. Mission accomplished!

Within the hour, the Grateful Dead played as the sun shone on a wonderful day, and the city of brotherly love blossomed contentedly. Several thousand extra people turned up and it entered local folklore as one of the highest gigs people had ever attended. The Dead played for over four hours and from that gig their popularity in Pennsylvania was assured. Everyone got paid, we got out in one piece, and we headed for the hotel, where I stood in a shower for what felt like hours trying to wash out my brain. At six in the morning we would be leaving on a flight for Connecticut, but I don't remember being able to sleep.

The money was in my saddlebags, though, and the band was happy. Tomorrow was another day.

CHAPTER 41

Don't touch anything

On March 20 and 21, 1970, the Grateful Dead played the Capitol Theatre in Port Chester, New York, our first gig for the promoter Howard Stein. It was a well-organized gig in a small theater with wonderful sightlines leading down a gently sloping auditorium to a proscenium stage. Just the kind of place the Grateful Dead loved to play.

The ritual of getting high before going on stage had always been a part of the Grateful Dead's thing, but in the early days it had been accompanied by a barrel of acid-laced Kool-Aid put in the audience so people could help themselves. Those days were gone, so that "taking the sacrament" was now a more private affair. Gathered together in the dressing-room, we would partake of the magic elixir. It was a part of being a member of the Grateful Dead's family and I held it to be absolutely sacred, as did most of my brothers. All of the equipment guys got high, as did the Pleasure Crew, and we would all usually be with the musicians in the half-hour before the band went on stage.

I remember the second night at the Port Chester theater very well. On the opening night I had been too preoccupied with arrangements and details to get high with everyone else in the family, but I knew the second night was coming, and that would be my chance to join the merry throng in la-la land. The evening began with the band playing an acoustic set, which was very well received by the audience and a lot of fun. As the stage was prepared for the electric set that was to follow, I made my way backstage and waited for an opportune moment to talk with Ramrod. He and I had an arrangement whereby I would stash my briefcase with the money in a flight case on the stage, the safest place in the building. Then I could wander off and get high and didn't have to worry about getting mugged or losing the money.

While the band was playing, it was my habit to wander through the auditorium checking on what was going on. It was a routine I had at every gig.

I would start out the front of the venue. Were there people hanging around outside, hassling and still trying to get in? Was everything cool or were there fights going on and people trying to smash their way into the building? Was security on duty outside liaising with local police, or were the cops harassing our patrons?

We had a "duty of care" to our people and a tour manager cannot know what is happening outside a building unless he physically gets off his butt and goes and looks. Same goes for the inside of a building: if he really wants to know what's going on, the tour manager has to visit the whole environment of the gig, not just hang out in the promoter's office or backstage.

There are many questions a tour manager has to ask. For example, are the front doors to the building locked? There have been numerous instances in which a venue has been filled to capacity and in order to secure the premises the promoters have chained shut the doors. Many people have died as a result of this stupidity, for in the event of a fire patrons cannot escape the building. When you lock doors so that people cannot get in, you create the unintended side effect of ensuring that people cannot get out.

Are the prices for food and drink reasonable, or are people being ripped off? We were not in the business of attracting people to a place so that they might be crudely exploited, so this was a legitimate concern. These and a million other small but vital issues I addressed and assessed as I walked around taking care of business.

In the back of the auditorium, I noticed a police officer. He seemed out of place in the midst of the partying and I wandered over to say hello. I asked him if anything was wrong and he said no, so I asked what he was doing there and he said he was from the police department and "just checking things out." There was a noticeable smell of marijuana burning and I wondered if it had registered with him.

"I'm from the band," I told him, and he looked unimpressed. "We don't usually have uniformed police officers in the auditorium at our gigs and I wondered if there was any way I could be of assistance?"

He looked at me strangely and said in a belligerent tone, "When we need your help we'll ask for it."

This did not sound too healthy, so I made my way backstage to ensure that security was in place and that there was no way a uniformed officer was going to be able to enter the backstage area unannounced. Who knows what he might have found going on back there! I decided that I would keep an eye on our floating policeman, who didn't seem to have any legitimate reason for being in the auditorium. Why, I asked myself, isn't he out there catching criminals? Why has he been assigned to the inside of the building?

High on LSD, I wandered around the outside of the building. Our equipment truck was parked in the alley by the stage door. Was it secure? Was anyone hanging around checking out the truck to see if it was worth breaking into?

Security within a building is only of value if it is closely coordinated with security around the outside perimeter of a building. The one without the other is virtually useless.

I'd always check in with the police on the streets. They were generally very civil, as my appearance must have startled them. A long-haired hippie in a good suit with an expensive briefcase is not an everyday occurrence for most police officers. I never ever had a problem with the police as people and always looked beyond the uniform. I thought that the law's attitude to drugs was simply wrong, but the police had a job to do just like me. A different job, but a job nonetheless. My job involved me having fun, whereas one would be hard put to describe the policeman's lot as a happy one.

I'd walk up to the police on the street outside the theater smiling, and introduce myself as the tour manager from the band and ask them if everything was cool. Asking the cops on the street how things were going hours into a Grateful Dead show allowed me to judge their mood. Were our people likely to be hassled on the way home because the cops were uptight and fed up, or were the cops pretty much cool with everything and laid-back? These were important judgments to make.

If it looked like people were going to be harassed by the cops on their way home, we could make elliptical announcements from the stage, telling people to be cool on the way out as "the man was about" and feeling frisky. Mind you, most people who came to a Dead concert didn't have much to be concerned about on the way home. They might well have arrived with drugs, but they certainly didn't leave with them. They were all consumed on the premises, so the chances of being busted going home were remote.

People have always been intrigued about my being a tour manager and taking acid, as if the two were not compatible. To which I reply, well, it depends upon the tour manager and it depends upon the acid. I only ever took the family's acid, which came from a highly reputable source — its absolute purity was a given. Plus, I always took a relatively small amount. It is not advisable to act as a tour manager and at the same time conduct intimate conversations with God, so a small amount was the go — say, somewhere between forty and sixty micrograms. For conversations with the Almighty one would have to take closer to 250 micrograms.

Among people in the Grateful Dead there was a general feeling that while it was cool to get high, there was still stuff to take care of, business to attend to, so getting too out of it was considered to be somewhat irresponsible. Drugs of any kind were never to interfere with taking care of business and what had to be done.

On the second night of the Port Chester gig, high as a kite and feeling good, with the briefcase stashed and everything in order, I wandered back into the auditorium. The place was cooking, literally — it felt as hot as a baker's oven. The same policeman in full uniform I had seen earlier now stood at the side of the room with his back to a wall. Immediately in front of him, a couple of thousand delirious hippies were having the time of their lives. I wandered across to say hello.

I introduced myself, showing him my security pass, and asked how he was doing. He remembered me from before, but seemed a little friendlier this time. "Man, I been here for over two hours and I'm sweatin' and I ain't had nothin' to drink and I need a break," he told me.

I smiled at him. "You fancy a beer? I'll get you a beer if you want one."

He looked horrified. "Man, it's more than my life's worth to drink a beer. I'm on duty."

I sighed sympathetically and apologized, saying, "Of course you are, sorry about that. Anyway, what d'you think of the show?"

He smiled. "That's one hell of a band you got there; the acoustic set was great." I thought to myself, well, at least he likes the music. He motioned with his arm to the kids boogying like mad in the auditorium. "Nice buncha kids, no problems here, these kids are having fun."

I looked at him and smiled. "Tell you what, buddy, I know you're on duty, but you surely could drink a Coca-Cola, couldn't you?"

He sighed. "You know what, I'd love one, but before we

came on duty we had a briefing from the captain and he told us all not to touch anything, 'cos it was likely to be contaminated with that LSD."

I was as high as the Empire State Building, and I smiled at him again. "Seems a pity a man can't have a drink on such a hot night."

He nodded and looked glum. I pretended to have a flash of inspiration.

"Tell you what. I could get you a Coca-Cola unopened. That way you'd be safe. There's no way anyone can mess with a Coca-Cola in an unopened can. You can open it yourself."

"You know what," he said, "I reckon that would be okay."

I fetched a cold drink from the garbage can that stood on the stage and wiped away the excess water. Between the tab and the lip of the can a small drop of magic was applied, and I wandered back into the auditorium to find my thirsty policeman. I handed him the unopened can and he pulled the tab and drank with a gasp of satisfaction.

I gave him a wink and told him, "You want another one, you just let me know." I leaned against the wall with my new best buddy and looked at the audience, checking out the view.

A short time passed and the policeman took off his hat. Then he loosened his tie. It was, after all, really hot in the building.

"Would you like another Coke?" I asked and he nodded appreciatively. I wandered backstage and grabbed a couple, though it was no longer necessary for the magic ingredient to be applied. He smiled as I handed him the Cokes and nodded toward the audience.

Less than five feet away, a lovely girl danced. She moved like a flower that stands in a soft breeze, her arms like petals wandering above her head, and her whole being shining with a serene light. She danced for herself; she danced for creation; she danced with the music; and she danced quite naturally and effortlessly for the policeman, who thought of himself for once as the luckiest man in the world.

I returned backstage to stand behind the amplifiers, to lose myself in the music of the gods and to relax. Over the stage apron I could see the policeman: he was smiling. In front of him, several beautiful girls were dancing as if for his pleasure. He was like a Pasha with his harem. He was no longer the outsider but was now the same as all of us in the auditorium, at one with the people and the music.

Garcia noticed the cop and smiled knowingly at me. I grinned to myself as a voice in my head softly whispered the words: "Game, set, and match."

CHAPTER 42

All aboard that train

By the middle of 1970, things on the Dead financial front were looking brighter. I would arrive home with the funds from one tour and drag myself into the office to organize the next one. There was a constant and unending demand for funds from the organization, which seemed to be growing exponentially, and the only way to satisfy this demand was by doing gigs. Thankfully we all loved the gigs and I loved being the tour manager, but after six months everyone was tired and badly in need of either a rest or a party.

A Canadian Deadhead named Thor Eaton came to our rescue. He was the heir to the vast Eaton fortune. He liked rock-'n'roll, and specifically the Grateful Dead, and wanted to bring a group of the best musicians he could find to Canada. He would take them coast to coast on a train while they did a series of concerts in football stadiums. To the Dead, who'd just spent months working their butts off at relatively conventional gigs, the idea of the Canadian tour sounded fabulous. We couldn't wait to get on board.

We duly arrived in Toronto to have a look at the train and were delighted to find a huge, full-size locomotive, with dining, sleeping, and bar cars and all of the accoutrements of a genuine

Canadian Pacific beauty. I marveled at its size — it seemed to go on forever.

People swarmed aboard and claimed bunks and got organized with smiles and grins all round. It was a great start to the gig, and we were joined by bluesman Buddy Guy, Ian and Sylvia Tyson, The Band, Janis Joplin, the New Riders of the Purple Sage, Elephant's Memory, Sha Na Na, Delaney & Bonnie, and the Flying Burrito Brothers.

The sight of all those musicians running excitedly up and down the train corridors is not one I'll ever forget. It was like a crazy school outing; people couldn't believe their luck. Everyone was convinced this was going to be one hell of a party.

The first gig would take place in Toronto, before we set off. I met Ken Wallace, the promoter, at the stadium, and things unfortunately were not looking good. Insufficient tickets had been sold to cover expenses (or so I guessed) and there were a substantial number of people outside the main gates ready to fight the police to get in. Some of the kids were adamant that the $14 ticket prices were too high and certain sections of the press were claiming that the promoters were greedy. Once again the word "free" was being bandied about, with people claiming the music should be free. Even more radically, some were claiming that dope and food should also be free! The protesters were actually demanding that the promoters hand over 60 per cent of their ticket revenues for the protesters to distribute as they saw fit.

Things were going to get ugly within an hour, I estimated, as the sun beat down and tempers frayed.

I talked to Thor Eaton and Ken Wallace and they seemed to think that the Grateful Dead could mollify the protesters, as the Dead were the "underground" band on the bill and most of the people fighting the cops were long-haired activists.

Wallace wanted Garcia to talk to the people at the festival, to promise that we would do something, but I had my doubts. Garcia had no real announcement to make, other than that we would look into things and report back to the audience, which seemed a bit lame.

Garcia agreed to speak and made a brave attempt to justify the ticket prices, but didn't really sound convincing, and a question and answer session with hecklers ensued. A protester was given the microphone in a conciliatory gesture and immediately lambasted the cops as "pigs" who were doing the promoters' dirty work for them. I was forced to grab the mic and make the limp promise that we (the musicians, not the promoters) would come up with something.

Only moments before, I had seen a policeman receive a serious skull injury and protesters being hurt as several hundred people fought to get in. The skirmishes at the front gate looked as though they were going to develop into full-on pitched battles. It almost felt as if the police were fighting on the musicians' behalf — which made us feel very uncomfortable.

Garcia and I talked about the alternatives and I told him there was no way that the promoters should open the gates. They were already going to lose a lot of money, and I didn't feel it was fair of the protesters to demand that they lose even more. What we should do, I thought, was play outside the facility, removing ourselves from the environment where all the confrontational bullshit had been happening. We should, I argued, take the music away from the police on horseback, who were spoiling for a fight with the hippies, and put it in a neutral setting.

Fortunately, a small city park was close by and I literally ran from the stadium to have a look. Coronation Park was typical of the municipal parks in cities throughout the former British Empire: neat and tidy, all mown grass and flowerbeds, and perfect for a small concert. I reported back to the Dead that with two flatbed trucks and a small amount of sound gear, the Dead could play there and save the day.

Back at the stadium the festival was grinding along. Those inside the facility were having a good time and those on the outside were involved in running skirmishes with the police. Every so often, a protester would manage to break through the police lines and fling himself over the barricades and into the stadium, to the delighted cheers of his compatriots.

There was an urgent need to defuse the situation before more people were seriously hurt. Several protesters and two policemen had already been taken to the hospital, and there was a very real prospect of someone being killed. The Grateful Dead agreed with me that after they had played in the stadium they would then go to the park and play there, for free.

It was a noble and magnanimous gesture on the Dead's part, for the band deeply resented the violence that was happening, but they had little choice. No free music would inevitably increase the aggression of the protestors.

We would play once for money and once for free — and both times for peace and love and fun and humanity and decency, not for violence. At this first concert of the Canadian tour I was proud to be a member of the Grateful Dead. Somehow or other we managed to keep everybody happy and with music we soothed the savage breast.

I went on the microphone and talked to the crowds inside and outside the stadium. For a moment there was a lull in the fighting. I announced that the musicians abhorred violence and that no music was worth hurting one another for. We supported the promoters' rights to put on a show and charge money to come to the show. People had a simple choice. They could pay to come in, or they could stay away. We would play in the stadium, and sometime later we would play in Coronation Park. We would not play in Coronation Park if the protests continued, and we looked forward to a sweet event, both here and there. The announcement was greeted by desultory cheers, but eventually people started wandering over to the park where we had announced we'd play.

I liaised with the equipment crew about how we were going to play two gigs on the same day. The Dead had gone on first in the stadium, and on the periphery of the stage stood some of the finest musicians of their generation, listening to Jerry and the boys, who were very conscious of the impact they were having. Slowly the smiles returned and while we all got high, the Dead played superbly.

At long last a decent vibe descended, and the Grateful Dead set the tone for the whole adventure: it was to be fun, a celebration of life through music. By lugging the band's gear on and off two different stages we managed to play two gigs in one day, while keeping both sides of the equation happy.

All in a day's work!

The idea that charging for music was somehow a rip-off never ceased to amaze me. What happened to the principle of a fair day's pay for a fair day's work, central to the working-class culture of the western world? Weren't musicians entitled to earn a living from their craft? Or was it the commercialization of music that bothered people, the emergence of financial considerations controlling this creative thing that was now being turned into an industry?

Whatever it was, in my estimation music wasn't worth fighting and dying for.

The demand from a small minority that music should be "free" haunted the tour. This absurd demand was to follow the train as it made its way across Canada, spoiling ticket sales in the other cities we were due to visit. Consequently, the tour had to be shortened and never made it through to Vancouver, ending prematurely at Calgary. The demands of the East Coast radicals, in effect, denied their West Coast cousins the chance to see the finest bill of music that had ever been put together in Canada.

Thor Eaton, who underwrote the whole thing, approached the tour's eventual losses with spontaneous generosity and declared that "the show must go on," so we all boarded the train that evening ready to set off for Winnipeg. We had weathered the inauspicious beginnings to the tour and now, thanks to Thor's generosity, it was time to party.

CHAPTER 43

Memories are made of this

What felt like the longest train in the world was parked in Toronto and a collection of crazy musicians was on board and ready to roll. By the time I got to the train it was evening, but some people had been there most of the afternoon. As I walked through the train I came to the bar car and there were two of the prettiest ladies, Bonnie Bramlett and Sylvia Tyson, with their arms around one another's shoulders, singing away. I was enchanted. Delaney Bramlett sat on a sofa nearby, playing his guitar and singing along with that voice of his — a voice to die for. No wonder Eric Clapton wanted to run away from Blind Faith and play with Bonnie & Delaney! Delaney had more soul in his little finger than most musicians on the planet. It was just so great seeing him and his lady; they sweetened the musical vibe from word go. Delaney Bramlett was sitting there singing "Going Down the Road Feeling Bad" before the train had even left the station — I was blown away.

It was amazing to think that we had boarded a train that was not going to stop for over forty-eight hours. We had a lot of fun deciding what was necessary for the journey.

Contrary to some reports, the Grateful Dead family, at least, were prepared for any eventuality. We realized that scoring something to smoke in the middle of Canada was highly unlikely and we had made arrangements accordingly. Rumor had it that a sizeable quantity of local grass had somehow magically appeared in Toronto. Some said it was a peace offering from the Toronto dealers, who felt bad about the violence in what is normally a laid-back and mellow city.

People boarded the train with what looked like enough supplies for a week — bags of oranges, a kilo of Brazilian nuts, endless varieties of vegetarian food, and even a propane gas cooker. I asked the man with the cooker why he brought such a thing. "What if the train breaks down?" he asked. "What we gonna do then, in the middle of nowhere?" I admired his foresight.

The musicians had brought along wine and spirits sufficient to tide them over. Equipment guys tended to favor cases of beer. There were several large bottles of water and enough biscuits for a thousand people. One lady boarded the train with three heads of lettuce. I got on board with nothing to eat, plenty of money, and enough cigarettes to last for a year. If the train had broken down in the middle of the woods I reckon I would have lasted forty-eight hours at most, but with the welcome consolation of being able to smoke myself to death.

Finally, the train departed, and as our new home chugged away the realization hit everybody that we were together for the next couple of days. Within half an hour of leaving Toronto, while we were still going slowly through the suburbs, guitars were pulled from cases and instruments were tuned. Drummers were getting their kits out, a pedal steel was set up, glasses of whiskey were being poured, the first joints appeared, and things began to roll. On either side of the bar car were cars with seating, and these three cars were central to the train. Very few people were thinking about sleeping.

I met The Band's Rick Danko in the dining car, where he was talking to a cat from Buddy Guy's band. I introduced myself and got some beers. I asked the guys if they'd like to smoke a joint and they looked about, nervous. I laughed and told Rick that from here to Winnipeg we could do what the hell we liked, and everybody relaxed. Rick was an adventurous cat. The Band had been given the opportunity to come on the train, but the only one who had wanted to ride along with everyone else was Rick, who loved to party. He was going to play with Buddy Guy, he told me.

Rick was one of the truly great players, a man with a voice that sang the truth, a bass player of prodigious technique, and now he was going to jam with the hottest bluesman around.

This tour had Buddy Guy, Jerry Garcia, and Robbie Robertson on the lineup, three of the greatest guitar players of the '70s. Robbie wasn't on the train, though. He thought himself far too gifted to slob around with a bunch of other musicians on a train and was far too world-weary and sophisticated to know what he missed.

The train was crawling with talent, truly fabulous musicians, and there was booze and dope. As my Deadhead friend Craze used to say, where there's booze and dope, there's hope. Add a sprinkle of the world's finest musicians and some would say you've got an earthly version of paradise.

Rick Danko and I sat in the dining car having long raps about music and laughing about the sordid music business. Various members of the Dead family would come through and introduce themselves to Rick. The Dead knew of The Band and their music, of course, and held them in the highest regard. It was here on the train that I first talked to Rick Danko about Albert Grossman, the manager of Dylan, The Band, and Janis Joplin. From our initial meeting over a sandwich all kinds of collaborations between The Band and the Dead would develop, eventually culminating in the two bands playing with the Allman Brothers at Watkins Glen for 700,000 people.

Three carriages were packed with musicians and instruments and slowly the train had begun to establish a rhythm and a speed to which people became naturally attuned, as if they were playing together in time to a beat.

It was dark outside. Canada and the world and its worries were slipping effortlessly by, and no one needed to have a care for days. I have never seen people look so relaxed and happy.

In the railroad car where I was sitting, the most beautiful thing was happening. Buddy Guy was playing and singing the blues with a whole slew of musicians from different bands. The sax player from Buddy's band was just playing his heart out and having such a good time. Next car along Bonnie and Delaney Bramlett were picking with people from the New Riders of the Purple Sage, and one wagon further along, there were Garcia and Weir, playing with Janis Joplin.

I went back to my bunk in the sleeping car for a nap, as I knew this was going to be a long night (or two). On the way to my bed, at the end of the dining car, I came across the "promoters' table," as it came to be called. Sitting there were the two promoters, Ken and Thor, and the head of security seconded from the Toronto police department. He was as nice a fella as one could wish to meet. I stopped off for a chat. I soon concluded from the promoters' long faces that the tour was losing a fortune, but there was little I could do to rectify that on a train whizzing through the Canadian night.

We talked about extra radio advertisements and the like, and they told me of the problems with the "free music" brigade, and how the Toronto violence had been widely reported in the national media with lots of graphic photos. The negative publicity was hitting ticket sales. I felt glad I wasn't a promoter, something I've never wanted to be.

Thor Eaton was cool about the whole finances thing. He said he was prepared to cover the costs up to Calgary, and that things would be reassessed after that. He wanted everyone to have fun.

I made a point of telling him, "You have fun and you should come to the other cars and dig the music," but he seemed content where he was, counting his losses. I made my excuses and headed to my bed to lie down for a minute and get my bearings.

The acid I had taken that afternoon had come back to visit me a second time, and for a moment I felt fragile.

A window stretched the length of my small bunk. I rolled open the blind and lay looking out as the train ran deep through forests, trees rushing by like an endless black wall tipped with shadowy spikes stabbing into the stars and the sky. The train's rhythm was insistent, purposeful. This was a train powerful enough to drive to the ends of the earth and back again. It had the precise, confident, mechanical rhythm of an expensive watch. I fell into a light sleep.

I awoke with a start to see an identical panorama of trees standing motionless at attention as the train sped past through the night. The stars shone, a pleasant crescent moon hung in the sky, and I was ready to check things out. It was three in the morning.

The first music car I got to was cooking. Rick Danko was singing with Janis, Jerry and Weir, and Marmaduke from the New Riders of the Purple Sage. Other musicians were playing all kinds of percussion and Buddy Cage, also from the New Riders, was sitting at a pedal steel joining in the fun. The music was loud and people were slightly drunk, but it sure had soul. I think they sang the song "Long Black Veil" at least a dozen times between Toronto and Winnipeg and to me it felt so good that half the wolves in Canada must have howled along to its mournful chorus.

Janis was in her element, surrounded by boys. She had no competition in sight, as Bonnie Bramlett was at the center of things in another car with Delaney, while Sylvia Tyson floated between all three cars and joined in when the feeling took her.

This left Janis firmly wedged between Garcia and Rick Danko while they sang the most heartrending blues songs and generally had fun. It was the only time I ever saw Garcia drunk. He handled it impeccably, though I noticed that between Toronto and Winnipeg he told Janis he loved her many times, and may have arranged to marry her two or three times as well.

Janis was, of course, practiced in the art of drinking, unlike several of the musicians who surrounded her, so she had the slightly naughty pleasure of getting them all well and truly smashed. Garcia was what we used to call "legless." Bless 'im.

With Janis the only woman in town one would have thought the competition for the lady's favors would have been fast and furious, but people were more interested in the music than seduction. The chance to jam with so many musicians was so attractive that Venus herself would have been hard put to drag people away from the fun. As the hours and the kilometers passed and the alcohol flowed, people realized that they could go to sleep, get up, and the party would no doubt be kicking on — and that there was still a day and a half to go before we got to Winnipeg.

As we looked out the windows, dawn broke, with the train carving its way methodically through the Canadian wilderness. With several drinks in my belly I made my way back to my bunk to catch up on some sleep and recharge my batteries. It was a long way to Winnipeg and I would need all of my stamina and strength when we got there.

By the time I awoke, half the train was looking for cigarettes and the party hadn't stopped for a moment.

CHAPTER 44

Running like clockwork

Breakfast was interesting. I sat with a large, bearded man from Buddy Guy's band, who I subsequently discovered was his rhythm guitar player, and we discussed the whole festival trip. The musicians from Buddy Guy's band were the only African-Americans on the train and had been amazed and delighted by the genuine warmth they had experienced. They hadn't yet managed to break out of the black music scene, but in Buddy Guy they had a guitarist of genius and this was their first in-depth exposure to the white rock'n'roll scene.

They were having a great time and had stayed up until six in the morning playing with Pigpen from the Grateful Dead and all kinds of other musicians, drinking booze and jamming the blues. It was the first time they had experienced such a loose scene amongst white guys. Buddy Guy and his band got higher than they'd ever been and it showed in their faces; they grinned and laughed their way happily across Canada and had a ball.

It was incredible how quickly the word spread that I was the man to see about cigarettes. I should have set up a black market operation and cleaned up, but I didn't have the heart, so instead I donated a carton to each of the music cars and the cigarettes sat there in the middle of the crowd and people smoked when they wanted.

Within forty-eight hours of leaving Toronto I was down to my last few packets from a stash of five cartons, and by the time we pulled into Winnipeg half the guys on the train were frantic to find a tobacconist. What a disgusting habit we all had. The Bear used to ask me, "How come you smoke something that kills you and doesn't get you high?" I often ask people this question myself now, but I have yet to receive a satisfactory explanation and unfortunately I am still a smoker.

Toward the rear of the train there was an observation car, and attached to the final carriage was a caboose. I went right to the end of the train and sat looking out across Canada and the hundreds of miles we had already traveled. The track ran straight for as far as I could see, a hypnotic ribbon that disappeared into infinity beyond the horizon. Sitting in that solitary place less than a meter above the rails gave me the opportunity to think and to reassess my life in music.

Just before boarding the train I had heard that process servers were seeking to serve a writ on Mick Jagger and the Stones on behalf of the owners of Altamont and the surrounding ranchers. My name was high on the list of people upon whom summonses were to be served. I had been told that we were to be sued for over $20 million. People had been to the Grateful Dead's offices looking for me, and apparently John Jaymes had left a message for me to call him in New York.

Altamont wasn't over yet, clearly. Mel Belli and his office were out of bounds to me; the lawyers were in dispute with the Stones over fees, while the Stones themselves refused to accept my calls. It had been over six months since the disaster, but there were still plenty of issues to be sorted. I had to make all kinds of decisions, and not just about Altamont.

The Grateful Dead had welcomed me into their family, and a commitment to the family could be lifelong. Was I going to live and work with the Grateful Dead for the rest of my life? Should I stay in America and live happily ever after?

I had grown to love the Dead, the music, and the people, and the thought of returning to Europe left me cold. To meet the Grateful Dead had been a dream and there was no reason why my relationship with the band should not go on for as long as we both wanted — if they felt the same way.

I realized that the only one I would get much sense from was Pigpen. Everyone else on the train was smashed on alcohol, but for Pigpen booze was no big deal, and because he didn't take acid he didn't have strange mystical ideas about the future. In fact Pigpen didn't have strange mystical ideas about anything, and was as far removed from what he called "hippie shit" as one could imagine.

Pigpen agreed to have a chat at the end of the train, and immediately liked the view back down the track from the platform at the rear of the caboose. As soon as he saw the spot where I went for a bit of solitude he sat down and pulled out his harmonica and played a great train blues in time with the clack of the wheels and the humming of the track.

I asked him what he thought I should do with the band, and what he saw as the band's priorities for the future. If I had talked like this with anyone else in the band, they would have laughed at me and said that the future was merely a matter of "riding the tiger" and hanging on long enough to see which way the critter went. I wanted some more down-home advice than that, and in the Grateful Dead there was no one more down home than Pigpen.

My relationship with Pigpen had begun when I was sorting out the room lists for going on the road with the Grateful Dead. As a matter of economy people had agreed to share rooms while on the road, but Pigpen was somehow not included in the deal. No one wanted to share with Pigpen, and vice versa. This was a somewhat delicate issue. He came to see me a couple of days after I had first started hanging out at the Dead's offices and we sat on the porch, just as we were now sitting on the train's caboose, and we talked things over. Pigpen revealed why he didn't want to share rooms and he made me promise to keep what he said to myself.

Pigpen was very afraid of acid, and convinced that if he shared a room, sooner or later he would get dosed. I can happily confirm that both the Stones and the Dead enjoyed their sybaritic pleasures enormously, but Pigpen from the Dead and Bill Wyman from the Stones were the exceptions to the rule. They were not into drugs, which in my estimation made them somewhat less interesting than their fellows. (Though there is absolutely no truth to the rumor that his fellow musicians called Bill Wyman "boring Bill.")

Pigpen had been high before on acid but hated the experience and there was no way he wanted to risk it by sharing a room. He liked booze, that was his trip, and as everyone knows LSD is anathema to an alcoholic. Pigpen's paranoia about acid extended to his time on stage, where he would only accept things from the equipment guy Steve Parrish, as he and Parrish disapproved of people being dosed on LSD. So when Pigpen got a drink on stage from Parrish, he felt that it was safe from unwanted contamination — and it always was.

Pigpen roomed alone when we were on tour, and so did I. I'd volunteered to share a room with someone just like everyone else, but after a couple of weeks none of them wanted to room with me anymore. What people in the Grateful Dead had forgotten was that a tour manager's job is twenty-four hours a day. Musicians work hard on stage and then their work stops and they can "play." It's the same for equipment guys; however hard they work, eventually it stops and they can get some rest. A tour manager never stops, even when he's lucky enough to get some sleep.

If someone wants to call him at four in the morning, and people often do, then he has to be available. It could be a crisis — someone being arrested, someone being harassed, someone in need of money. A tour manager cannot be unavailable. The phone never stops ringing. The Dead's Rex Jackson once told me I was the only person he knew who would answer the telephone at any time and immediately be 100 per cent lucid regardless of what was happening. Several lady friends over the years have become most upset when in the midst of canoodling I insisted on answering the telephone; those old tour manager habits die hard.

Pigpen didn't look well to me. In fact, he hadn't looked well ever since I first went to work for the band. He had that pale-skinned look of a serious drinker, and he stank of alcohol. People who really drink have the stuff coming out of their pores, so if you get close to them they reek of whiskey or brandy or whatever their choice of booze. Pigpen drank Southern Comfort. Speeding through Canada I asked him how he felt and he told me that the constant vibrations of the train made his stomach hurt, and he placed his hand over his liver. Pigpen died in 1973, but he knew he wasn't well long before, and seemed resigned to whatever would happen. There was no way on earth that he was going to give up drinking, and I had no problem in getting him a bottle if supplies were low. I bought him four for the train ride, and that kept Pigpen and me pretty tight.

I asked him where he thought the Grateful Dead's trip should direct itself and he said something that was to have a big effect on me, and on my understanding of the band. He told me that ever since the band had begun he basically had no money. He still had no money — just about enough to live on, to buy a bottle of booze, but no real money. Now he didn't mind, he told me, set-tling all those debts and paying everybody, but he was tired of being so broke, and he'd like to see a bit more of his money.

Pigpen, in his rundown state, reckoned we needed to make more money and work less. We were working too hard; it was getting to be too much for him. Pigpen was a straightforward man and things to him were basically uncomplicated. In July 1970 he was on $200 a week, plus ten dollars a day per diem when he was on tour. He received the same as everybody else in the family. It was not enough.

Pigpen's experiences with his band struck me as a little like what Brian Jones had gone through. Pigpen was the founder of the Grateful Dead — they were in many ways his band, in much the same way as Brian Jones had founded the Stones. And just as the Stones had fired Brian from the very band he'd started, Pigpen recounted bitterly to me that Phil and Jerry had considered sacking him and Weir from the band. They had talked it over with Scully but had never broached the subject directly because of a failure of nerve on Garcia's part.

This had hurt Pigpen deeply. The band had started out as a blues band, a "jug" band, and he was a blues man. When the Grateful Dead wandered off down the byways of psychedelic musical doodling it left him feeling ambivalent at best. As he put it, he couldn't "play that shit," so when the band went musically intergalactic, he remained very much earthbound and would shake a rattle or walk off to the side of the stage and wait for his turn to play something.

Deep fissures had appeared in the fabric of the Rolling Stones when the band decided to move away from their original rhythm and blues material and write their own songs. Brian Jones, the founder and leader of the band, who'd been a brilliant musician capable of playing virtually any instrument, didn't know how to write songs. As a result his leadership position was eroded and other people in the band came to prominence. The Grateful Dead had started out with jug band music and rhythm and blues, and had originally played plenty of covers. When the need had arisen to write their own material, Pigpen, like Brian Jones, began to feel isolated.

Pigpen couldn't write songs. Neither could anyone else in the band when they had begun the trip, but slowly Hunter and Garcia had emerged as the songwriters. As others had stepped up to carry the creative load, Pigpen's musical contribution had diminished. During a Dead set he might only appear at the front of the group once or twice in a whole evening. I think this hurt Pigpen. He never complained, but one of the ways his pain manifested itself was that he would be less involved in what was happening on stage. In his unhappiness he'd also hit the bottle.

We sat at the back of the train, watching the silent army of trees disappear behind us. I told Pigpen I had a surprise for him, and handed him a bottle of his favorite booze. He grinned and thanked me and even offered to pay for it, but I'd managed to get the cost covered by the promoter in Toronto. A bar was fine for other people. Pigpen needed the "security" of his own booze.

We sat and stared at the disappearing tracks and I had a slug of his Southern Comfort. I thought it pretty disgusting, but shared it with him anyway. We talked about our lightning visit to the U.K. to play a festival in the north of England, and we laughed when we remembered a rather cruel joke I had played on the band.

We had flown into London and were then to travel to the north of England by bus, and as we waited for the bus I regaled the band with tales of the English music business. I told them that we were to drive up the first motorway in England (the M1) and that on the way we would stop at a famous old coaching inn called the Blue Boar.

There, I said, I had met all kinds of musicians as they traveled the length and breadth of England. It was famous. People would meet there and exchange information on promoters and gigs and it was known as a hangout to all the bands. The Grateful Dead couldn't wait to experience what all those famous bands had experienced, so we set off northwards in the bus in great spirits. I am sure the Grateful Dead had pictures on their collective mind of the Blue Boar being a seventeenth-century coaching inn, where they could take photos and marvel at the general antiquity of everything.

In due course our bus pulled off the motorway and the band trooped into the Blue Boar. It was exactly like places in America. All strip lighting, sterile and soulless, with food wrapped in plastic that looked singularly unappetizing. People complained bitterly. It took me hours to explain that this was indeed the famous Blue Boar and that it was where the bands all stopped because quite simply there was nowhere else. My little joke was not appreciated by anyone — except Pigpen. When I asked him what he had expected he said, "Just the same ol' shit." He was a wise old bugger.

Pigpen and I talked money. He felt that the band should be getting a larger slice of the pie. He was shocked when he found out that I was getting the same as the equipment guys and himself. I asked him if he'd been at the meeting where the decision had been made that we should all be paid equally, and he agreed that he must have been — he just couldn't remember it. It was Pigpen's unreliable memory that made me decide in future to draw up minutes from our meetings to outline what had been agreed.

He and I commiserated with one another. Pigpen needed a car, while I needed money to fix my teeth, which were in a woeful state. It was pretty obvious that we were not going to be able to live on $200 a week indefinitely, and I promised him that I would see how we could increase the money in our pockets.

CHAPTER 45

The end of the line

After a massive booze-fueled party and an excess of gluttony, about a hundred of the world's worst hangovers pulled into Winnipeg.

People looked a mess. The musicians were pale and exhausted. As the train finally came to a halt, it was with a sense of palpable relief that they got off the bloody thing and finally stood on firm ground. Several of them were throwing up.

The promoters knew a thing or two about musicians and had wisely guessed that they would arrive in Winnipeg trashed. They had come up with the sensible idea of taking everyone to the local swimming pool. People certainly needed a wash, and were transported to the pool in buses, whereupon they entered the place, stripped off, and ran stark naked into the water, led by a hysterically laughing Janis Joplin.

The pool visit was the perfect recovery session, a credit to the promoters, and great fun. Thankfully, the pool was hired for a private session, otherwise God knows what the response of the public might have been. Hung-over musicians getting naked in broad daylight and jumping in a municipal swimming pool is not a pretty sight. The good time at the pool ensured that the musicians' heads were in a great place when it came time for them to play and that everyone was clean enough to get back on the train and enjoy living in close proximity for a few more days.

The Winnipeg gig was one of the truly great gigs of the early '70s, with one of the greatest lineups of those times: The Band, Janis Joplin, the Grateful Dead, Buddy Guy, Delaney & Bonnie, Ian & Sylvia, the Flying Burritos . . . the list of major artists went on and on, and in perfect weather all of the bands played their hearts out.

Unfortunately the "music should be free" pressure groups had been active in Winnipeg. People assumed that eventually they would be let into the concert without having to pay when the promoters opened the gates. Many wondered if the unpleasant scenes from Toronto would be replicated in Winnipeg.

Once again there were meetings with promoters and protesters, but by this time the musicians' attitudes had changed and they were no longer sympathetic to the protesters' cause. The promoters had lost a fortune and had paid the bands their fees, so why shouldn't the audience pay to hear the music? Happily the violence that had occurred in Toronto was not repeated in Winnipeg, so about 8,000 people got to hear some amazing music in a facility that could easily have held 40,000. The bands played wonderfully, the crowd had a ball, and soon after nightfall we were all back on the train and getting ready to head for Calgary.

People arrived at the railroad yards with enough supplies for what looked like a couple of weeks. Cartons of cigarettes and cases of beer, mountains of fruit, bread, and other supplies were packed on the train for the journey, as well as several young ladies who were smuggled aboard and came along for the ride.

I must say musicians are very similar, regardless what part of the world you live in. When they have to think of the necessities of life they always seem to come up with the same answer: "Booze and broads."

From Winnipeg to Calgary there was plenty of booze, tons of cigarettes, and some rather delicious-looking creatures who were hot to have fun. The numbers onboard had doubled; half the people didn't have bunks, but what the hell, they decided, let's stay up until Calgary, the last gig of the tour. That trip was certainly one of the great parties of my life.

In 1970 there was no such thing as mobile phones, so I had spent the time in Winnipeg frantically making last-minute arrangements for the band. The numbers in the Grateful Dead party had increased, as various family people had now joined the train.

People were looking to have the kind of party that reduces you to inane grinning whenever you think about the fun that you had. Security had to be stepped up; otherwise there would have been too many people on board.

Finally, with everything packed aboard, the train strained and groaned its way out of Winnipeg, and all of the musicians slipped effortlessly back into the journey. As the train started to move, a hundred hands reached for a hundred bottles and snapped at their tops. If synchronized drinking were an Olympic sport, I was about to witness some gold medal performances.

Toasts were drunk, guitars were tuned, and then people got down to the serious business of consumption. Within a hundred miles of Winnipeg everyone was as pissed as a sailor on shore leave, playing music and having a wonderful time.

Many hours passed and we realized that we were going to run out of booze. Almost everything brought on board had gone. The promoters immediately held a war council. As it was in effect their train, they were able to perform a miracle. They had the train stop in the middle of nowhere so that we could make a massive booze run.

It was one of the craziest scenes ever, as a horde of us descended on a small liquor store in a one-horse town and purchased several thousand dollars' worth of booze. This huge stash included a demijohn of Canadian Club whiskey from the store's display window and countless cases of beer — enough booze, everyone reckoned, to get us safely to Calgary. Even the journalists on board, hard drinkers to a man, reckoned that we probably had enough to see us through. We all clambered back on the train and filled our glasses.

Before the train had even begun to move we were back in the groove.

The communal demijohn of Canadian whiskey was set up in the music car and it had been "seen to" by some benevolent psychedelic assassin. One would have thought that acid and alcohol could produce some strange effects, but the musicians plowed on without a care in the world and the huge whiskey bottle slowly emptied. The singing grew rowdier, the boozing more enthusiastic, and the ladies looked even more beautiful. Rick Danko on the one side and Jerry Garcia on the other once again supported Janis and they seemed determined to sing every mournful country blues song in the book. Various musicians added their instruments to attain that high ol' lonesome sound.

The train had an unusual effect on the ladies, I noticed. They seemed to be particularly amorous, an effect I put down to the alcohol and acid and the incessant beat of the train as it headed west.

I observed Janis sliding off to the sleeping car with Marmaduke from the New Riders. Her shrieks of pleasure could be heard wafting down the corridors. After half an hour they returned to the music car; Marmaduke wore a smile the size of a Cheshire cat's.

A dark-haired lady let me take her to the caboose and she spent what seemed like hours demonstrating the difference between American and Canadian girls. She finally crashed out in my bunk while I went back to the party.

There were girls with girls and girls with boys and it seemed like people ran promiscuously from bed to bed and did their best to keep up. Some serious loving was mixed with some serious music and everybody seemed very happy.

Eventually, the train stopped and disgorged some very spent people. All of the Grateful Dead were on their hands and knees, puking and groaning beside the train and swearing that they would never ever touch alcohol again.

Our equipment guys looked like they'd been on tour non-stop for two years and began to unload the gear from the train with all the enthusiasm of slave laborers.

Various confused-looking girls were hunting through the sleeping cars for items of clothing they had somehow misplaced. Musicians were trying to untangle guitar leads and find instrument cases and the train doctor was busily explaining to one and all that the only thing that he could do for a hangover was to give people a shot of B12. Rick Danko and I tried it out and it seemed to help, though I could never quite identify its specific effects.

Slowly I managed to rally the troops and a chastened and seriously hung-over bunch of musicians made their way aboard a fleet of buses to the football stadium in the middle of Calgary.

The only people who seemed completely unfazed by the excessive boozing were Pigpen and Janis, who had a great time laughing at all the amateurs puking by the railroad track. The two of them were already swigging Southern Comfort at ten in the morning after drinking all night.

On the bus Janis told me it was her birthday and as soon as I got to the stadium I went in search of the promoters, because Janis's birthday definitely deserved a celebration. The promoters came up with a huge cake that had "Happy Birthday Janis" written across it.

I was to find out later that Sonny Heard had put a couple of hundred drops of LSD all over the icing. The cake was so big that four men had to carry it in on a sheet of plywood that doubled as a serving tray. As Janis began to play we prepared to give everyone on the stage a piece of her cake; first she would have to cut it in front of the fans while everyone sang "Happy Birthday."

Janis had the first piece of cake and made sure that everyone in her band got some. Taking the knife from her, I traced a bunch of grid lines on top of the cake and cut it as fast as I could, while what seemed like an army of musicians and stage crew and equipment and lighting people helped themselves. We carried the remains to the backstage area.

Several amiable members of the Calgary police department were lounging there and they had some cake too. I wasn't to find this out until later.

This is what happened.

The Full Tilt Boogie band was playing with Janis, and she was belting out her vocals facing a crowd of maybe 6,000 people. The sun was sinking over the stadium's rim and people were getting very high.

I noticed a police officer standing behind the back-line of Janis's band, obviously enjoying the music while he stared into the sunset with manic intensity. He removed his hat and undid his tie and dropped them on the floor of the stage. He began to unbutton his shirt and he took it off and also dropped it on the floor. He was standing there in a white cotton T-shirt.

I watched with a mounting sense of alarm as the man began to unbutton his gun belt and dropped his gun on the pile of clothes beside him on the floor.

I quickly realized that he must have had some cake, for no cop would take off his gun like that in public. Not our fault, right?

A quick check around me revealed several cops who were also off their heads and having fun, totally oblivious to their police responsibilities. They had abandoned caps and ties, unbuttoned their shirts, and were staring at the gorgeous hippie chicks who danced in front of them.

Two of the cops were dancing. It wasn't attractive, but it was definitely dancing.

Then there was a commotion backstage and three police cars pulled up. Out of the cars stepped a determined-looking bunch of fresh cops, who started rounding up their compatriots who had, as it were, strayed off the reservation.

The dancing officers were taken beneath the stands to a players' changing room. I wandered over to see what kind of progress they were all making. All the poor stoned cops, who could have been in the stadium having a good time, were sitting on a hard bench beneath the harsh glare of some hideous overhead fluorescent strip lights. A senior sergeant was yelling at them and telling them that he had warned them not to eat or drink anything. They all looked decidedly glum.

Janis came off stage after a set that electrified everybody, and was furious. She stormed up to me and angrily demanded to know who had dosed her. I told her truthfully that I didn't have a clue, but that I was just as high as she was and so were a couple of hundred other people, including the cops. The band was great, I told her. They wandered past looking somewhat confused and Janis decided that she was going on the warpath. She grabbed hold of my arm and insisted I take her backstage to her dressing-room. She was trembling and high and not a happy hippie.

Janis hated being dosed on LSD. When Garcia came to say hello and see if she was all right, Janis vociferously complained. Jerry looked uncomfortable as she moaned about the crew and how it was Jerry's fault because they were his crew and they were out of control, and she hated fuckin' acid and she was furious. Garcia gave her a friendly hug, and eventually Janis's anger subsided.

I sat there watching all of this with Jerry every once in a while giving me meaningful glances. Without saying a word, we accepted that things had gone too far. No one should be taking LSD without their informed consent.

Jerry had to go to the stage and Janis and I had a few minutes alone. I got her some herbal tea, which helped to calm her down. I also got her a couple of chocolate bars and she munched on these as I told her not very convincingly that they would help her to chill out. I gave her a cuddle and we giggled about how much fun the train had been, what a brilliant idea, and we promised one another that we'd look into getting together a similar trip in America.

With a final kiss, Janis left to go to the airport and I waved goodbye to her. I would never see her again. Just a couple of months later, on October 4, 1970, she died while on the road. It is no exaggeration to say that every member of the Grateful Dead family shed many a tear.

CHAPTER 46

Whistling in the graveyard

When I got back to the office in California I found several messages waiting for me from John Jaymes. It had been months since I'd last seen the man at the mess that was Altamont. Sitting in the last railroad car on my own, zooming across Canada, I had realized that sooner or later I would have to talk with Jaymes, if only to discover what he wanted. I called him from Calgary and arranged to meet him, as I would be in New York with the Grateful Dead within a week.

Since the end of my relationship with the Rolling Stones I had not been idle when it came to Jaymes. I'd met a private detective who worked for a San Francisco lawyer, and he and I had several debates about John Jaymes. The detective somehow managed to dig up the interesting fact that Jaymes had been a witness for the prosecution against some organized crime people in New England.

Through the detective I was introduced to another very serious and "connected" lawyer based in Cleveland, Ohio. The lawyer represented some of the heaviest people in the Midwest, people who would know whether a man was a full member of the fraternity, merely cooperating with them, or just some foolish wannabe. The fact that Jaymes seemed to have cooperated with federal law enforcement agencies in the past piqued the lawyer's interest and he promised to get back to me after a couple of weeks and report on what he had found out.

John Jaymes was what's known in London as a "kiter." Check kiting means writing a check on one bank account, even though there is not enough money in the account to cover it, and then depositing it in a second account with a different institution. Before the first check has time to clear, the kiter writes another check, this time on the second account, which now has an inflated balance. The money from the second account is paid back to the first, so that the original check is honored. It is essentially a way of borrowing funds without going through a formal application for credit, but when it is done on a grand scale, it can cost institutions millions.

The lawyer informed me that Jaymes (under the name of Ellsworth) had been imprisoned for this. It seemed likely, the lawyer said, that while in prison, Jaymes/Ellsworth had cut some kind of a deal with the authorities, because he had been released early. He then got involved with New England criminals who were being targeted by federal prosecutors. Jaymes was, as they say, playing both sides of the street.

The lawyer told me that Jaymes was not a "made man," but was working closely with members of Paul Castellano's family in New York. He was also a witness for the prosecution in a trial of suspected Mafiosi. He had testified against members of Raymond Patriarca's clan and other members of the New England mob. The lawyer was at a loss to explain how such a man could still be alive, let alone involved with one mob family while informing on another.

His participation as a prosecution witness in the trial was meant to be secret, but had easily been uncovered by the private detective in San Francisco, who in turn informed the mob lawyer in Cleveland, who would certainly have let people on the East Coast know. I was left in no doubt that John Jaymes had some heavy enemies and was unlikely to live a long life.

My old friend Goldfinger was also very interested in Jaymes

and had some strange stuff to tell me. Over lines of coke and Afghan hashish at his Mill Valley home, we spent an evening discussing some of the weirder aspects of Altamont.

Ken had been there for the whole day and carefully noted the behavior of various people, many of whom he suspected to be federal officers. Ken believed that Woodstock had seriously frightened the federal authorities and that they were determined that similar events would not become commonplace. I asked Ken to find out as much as he could for me. After a few weeks we met up again and the smuggler told me what he'd learned about Jaymes through his extensive connections.

Apparently Jaymes was well known to the San Francisco office of the FBI, as was Mel Belli, the flamboyant but useless attorney. According to Goldfinger, both men met regularly with FBI officials immediately prior to Altamont.

Goldfinger got this information from a secretary in the Belli offices who often scored cocaine from him. Why they were meeting the FBI the secretary had no idea, but she was pretty sure it had something to do with the free concert.

Goldfinger was absolutely convinced that after Woodstock the U.S. government became seriously concerned about the possible radicalization of the nation's youth at large pop festivals and he was sure that the government was determined to stop this happening by any means possible.

J. Edgar Hoover, the cross-dressing head of the FBI, was leading the fight to protect the nation's youth from the scourge of the fundamentalist left of the youth movement and the Black Panthers. He saw the whole business of festivals as part of some radical left-wing agenda designed to subvert the healthier interests of the youth of the United States.

Those sections of the various federal law enforcement agencies concerned with the fight against drugs were on Hoover's side, convinced that festivals were set up by drug dealers to facilitate the more efficient distribution of their product.

Altamont, coming so soon after Woodstock, was an immediate threat. When they couldn't stop the concert happening, Goldfinger said, they decided to use whatever means necessary to discredit the event.

It is worth remembering that at the time of Altamont, Richard Nixon was president and the attorney-general, John Mitchell, was a man who, though sworn to uphold the law, was instead breaking it at virtually every possible opportunity in order to protect Nixon's political interests.

The FBI cooperated in their endeavors with the BNDD (Bureau of Narcotics and Dangerous Drugs, the precursor to today's DEA), and according to Goldfinger, it was narcotics agents who had been responsible for the distribution of thousands of tablets of tainted acid at Altamont.

The pills in question were pale yellow and, according to Goldfinger's source, contained some 1,600 micrograms of LSD (almost seven times the normal "meeting God" dose). They had been poorly manufactured and may have been contaminated with adulterants. Tablets are as readily identifiable as fingerprints and a skilled forensic chemist can tell immediately by examining any tablet what kind of machine was used in its manufacturing and processing. But these pills had been pressed in a tabbing machine that no one had ever seen before.

Several of the Bay Area chemists had managed to get samples of that batch of bad acid and were adamant that it was not manufactured by any of the California street chemists, all of whom formed a pretty tight little underground cabal.

They all agreed that the bad acid given away at Altamont was pressed on a machine of a type that can only be found in the upper reaches of the legitimate pharmacological industry. Such a machine would have cost hundreds of thousands of dollars, which was beyond the reach of the underground chemists.

And even if the underground chemists had been able to afford such a machine, the federal anti-drug agencies were monitoring the manufacturers of these machines and would know of anybody who had purchased one. To purchase such a machine would make being busted an absolute certainty. Of course, such a machine would have been readily available to federal agencies if they required it.

Goldfinger had been responsible for the distribution of many thousands of trips over the years and scoffed at my suggestion that the bad acid was simply a batch that had been manufactured poorly by some inefficient street chemist.

He gave me a rapid rundown on the underground manufacturing process. No one, he insisted, would have released such bad acid onto the street. After a chemist made a bunch of acid, he always checked its purity. Indeed, while manufacturing acid it was impossible, Goldfinger explained, for the chemist not to get high on his own product. If the product had been tainted there would have been one very sick chemist.

As he also explained, there were some super-healthy egos involved in the chemistry side of the drug scene and they were all competing to produce the "purest" acid. It was a small scene: the chemists all knew one another and considered themselves members of an elite who were changing the consciousness of the world. None of them would have dreamed of being associated with something so substandard; it would have been bad for their reputation.

The arrival of these little yellow hell pills at Altamont, Ken explained, was deliberate. They were intended not to get people high, but to fuck them up and discredit the counterculture.

Goldfinger also told me that the head of the FBI office in San Francisco was at the Altamont festival and had been in communication with several of the people who worked for Jaymes. The Feds had a motorhome parked near the Altamont racetrack offices and had used it to hang out. Ken said he knew the head of the FBI in San Francisco, so when he said that he had seen him talking quite openly with some of Jaymes's people, I had no reason to disbelieve him. When I told Ken that Jaymes knew exactly who he was and was freaked out about his hanging out with the Stones, Ken laughed grimly.

The wealthy drug smuggler viewed the Stones as a bunch of naive English fools who had been out of their depth in the U.S. He thought it hilarious that a man like Jaymes had been able to worm his way into the Stones' inner circle.

Did I know, he asked, that the Stones had been surrounded in the end by people from the Mafia and the federal police, and that in effect these two groups of people were cooperating with one another? The people who John Jaymes had brought in to look after the Stones at Altamont, who had been singularly unsuccessful in doing anything but covering themselves, came from Sam "Momo" Giancana's mob in Chicago.

These were the same boys, it later transpired, who were cooperating with the intelligence agencies to bump off Castro. These guys were truly heavy, and yet they looked like anyone you'd see on the street. Their appearance was completely "normal," anonymous, and they went out of their way to seem utterly unremarkable — yet to a man they were trained killers. These were the guys who didn't see the point in taking on the Hells Angels at Altamont and who simply melted away when the violence got out of hand. Perhaps they thought it was more important to remain invisible. I never did quite understand their "no-show."

Whenever we met, Ken was enthusiastic about me getting together with Jaymes and wanted me to get him out to California. Ken had a mad scheme: he wanted to lure Jaymes into a "honey trap," where a chick would get him talking in a wired house. He even talked about kidnapping the man. It all sounded dangerous and far too crazy for me. I wanted no part of anything to do with Jaymes, but was concerned about his Mafia association. The Rolling Stones would never have let him get so close to them if they had understood about his background.

At the end of the train ride in Canada I called Ken in California and told him that I had a phone number for Jaymes in New York, and that we were going to meet while I was in town for the Dead's shows at the Fillmore East. Ken immediately said he was coming, as he'd missed the Canadian party and didn't want to miss this high old time.

He wanted to bring a wire for me to wear when I met Jaymes, but I absolutely refused. I only wanted to establish the truth insofar as it affected me and the Stones, and did not want to go in for any kind of heroics.

I had first begun my rock'n'roll journey, like so many of my generation, thrilled with the spirit of joyful self-expression that the music represented, and threw myself into the fray with idealistic enthusiasm. This was the music of my people and, as the Who claimed, it talked about "my generation." Slowly I had come to realize that what had once been fun for so many had been reduced to the sleazy realities of commerce, and little but the craving for material wealth seemed to have any meaning.

Some dark forces were now at work in the marketing of music. These people were out to control bands and stadiums — anything they could get their grubby hands on. Music was being taken over by gangsters and major corporations, and any idealism was fast being eroded in the search for big bucks. John Jaymes and his mob were just the forward guard in the commercial takeover of the counterculture's music. I could see it coming from miles away.

And I wanted no part of it.

CHAPTER 47

An unsavory meal

One evening, prior to the Dead's series of concerts at the Fillmore East, I went to have dinner with Jaymes. I went alone, unarmed, and without the wire that Goldfinger had urged me to wear. Ken had been keen to entrap Jaymes and to expose the work of the police in wrecking the Altamont concert to the underground press, but I didn't feel courageous enough to go through with such a dangerous scheme.

Jaymes had invited me to dinner at 21, an expensive and fashionable restaurant in midtown Manhattan. It had a small set of stairs that led down from the street and was obviously popular with the upper classes. As I walked into the place I felt like the poorest person there by a country mile. I was shown to a table at the back of the restaurant, where I found John Jaymes, sitting alone and perspiring slightly, surrounded by Manhattan's wealthiest citizens. He was obviously stressed and didn't look well.

I decided I would tell Jaymes as little as possible about what I knew of his previous exploits. I began by asking him how the film was going, as I assumed he had a share in it.

"The fucking film's going nowhere without me," he snapped, and went into a long tirade about how it was being held up by the police and the lawyers because of the murder that had been captured on camera.

I asked him about the lawsuit and said I was concerned that I was one of the people being chased by the process servers. He didn't tell me if he'd been interviewed himself, just grimaced and moaned about the filmmakers and how he was going to sue them if they included his face in the film.

I asked whether he'd been in touch with the Stones, and he tried to ignore my question. I thought I'd try a new tack, and complained bitterly about being owed money from my work on the tour, but it produced precious little response. He seemed preoccupied, and kept looking around the restaurant as if he expected someone to appear. I wondered if we were under surveillance. It was highly probable.

I asked Jaymes why he had wanted to meet with me. He told me he was going to start producing concerts, beginning with a rock festival in Florida. He wanted to know if I would like to be involved. I was speechless.

Jaymes told me he had the financial backing to do a series of shows, and had all the security he needed, while through "connections" he could get Indian land in Florida that was not subject to any state or local controls. The thought of John Jaymes doing concerts without any controls was astounding. I was filled with admiration at his almost suicidal recklessness. The man was as deluded as his gangster cronies, who no doubt he envisioned handling the "security" with the same miserable aplomb they'd displayed at Altamont.

I asked him how he expected to produce shows when the last one he'd been involved in had been such a spectacular failure. Jaymes refused to accept any responsibility for the events at Altamont, though I knew that legally he was liable, as Young America Enterprises had actually signed the contract for the site, not the Rolling Stones. As far as Jaymes was concerned, though, it was all the fault of the Hells Angels. His people had been there, he said. They had been more than capable of handling the security, but when the Angels interfered, that had screwed up the whole scene.

I put it to Jaymes that his people had left the concert early and were next to useless. It was only the fact that the Angels had intervened that saved someone on stage from being killed.

Jaymes looked thoughtful for a moment, then told me the most incredible tale.

Meredith Hunter was a patsy, he explained. He was at Altamont to do "someone else's" bidding. He claimed that Hunter had been given some unspecified task and it had all gone horribly wrong, but Jaymes didn't furnish any further details. He warbled on about the San Francisco police and what cordial relations he enjoyed with the department. He claimed that the only reason Meredith Hunter had even been on the street was by virtue of the good graces of local narcotics officers.

I didn't believe anything he said.

I wasn't even paying attention to what he was saying now, but thinking about something else. For the first and only time in my life, I decided to take revenge. This man represented everything I loathed and despised, and his greed shocked me. In the past I would have walked away, but now I had to act.

In my pocket I had a small eyedropper bottle given to me by a friend. In the bottle was enough acid to turn all the gangsters in New York into ballet dancers.

I stared at Jaymes as his lies became more and more preposterous. It was time he understood that the people whom he had attempted to righteously screw were not to be messed with. The whole underground scene and 300,000 people at Altamont seemed to be calling me to action.

I lied to Jaymes, telling him that I had to be at my hotel before 11 p.m. to check out, and that surely it was time we ordered our food, otherwise I would be late. I was on the late-night flight to the coast. He asked me to wait a minute; he'd forgotten his wallet and would have to make arrangements about paying.

He waddled off to talk to the maître d'. In front of me, beside his place setting, was an expensive Waterford crystal glass half-filled with drinking water. Beside that was his glass of brandy.

I pulled out the eyedropper and quickly squirted eight or nine drops of acid into his drinking water.

Jaymes returned and waffled on about how he'd spoken to the owner, who was going to send the bill to the Plaza Hotel, where Jaymes was staying with the Rolling Stones, and how (of course) the Stones weren't registered there under their own names but in the name of some record company. He sat down and took a long swig of his water. I looked steadily at him and said nothing as he continued with his preposterous tale. "Yeah, that black man was a little shit that my people controlled," he said, and peered at me convincingly. "We would have taken care of him, but the fuckin' Angels got involved. Your hiring the Angels fucked up a lot of things, Sam."

I was about to argue with him when I remembered that Jaymes was just about to get very high. I poured us both some fresh water, lifted my own glass and said, "Cheers."

Jaymes was no longer talking. He swigged the fresh water I gave him and held out his glass for a refill. I graciously obliged. This too went the way of the previous glass; he seemed to be very thirsty.

He tugged at the tie at his throat and loosened it, and asked me if I thought it was hot in the restaurant. I shrugged. "Not particularly."

He looked down at the table and began to fastidiously rearrange his knives and forks. He seemed unsettled by the arrangement of them, blissfully unaware that it was the Cutler — not the cutlery — that was intent on unsettling him.

As Jaymes considered the fork in his hand for the umpteenth time I smiled cheerfully at him and stood up, pretending I was heading to the bathroom.

"John," I said, "I'll be right back," and I strolled off toward the toilets. Once I was out of his sight I swiftly left the restaurant.

I had exacted what I thought to be an appropriate response

to his greed and duplicity. Jaymes was now "free" and would soon be making an interior journey where all would be revealed to him. I must confess that in my foolishness, I felt very pleased with myself.

In those days I truly believed that LSD was the answer to a number of society's problems. I was deluded enough to think that if only the leaders of the world took acid, the prospect of nuclear war would be unimaginable and they would turn from aggression to peace and love. If a man like Jaymes took an inner journey, had a conversation with God, he would surely see the error of his ways.

I hasten to add that I was not alone in my foolishness and that many people shared my views. Needless to say I was seriously misguided. Like a fool I was convinced that what I had discovered for myself was what everyone else needed to have revealed to them. It took me a few years to rid myself of these delusions.

And so it was that I left John Jaymes, the gangster, in one of the most expensive restaurants in New York without a cent in his pocket, on his first trip — and hopefully reassessing his career in crime.

I never did discover how that little episode played out, but learned several years later that Jaymes had been thrown from a fourth-floor window by his Mafia cronies and spent some time in hospital after he had successfully conned Rosalynn Carter, the president's wife, in one of his scams and managed to relieve the United Nations Children's Fund of hundreds of thousands of dollars.

John Ellsworth Jaymes is now dead.

CHAPTER 48

The Fillmore East

After abandoning John Jaymes to his fate at the restaurant, it was a relief to walk to the Navarro Hotel and be greeted by the staff, whom I regarded as old friends. I felt as if I had made the transition from darkness to light. The Grateful Dead loved New York City and I loved being there with them. It was all such an adventure. It felt like it was the place where the future began. There was also the happy and slightly mischievous feeling that we were in town to show those East Coast people a thing or two, to lay out our West Coast musical wares with humor and panache and to generally get inside the city slickers' heads California-style. Did we have fun!

We always stayed in the Navarro hotel on Central Park South and one of my first duties was to sort out our domicile so that everything was cool. The Navarro was owned in part by the English band the Who, and the staff there were well used to the excesses of rock'n'roll bands — but no hotel in the world is necessarily equipped to deal with the Grateful Dead.

There was a range of practical reasons why we loved doing shows at the Fillmore in New York, and top of the list for me was the fact that for a few days we would be staying in the one place, playing in the one place, and getting off our face in the one place. Added attractions were the standard of show production at the Fillmore, which was always first class, and the wonderful opportunity of playing in the very heart of Manhattan.

The first working day in New York always began with the dreaded wake-up call for the crew at 7 a.m., which allowed everyone to get in a good breakfast before a long and tiring day. We would then head for the Fillmore East in cabs, arriving for a 9 a.m. crew call and the start of the action.

At this stage in the development of the Grateful Dead we were still using in-house sound and lights, and it was a blessed relief to be in the hands of the Fillmore's professional production crew. Both band and crew could relax and focus on the music rather than wondering what the hell things were going to sound like.

The Grateful Dead always sold out the Fillmore East. People from all over the eastern seaboard would come to New York solely to make the pilgrimage to Bill Graham's place, hoping to be at every show we played. After the gigs sold out, the only way of getting in was to be on the guest list.

With each successive show the list would get longer and longer as our friendship pool expanded. By the time we had actually arrived in New York there might already be some hundred names on it, with the numbers growing by the hour.

The guest list always gave me more headaches than anything else. It made me instant friends with those who were fortunate enough to get on the bloody thing and an enemy to those I had to refuse. It was a thankless task administering the list and at times it drove me crazy, but I had to do it — there was no one else I could trust to keep the numbers in any kind of reasonable proportion.

By not very happy mutual consent I would limit each musician to five guests. The same went for the crew. That meant we already had some sixty people on the list before we'd even left San Francisco. The people from the office would add to the list, the record company would add names, and slowly and surely the list would begin to grow. By the time I actually arrived at the

Fillmore it would fill several sheets of paper.

The system was unsatisfactory, but in my time with the band we never did manage to come up with an alternative. The problem with "friends of the family" was that they seemed singularly ill equipped to purchase tickets like everyone else — but as these people really were our friends, how could we refuse them?

Sometimes it also fell to me to get people in who had been overlooked and weren't on the "inventory." I became an expert at such maneuvers and reckon that between me and the crew we could have smuggled someone into Fort Knox if we'd really put our mind to it. In the end it all became a crazy game of outwitting Bill Graham and his staff and circumnavigating whatever controls he had in place. The "weak spot" was the stage door, and there my attentions would be focused.

One of the easiest tricks was the "flight case scam." Our truck would be parked in the alley at the back of the Fillmore and I would slip out, taking a couple of empty flight cases from the truck. These would then be wheeled into the backstage area by whoever had not managed to make the guest list. The unsuspecting security guy would wave them through, convinced that the equipment was urgently needed. It never failed to amuse me that the security guys didn't notice that the people pushing the cases were dressed in their Sunday best. This ruse could only be used a few times before the man on the door got wise; then we'd resort to other stratagems.

One of my simple techniques was to tell the man on the door that the particular pretty lady I was trying to get in was one of the band's "old ladies." Many a lovely one became Garcia's or Phil's nominal old lady and there was no way the man could refuse her, especially as she had been "identified" by me.

Another strategy I used was to arrive at the door with the list, by now five or six pages long, and in flustered fashion run my eye down it, looking for some name. With perfect timing a crew member would tell me, "Sam, you're needed at the box office." In exasperation I'd tell the man on the door I had to rush, Bill Graham wanted me — and he would relent and one more person would enter. The poor guy didn't stand a chance.

Then I'd ask one of the ladies from the family to take over the guest list and this charming creature would begin a slow and sneaky "seduction" of the security man. First she would chat to him and generally make him feel loved and appreciated for the great job he was doing. Then she'd ask if he'd like a drink. A tiny amount of psychedelics would mysteriously find its way into the drink and the man would begin to relax and not take his duties quite so seriously. Slowly but surely, the backstage would fill with people and everyone would be happy — except Bill Graham, who frequently went ballistic as the evening progressed. In the end, though, even he would give up the uneven struggle.

The Manhattan chapter of the Hells Angels were our friends, and happened to live just around the corner from the Fillmore, so there was no way that they were not going to come and party with us. Bill Graham hated the Angels with a passion, but what could he do? The band would be playing and several Angels would show up at the back door. The idea of refusing them entry was obviously not wise. The security man would look at the bikers and then look at me, shrug, and decide he didn't care anyway, then in they'd come.

I made a private deal with Bill Graham: while the bikers were our guests Bill had my word and theirs that nothing untoward would happen backstage, and thanks to the discipline and sagacity of the Angels the deal was never broken. It was also part of the deal that I negotiated with the president of the chapter and Bill Graham that the Angels would never expect to gain entry to the Fillmore except when the Grateful Dead were playing. This deal held good until the Fillmore closed.

The demise of the Fillmore East came at an opportune time for the Grateful Dead, as we had basically outgrown the place. Bill Graham had outgrown the venue as well: simple economics dictated that the same crew that ran a 3,000-capacity venue could do shows in venues that held 10,000 or more equally well. The Grateful Dead looked for a larger port to continue with their trip.

But the Fillmore East was without doubt the best facility for rock music I have ever experienced. It had great sound and lights and a wonderful crew. It was a credit to the Bill Graham Organization. The Dead went on to bigger things, as did Bill Graham, but in many respects the intimate lunacies of our gigs at the Fillmore were never to be replicated.

The closing of the Fillmore marked the end of my first year with the band, a year in which we had worked harder than we had ever done, playing over a hundred gigs. The Dead's finances had been straightened out and the continuation of our journey was assured. People in the band pursued their own musical projects and the crew began to assemble the "wall of sound," a massive PA designed by Bear and Alembic. There was no rest for the wicked — at least not for me.

CHAPTER 49

Europe

The Dead dreamed of touring Europe, and it made sense com-
mercially, as the band was virtually unknown outside the U.S.
Not that the band cared about commerce: they wanted to find
out what it was like to play for people other than Americans.

I put together a tour for them that encompassed Britain,
Denmark, Germany, Luxembourg, Holland, Switzerland, and
France; forty-nine members of the family came on the subsequent journey. We left on April 1 (April Fools' Day), taking with
us a sixteen-track recording machine, more than fourteen tons
of equipment, and enough magic elixir to keep all of us seriously high.

The results of that trip can be heard on *Europe '72*, the
band's triple live album. In my opinion, that album captured
the band at its tightest and is a supreme example of the Dead's
onstage art. While we were performing in Europe, the Stones
were doing it big time in America; their efforts can be heard on
the album *Exile on Main Street*. It's instructive to listen to both
albums and let the music show you the difference between the
bands.

In London, we played the Lyceum Theatre on the Strand.
The band was to play there for three nights and I decided that
my mother and her husband Mel just had to see who I was

working with. I sent a limousine to Raglan Court in Croydon to bring them to the theater.

They came on the third night, which was as high a night as the Dead ever managed. By the time they arrived we were all happily climbing our way to paradise, but the music was yet to start. Tripping like crazy, I more or less managed to keep a straight face, and ushered my mother to a seat in the front row of the balcony, right next to where Bob Mathews was mixing the sound. I then beat a hurried retreat to the dressing-rooms lest my psychedelic state alarm her.

The band played an absolutely blistering first set, and I completely forgot about my mother. Bob Mathews kindly brought her backstage in the interval. The poor woman appeared at the dressing-room door and I hurriedly pulled myself together as best I could. All around her were people out of their heads on acid and she looked decidedly uncomfortable.

I formally introduced the little white-haired lady to Garcia: "Jerry, this is my mum."

Garcia peered over his glasses and looked surprised. "I didn't know you had a mother, Sam." Everybody burst out laughing. My mother did not look at all pleased.

She then berated the musicians for playing music that was loud enough to be life-threatening and demanded that she be driven home. I placed her in the car and waved goodbye. It was the only time she was ever to see a band I worked for.

Another episode from that tour that I clearly remember occurred in the Hotel Berlin, our lodging in Hamburg. The original Hotel Berlin had been flattened in the war by Allied bombers and all that had been rescued was a small, oak-framed mirror that now had pride of place in the hotel's ornate elevator. One of our unruly mob had returned from a bit of a blast on the town, seen his reflection in the mirror, and punched himself. The mirror and frame had shattered into a thousand pieces. The manager called my room and demanded that I come to the office immediately.

He was furious, informing me that my people were "animals" and unfit to stay in such a splendid hotel. The whole business threatened to become a diplomatic incident, but I laid a thousand deutschmarks on his desk as reparation and slowly managed to smooth things over.

As we talked of music and how much I loved Beethoven and Mozart, he offered me a glass of schnapps. We raised our glasses to international understanding and at the very moment we said *"Prost!"*, a television set shot past his window and shattered into a million pieces on the pavement outside.

The offending object had been launched from the eighteenth floor by one of our happy band of travelers. At the moment of impact it was a close call as to whether the manager was going to die of apoplexy or I was going to expire from shame. He threatened to call the police, gave us five minutes to leave, and then called the police anyway. In front of the Hamburg riot squad, fifty-odd unhappy Americans assembled in the lobby while I frantically tried to find alternative accommodations.

It's strange the things one remembers down the years. On that tour we traveled on two buses. Our merry band instinctively divided themselves between the vehicles, one group being very much rowdier than the other. In Europe I had introduced people to the joys of hashish and the rowdy bus soon had bloody great lumps of the stuff, which people happily smoked at every opportunity. Five minutes before we reached the Danish–German border, I gave a stern lecture, explaining that Europe was a series of different countries, and we were about to pass through a customs checkpoint. Everyone stashed their lumps of hash and I collected all the passports for the border guards.

I raced through the bus as it slowed, spraying Ozium frantically in all directions. Ozium is used in hospitals to cover the smell of vomit and is powerful stuff. When we arrived at the border, the officials took one look at us and demanded that everyone get off the bus: they wanted to conduct a search. Five particularly nasty-looking border guards got onboard and began to look in people's bags and under the seats. The wait was excruciating and I was already thinking about who I could call; I was convinced that we were all going to get busted.

Sven the Danish bus driver sat in his seat with a glum look on his face, preparing himself for a visit to some German jail. I walked nervously to the door of the bus and stood on the steps listening to the police talking to Sven, then asked him what they were saying. Sven looked pale. "They are saying the bus smells of hashish," he told me. I decided to act.

I marched back onto the bus and with my Ozium spray secreted in my hand wandered down the aisle giving fresh squirts to the left and right of me, praying that the police wouldn't notice. "Is everything all right?" I innocently inquired, explaining that I was the leader of the group.

Thankfully none of the guards could speak English, so I prattled on, doing my best to distract them from their search. Finally they allowed us all to board, which we did in silence. We took to our seats, our eyes averted as we drove into Germany. No sooner were we a hundred yards from the border than people started retrieving their lumps from the curtains, where the hash had been hidden. The police had looked everywhere except the curtains and thus we were saved.

We reached Munich, that most civilized of towns, and were to play in the music hall, a glorious baroque masterpiece where Mozart had once performed. The backstage area was patrolled by an ancient gentleman who was the fire marshal. He wore a brass helmet that apparently dated back to the Napoleonic era and a uniform with more braid than a general. He also sported a Hitler moustache. The crew thought him hilarious, but they didn't have to deal with him. I did.

Through an interpreter, the fire marshal told me in no uncertain terms that cigarettes were verboten. We assured him that we would of course comply with his wishes.

The lights in the building went down and 2,000 people in the audience reached into their pockets and took out their lighters and held them in the air to welcome the band. The poor fire marshal started screaming at us all in unintelligible German.

Nobody took a blind bit of notice of him. Garcia pulled out a big fat spliff, lit it, had a wonderful toke, then carefully placed it on top of his amplifier. The fire marshal totally lost his cool and before anyone could stop him grabbed a bucket of water and dumped it over the amp. Half of Munich was plunged immediately into darkness as transformers could be heard popping all over the town's electricity grid.

In the ensuing melee, somehow or other the poor old fire marshal lost his beloved helmet and received, I suspect, a few well-aimed slaps. It was an absolute miracle that no one was killed.

Eventually a deathly hush descended upon the hall, and no one quite knew what to do. The equipment guys whispered to one another and a quick check confirmed that we were all okay. After an agonizing wait the emergency lighting came on; somewhere in the distance a generator could be heard humming away. The fire marshal was lying on the floor looking stunned and I helped him to his feet. He had no helmet and looked very shaken. I led him away from the stage as the director arrived. Thankfully, Herr Direktor didn't know what had happened and the old man was so shocked and disorientated that all he could do was bemoan the loss of his helmet. The director took me aside and explained.

The fire marshal's brass helmet was nearly as old as the hall itself, an irreplaceable relic of inestimable value. It had been at the hall since the early 1800s. The director looked me squarely in the eye and told me that I would be doing him a personal favor if I retrieved the ancient artifact and that all could then be forgotten. I promised to do my best.

The crew were mopping the stage and changing amplifiers, ready to kill the halfwit who had done so much damage, and in no mood to compromise, but I pleaded that unless we returned the helmet, the show would not be allowed to continue.

Reluctantly the crew started a search and I diplomatically turned my back. As if from nowhere, the helmet appeared. I approached the fire marshal, who was still looking dazed, and placed his hat upon his head.

Finally the electricity was restored and as the band ground into action the director was all smiles. The fire marshal decided that he was no longer young enough to withstand the rigors of his position and we didn't see him again. It was a night that Munich would never forget and one that is seared in my own memory.

One final anecdote from that tour bears telling. It involves Queen Juliana of the Netherlands, who was on a state visit to Denmark at the time. I had arranged for the Grateful Dead to play the Tivoli Theatre in the Danish capital, Copenhagen, which was being visited by the Dutch monarch amid much pomp and circumstance.

A state reception was being broadcast live on Danish television one evening. In a considerable coup, I had persuaded the TV station that immediately afterwards they should cut to the Tivoli and go to the Grateful Dead live, a first for them — no rock 'n'roll band had ever appeared live on TV in Denmark before. The television company was taking a massive leap into the unknown.

On the night of the show, everything was ready for a split-second changeover from the royal visit to pictures beamed from the Tivoli. My band and crew had been briefed and were standing ready to go when I slipped out of the backstage area to watch the historic moment from the "outside broadcast" truck.

Inside, a very nervous producer waited for the moment and a group of technicians hovered over the controls as the countdown began: "5 . . . 4 . . . 3 . . . 2 . . . 1, action!" With our eyes glued to the monitors, we saw the picture lurch about as the camera desperately searched for the announcer. The producer threw his hands in the air and screamed.

The announcer appeared on screen and managed to deliver

the first two or three words of his script before an almighty fist appeared, as if in slow motion, from the side of the screen — and the announcer was no more. He'd been literally punched out of the picture. The camera bobbled about frantically searching for the missing man. Finally, it threw a 180-degree spin and alighted on Garcia, who realized what was happening and began to play. The whole band followed and began the first tune as the producer collapsed, crying, "I'm ruined, I'm ruined," while various people tried unsuccessfully to console him.

This punch had enjoyed the largest audience in Danish TV history.

I sprinted backstage, and the first person I saw was the announcer, who was sitting on the floor among a pile of rubbish, ruefully rubbing his jaw. The second person I saw was our equipment guy Steve Parrish, who I was to discover owned the offending fist.

I steamed into Parrish and hissed, "What the fuck happened?"

The announcer was a short man and had been standing on his designated spot behind the amplifiers, awaiting his cue from the producer. Unfortunately, between the rehearsal and the live show, some equipment had been placed on the stage blocking the camera's sightlines. As the countdown began, the announcer madly tried to get himself into the camera's view and, having spotted a rubbish bin, he emptied it all over the stage and stood upon it so the camera could see him.

This was tantamount to an act of sacrilege in a church, for the Grateful Dead's stage is, to those on the crew, a sacred space. There was no way that Parrish was going to allow such desecration. A well-aimed punch had done the job and Parrish was happy that there was now one person in Denmark who understood you didn't lay your shit on the Grateful Dead.

That 1972 European tour was in many respects the best work that I did for the band, though Garcia complained throughout the tour that he was not getting enough playing time. He hated the two- or three-day gaps between gigs, but logistics dictated that we simply couldn't play every night — the one thing that would have made Garcia content.

Nonetheless, he smiled a lot and had some fun and there is little doubt that he was playing at his peak. Like everybody else, he found Europe weird and strange, and he loved weird and strange.

The European trip was the longest and the largest family outing the Dead were to make while I was around, and it served to reinforce those bonds that exist between people that cannot really be described in words. There was plenty of love and laughter, a little aggravation, and a whole lot of madness. What else could any self-respecting family desire? We also made a fabulous album.

We returned from Europe a different group of people: a closer and better integrated touring outfit for sure, but also a tighter group of friends. It changed people's perspective, gave them another slant on things, and (for me) it also gave the family the chance to show a London audience a high ol' time. There has never been a gig in London like the one at the Lyceum and those three nights remain one of my proudest achievements — even if my mother didn't approve.

At the end of it all I was exhausted, as sick as a dog, and felt like I was dying on my feet, but what the hell? Better a great dream realized than no dream at all.

CHAPTER 50

Out of Town Tours

We had been away for almost two months. I was exhausted and marked the holiday break with a stint in the Marin County hospital. I had returned home feeling unwell and went to see the doctor. He examined me, called an ambulance, and I was rushed to hospital with a bleeding stomach ulcer. I almost died. Stress, the tour manager's constant friend, had come to collect the rent.

Four weeks later, bent over like an old man and with a new seven-inch scar on my belly, I went away for a short break to recuperate and to recover my strength. The band had graciously paid for my hospitalization, as I had no personal funds or medical insurance. I was grateful to them for that.

It actually took me almost six months until I fully regained my strength, but in an absurd display of arrogance and personal pride I returned to work long before I should have.

I was happy to be alive and threw myself back into the fray. In fact, I had worked on the band's gigs while I was in hospital and received a stern admonishment from the medicos, but music and bands have their own momentum and there were things that simply could not wait. In the end the doctors refused to let me have a telephone in my room, but I got around that by having someone come to visit me every day to receive instructions and to make my calls for me.

I think I missed a week of work when the operation was done and the morphine took over. Other than that it was business more or less as usual, with some extra pain thrown into the mix.

After nearly dying I realized that things couldn't go on as they were, and I needed some help. The Grateful Dead had become too large for tours to be organized by their tour manager.

In conjunction with Chesley Millikin, and with the agreement of the Dead, I started a company called Out of Town Tours and found some offices at 1333 Lincoln Street, San Rafael, just down the street from the Dead's offices.

We had a great set-up. Gail Turner, who'd worked for Jefferson Airplane and had been the Reverend Lenny Hart's secretary, became the senior bookkeeper and was our in-house rock, upon whom we depended like children. A wonderful, feisty woman, Gail was the partner of Rick Turner, who was making electric guitars for Alembic. Gail kept meticulous accounts of where the money came from and where it went and nothing would have been possible without her. I only ever got involved when I was trying to get as much of the filthy stuff as possible out of a promoter for the Grateful Dead.

As my secretary I had "Mustang" Sally Dryden, who'd had fun being a naughty girl around various San Francisco bands but had then settled down and married Spencer Dryden of Jefferson Airplane. She was one spirited lady and I loved her dearly. We'd start the day with a spliff and a line of coke and then get down to business and Sally would do her best to organize me and make me more effective.

No one messed with Mustang Sally. She had a great mind and was the absolute soul of discretion, but could swear like a San Francisco longshoreman. Like everyone I worked with I trusted her implicitly.

Frances Carr, Libby Jones, and Rita Gentry initially made up the office staff, and eventually we were to add a couple of guys to book bands. Frances coordinated the money spent on

Grateful Dead tours and Libby took care of similar matters for the New Riders of the Purple Sage. Rita, who had previously worked for Bill Graham and went on to work for Santana, looked after the mountains of paperwork. When I went out on the road with the Dead, Chesley Millikin was in charge.

One of the first things I did when we moved into the new offices was to commission a local sculptor to build a conference table so that at long last everyone would have a place to sit when I met with all the members of the Grateful Dead family.

The oval-shaped table was massive, some twenty feet long, and the top was at least three inches thick. The sculptor crafted twelve huge "thrones" that sat around the table, and I purchased thirty Windsor chairs to complete the set-up. Each throne had an astrological sign carved in its back — every one was a unique work of art. At long last a semblance of order informed Grateful Dead meetings. Everyone got a chair and a chance to voice their concerns in a civilized manner. When the table was first installed, we sat proudly in the new conference room and smoked a celebratory joint or three and were mightily pleased with ourselves. As we lounged about we looked at the walls of the room, covered in framed photographs of the artists we were working with. Chesley said, "This is like a Hall of Fame."

I raced to the phones and promptly called Hal Kant, the Grateful Dead's lawyer, and asked him to register the name on my behalf. Thus was born the Rock and Roll Hall of Fame, at 1333 Lincoln Street, San Rafael, California, long before the one in Cleveland, Ohio, was even dreamed about. All of this was to lapse into abeyance when we split with the Grateful Dead and I closed the office, but it was fun while it lasted.

Over the next few years we would work with the Grateful Dead, The Band, the Allman Brothers, Mike Bloomfield, Merl Saunders, the New Riders of the Purple Sage, the Sons of Champlin, the Doug Sahm Band, and last, but by no means least, a personal hero of mine, Ramblin' Jack Elliott.

We had no contracts with any of our artists, preferring to deal with them on trust. They trusted us, we trusted them: simple. I never thought that contracts were necessary or desirable. Between bands and promoters we had American Federation of Musicians contracts, but between the bands and ourselves we had a handshake — and sometimes we didn't even have that.

It all worked really well and we were wildly successful. Several million dollars passed through our hands in just a few years, but in the whole time I was president of the company I drew a personal salary of $200 a week, just like everyone else at Out of Town Tours. We all got the same — except the band members. Now that the Dead's finances were on track, they had the luxury of buying themselves cars and houses.

Bill Graham and I remained sworn enemies, and continued with our screaming matches on the telephone. He was quite simply the most obnoxious man I have ever had to do business with. Bill was a brilliant promoter but in some respects, like us all, he was a fool.

Jerry Garcia came into my office one day and we were sitting having a joint when my secretary Sally buzzed and warned me that Bill was on the phone and steaming with rage. I had tricked him into agreeing to do a benefit the previous evening for Badger, one of the Richmond Angels. As I've noted, Bill Graham absolutely loathed the Hells Angels. He'd just found out what had happened and was looking for blood. I told Sally to keep him on hold for a moment so that Garcia and I could have a quick line of coke before the highjinks began, and then switched my phone to speaker.

"Cutler, you motherfucker, I'm going to break your arms and legs," Graham began.

Jerry blanched and I smiled to reassure him. He had never heard Bill talk like this and he was genuinely shocked.

"Hi, Bill!" I said in my most reasonable voice. "What's the problem?"

Graham continued his tirade. "You tricked me into doing a gig for the fuckin' Hells Angels and I'm going to come down there and rip your legs off and beat you to death with 'em."

Knowing that Graham worshiped the ground Jerry walked on, I sweetly told him, "Bill, I've got Jerry here — he can hear everything you're saying over my speakerphone. Please be reasonable."

There was a long silence and then the click of a phone as Bill Graham hung up. One more transgression was added to the long list of reasons for Bill Graham to hate me.

Though it may seem strange, that conversation was a turning point in my life. I realized that Garcia, and by extension the other musicians, didn't have a clue what I had to go through on their behalf.

Jerry had come to me over the years with various personal problems and I had always sorted them out discreetly, without anybody ever knowing what I'd done. Twice, with the help of friends, I'd intervened and saved his life when he'd been threatened with serious violence. On several occasions I'd got him out of legal scrapes. I was also the one who suggested to him that he use his palm print, showing the missing tip of his finger, on the cover of his first solo album, as a way for him to get over any lingering issues about his hand.

We were very close, but the man didn't have any real idea of what it took to cover his back and work for him. He hadn't even bothered to call or send a card when I was hospitalized, and neither had the other musicians. This realization made me feel deeply depressed.

Out of Town Tours thrived and our artists went from strength to strength but a worm of doubt began to gnaw its way into my consciousness. Were these people for whom I was working like a slave just a bunch of self-centered ingrates who only cared about their own trip and cared precious little for me? My stress levels rose with their success, so I experienced a diminishing of my own enthusiasms. Where before I had been able to get high and enjoy the whole scene, now I began to doubt. I worked on and tried to still the negative voices in my head, but they would not go away.

One evening in a quiet moment at the office I sat alone and wrote down the names of all the people who were relying upon my hard work. These were the musicians, equipment guys, secretaries, and the like, people who were buying houses and cars and living well. The people whose money, in the final analysis, came through my efforts. It came to over a hundred people.

My company was receiving 10 per cent of the income we generated for the artists, and the artists relied upon Out of Town Tours for virtually 90 per cent of their earnings. I didn't own a house or a car, and was living on $200 a week. If this was the California Dream then it wasn't really that much of a dream. At least, not for me.

I struggled on for a few months but I couldn't stop thinking about Jonathan Reister, a former tour manager of the Grateful Dead who had quit in frustration when the Reverend Lenny Hart had taken over. Reister, a loyal brother to the musicians, had repeatedly warned the band about Lenny and told them in a meeting that the reverend was not quite right. No one in that "band of brothers" had bothered to listen to him, though he was one of their own. Musicians are musicians and in the final analysis they are only basically equipped to care about their own music, their own trip. In frustration Reister had quit, though he later said he would regret that decision for the rest of his life. These thoughts gnawed away at my guts.

A tour manager is a solitary creature. He lives alone at the center of the maelstrom of a band's affairs and is blamed for what goes wrong, receiving little credit for any success. Being raised in England, I was never one to expect effusive gratitude or praise and, being a proud soul, I had never sought it from anyone in my life, even when I was a child. A thank-you would have been nice but wasn't actually necessary. A tour manager feels his own secret fulfillment at a job well done. Being a supreme pragmatist, he lives with his own quiet satisfactions and they're sufficient to keep him going.

The Grateful Dead were now successful and rich and making more money than they ever had before, but money isn't everything. Our relationship subtly shifted, until I was no longer getting the support I felt was my due.

In 1974 I was on tour with the Dead and the New Riders of the Purple Sage, and after a gig some of us gathered in a hotel bar. Dave Nelson from the New Riders, a musician whose skills I admired and a friend whom I loved, came to sit with me. He looked deeply unhappy.

When I asked him what was wrong he looked at me sadly and asked, "Are you stealing our money?"

I was so shocked at the very suggestion that I laughed in his face, but at that moment I knew. Trust no longer existed. Poisoned by doubt, things were never going to be the same again.

We returned to California from the tour and a meeting was scheduled for a few days later to discuss the next series of gigs. I got a call from Rock Scully, a man I had got high with, someone I considered a brother, and he warned me what was to happen. The Grateful Dead were going to ask me to take a cut in my 10 per cent commission. I thanked Rock for letting me know and it was to be the last conversation I had with him for many years.

The day of the meeting arrived and a solemn group of musicians entered my office and sat around the massive table. Everyone looked decidedly uncomfortable. Garcia cleared his throat and began the proceedings. This was a man I dearly loved, for all his faults, a man whose life I had literally saved on two occasions.

Without looking directly at me, Garcia said, "Sam, we have someone who can book the band for 5 per cent."

I stood up and simply said, "Good luck," and walked out of the room. That, as they say, was that. Ten minutes later my office was closed, and all those dear people who had worked so hard and been so loyal to the musicians and me were without a job.

I walked from the office with my feet not touching the ground. I had worked for the Grateful Dead for four of the best and highest years of my life. As I walked away my eyes may have been full of tears, but in my soul I felt no sorrow.

I was free. The Grateful Dead's problems were no longer my problems. No messy divorce, no anguished pleas, no begging, and no arguments. Stick 'em with the shit and split.

To this day I have no regrets. I remain proud of the work I did for the Grateful Dead, as I remain proud of the work I did for the Rolling Stones. I achieved all that I had first set out to achieve with both bands, namely to advance the cause and to nurture the dream.

Now it was time for my own dreams, to concentrate on myself, for someone had been living my life, but I didn't have a clue who that person was. I determined to set out upon the road to find him.

Don't look back?

I ran into the Stones for the first time in many years on the 2003 Australian leg of the "Licks" world tour. Charlie Watts telephoned me and invited me to the gig. I sat in the audience and a Stones employee came and asked me backstage before the gig started. I wandered back and there was Charlie making himself a coffee on an espresso machine he takes on tour. The backstage area was as quiet as a graveyard, with no one about but serious-looking security. Charlie was his usual sweet self and asked if I'd like to say hello to Keith. Mick, he explained, never saw anyone before he went on stage, including the band. We went into Keith's room and there was the main man sitting in a chair and messing with his guitar. He stood up with a grin and said, "Fuck me, Sam Cutler! Or should I say fuck you?" I grinned and laughed and told him, "Take your pick." He then asked me who my tailor was. (I was wearing a suit!)

Keith looked good and we exchanged pleasantries, nothing serious, just a bit of backstage banter. I left him to his guitar-tuning and wandered with Charlie into the dining room and met Bobby Keys, the Stones' main sax player, in the hall. After almost forty years Bobby slapped me on the back and grinned. "Fucking Sam Cutler! How ya doin', man?" I asked him, "How are *you*, man?" He grinned and told me, "Clean, man, clean," and I admitted to myself he looked really good. Ronnie Wood popped in, the perennial cheeky chappy, and grinned from ear to ear while Jo (his wife) fussed over his hair.

It was all very laid-back with not a groupie or a fan in sight. Small talk English-style was the friendly order of the day. Very civilized.

I made my goodbyes to smiles and handshakes all round and went back to my seat.

The band played a blistering show, the years rolled away, the Stones were *still* the Stones, the greatest rock'n'roll band in the world! I loved the music and loved Charlie for his consideration. A true gentleman.

The Grateful Dead? What happened to those guys? Who knows! I never made any attempt to contact them, and they never contacted me. They were kind to me in a distant, formal sense. I received gold records and copies of their albums as they appeared. It felt like the relationship one has with an ex-wife where no children are involved. We treated one another shabbily, we parted, we got on with life. Who calls their ex-wife?

Over the years I received tapes of their shows (I have hundreds of them) from Deadheads and I listened to the music as it ebbed and flowed like a river tumbling through different landscapes to the sea. Once in a while the music had the old magic, but often it seemed formulaic and uninspired, drifting where gravity dictated and lacking any sense of its higher self. The ex-wife had remarried, gone on to other relationships, expanded and contracted, lost husbands and offspring, and the family of which I had once been a member seemed (to me) no more. But to deny the family of which you were once a proud member is in a sense to deny yourself.

I'm one of those guys who, when he decides he loves someone or something, he loves it forever. I still love the Stones and the Grateful Dead, and I bear them no ill will. Let's face it: they're merely musicians, mere mortals, and most of them were not well equipped to deal with what the world threw at them.

I'm pleased that most of them survived, though Jerry Garcia, Ron "Pigpen" McKernan, and Keith Godchaux's deaths make me cry to this day. Some of the people of my generation paid a terrible price for our pleasures.

I remain proud of the fact that I helped my fellow human beings where I could. We crossed paths, we lived together, we got high together. What to say? Perhaps just this: If you meet a Buddha on the path, kill him.

ACKNOWLEDGMENTS

My book was written with the boundless love and encouragement of my wife and sons and the following people who have been kind beyond words.

Robert Altman, Jeff Apter, Elizabeth Cowell, Meredith Curnow, David Dalton, Baron Weighley De Demko, Charlie Demko, Marjoke de Vries, Patsy Dodds, Tommy Governor, Tony Grace, Dr. Howard Grainger, Steven Haas, Pat and Julie Hannagan and family, Annette Harris, Kay Harris, Mau Harris, Bill Horton, Dave Howell, Brian BB Hoyt, Dorry Kartabani, John Kenny, Jackie Marshall, Dauno Martinez, Dennis McNally, Suzie Mylecharane, Susan and Julian Neaser, Tim Page, Neil Rock, Claire Rose, Ethan Russell, Frances Salter, Ronnie Schneider, David Siler, Craig Spann, Bear and Sheila Stanley, Ben Stewart, Deb Suckling, Lance Tilbury, Bob Weatherall, and Ritchie Yorke. If I have forgotten anybody I apologize.

This book is dedicated to the memory of Rex Jackson, Peter "Craze" Sheridan, Ken "Goldfinger" Connell, Jerry Garcia, Chesley Millikin, Jimi Hendrix, Ramrod Shurtliff, Clifford "Sonny" Heard, Janis Joplin, Ron "Pigpen" McKernan, Tony

Secunda, Rick Danko, and all those other people who died doing what they loved.

I wish to publicly affirm the lifelong gratitude I feel to my adoptive parents, Ernest and Dora Cutler, who saved me from an orphanage. They would have hated this book and the lifestyle it describes, and in mitigation I can only plead that I am a certain kind of person because I have experienced a certain kind of life. If I could ask them to forgive me for what I did and what I became, then I would.

This book simply could not have been written without Nick Veltre, a brother and wonderful Deadhead whom I met in Australia. His wit, wisdom, and wacky enthusiasms were critical to my getting the story told.

Finally thanks are due to Jen Hale, my editor at ECW Press, for her patience and attention to the most minute detail, and Jack David at ECW Press, who had faith in my book when all the other North American publishers couldn't see the wood for the trees.

The poem at the start of this book was written in Mill Valley, California, a couple of hours after I parted ways with the Grateful Dead.